WHAT CAN THE HISTORY OF THE JEWISH PEOPLE and their kings and queens teach us? Much in every way! In these pages the author shows that prosperity, both temporal but especially spiritual, is closely linked with a relationship to God. But we learn much about the world yet future through the remarkable prophecies of Isaiah, Daniel, and Malachi—a truly modern book in its application.

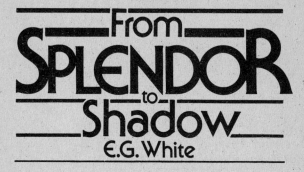

From SPLENDOR to Shadow

E.G. White

A condensation of
Prophets and Kings

**PACIFIC PRESS
PUBLISHING ASSOCIATION**
Mountain View, California
Oshawa, Ontario

This condensation is not a paraphrase. The author's own words are retained throughout, except when it has been necessary to substitute a proper noun for a pronoun to avoid confusion, to change a verb tense to maintain meaning and continuity, or to supply a word or phrase to make a sentence read more smoothly.

Copyright © 1984 by
Pacific Press Publishing Association
Printed in United States of America
All Rights Reserved

ISBN 0-8163-0559-5   84 85 86 87 88 89 • 6 5 4 3 2 1

Why You Should Read This Book

Does history have meaning? Does human life have lasting significance? Is God involved in events upon earth?

To these questions the author of this book answers Yes. Then, with deep insight into providential workings, she draws the curtain aside and reveals a philosophy of history by which past events take on eternal significance. Here is her philosophy:

"The strength of nations and of individuals is not found in the opportunities and facilities that appear to make them invincible; it is not found in their boasted greatness. That which alone can make them great or strong is the power and purpose of God. They themselves by their attitude toward His purpose decide their own destiny.

"Human histories relate man's achievements, his victories in battle, his success in climbing to worldly greatness. God's history describes man as heaven views him."

This volume opens with the account of Solomon's glorious reign over Israel. Here is traced the history of a favored and chosen people, torn between allegiance to God and to the gods of the nations about them. And here is seen vividly, through a crucial period of this world's history, the dramatic evidences of the raging conflict between Christ and Satan for the hearts of men and women.

This book abounds in fascinating character studies—the wise Solomon, who did not permit wisdom to keep

6 / FROM SPLENDOR TO SHADOW

him from transgression; Jeroboam, the self-serving man of policy; Elijah, the mighty and fearless prophet; Elisha, the prophet of peace and healing; Ahaz, the fearful and wicked king; Hezekiah, the loyal and good-hearted ruler; Daniel, beloved prophet and statesman; Jeremiah, the courageous prophet of sorrow; Haggai, Zechariah, and Malachi, prophets of the restoration. And beyond them all rises God's only-begotten Son, the coming King, the Lamb of God, in all His glory.

Under the title *Prophets and Kings*, this book has been circulated worldwide and has been translated into many languages. It is now presented in this condensed edition with the hope that it may reach an even larger audience.

It is our belief that this volume, with its rich lessons of faith in God and the stories of His providence in the lives of men and women of Old Testament times, will enlighten the minds and deepen the religious experience of all who read its pages.

The Publishers

The Glorious Destiny Israel Might Have Had*

To bring the best gifts of Heaven to all peoples, God called Abraham from his idolatrous kindred and bade him dwell in Canaan. "I will make of thee a great nation, and I will bless thee, and make thy name great; and thou shalt be a blessing." Genesis 12:2. It was a high honor to which Abraham was called—to be the father of the people who were to be the preservers of the truth of God, the people through whom all nations should be blessed in the advent of the promised Messiah.

Men had well-nigh lost the knowledge of the true God. Their minds were darkened by idolatry. Yet God in His mercy did not blot them out of existence. He designed that the principles revealed through His people should be the means of restoring the moral image of God in man.

God's law must be exalted, and to the house of Israel was given this great work. God separated them from the world and purposed through them to preserve among men the knowledge of Himself. Thus a voice was to be heard appealing to all peoples to turn from idolatry to serve the living God.

God brought His chosen people out of Egypt that He might bring them to a good land He had prepared as a refuge from their enemies. In return for His goodness they were to make His name glorious in the earth. Miraculously preserved from the perils of the wilderness wandering, they were finally established in the Land of Promise as a favored nation.

* *Author's Introduction*

Isaiah told with touching pathos the story of Israel's call and training: "My wellbeloved hath a vineyard in a very fruitful hill: and He fenced it, and gathered out the stones thereof, and planted it with the choicest vine, and built a tower in the midst of it, and also made a winepress therein: and He looked that it should bring forth grapes." Isaiah 5:1, 2.

"The vineyard of the Lord of hosts," the prophet declared, "is the house of Israel, and the men of Judah His pleasant plant." Isaiah 5:7. This people were hedged about by the precepts of His law, the everlasting principles of truth, justice, and purity. Obedience was to be their protection, for it would save them from destroying themselves by sinful practices. And as the tower in the vineyard, God placed in the midst of the land His holy temple. Christ was their instructor, their teacher and guide. In the temple His glory dwelt in the holy Shekinah above the mercy seat.

Through Moses the purpose of God and the terms of their prosperity were made plain. "Thou art an holy people unto the Lord thy God," He said; "the Lord thy God hath chosen thee to be a special people unto Himself, above all people that are upon the face of the earth." "The Lord hath avouched thee this day to be His peculiar people, as He hath promised thee, and that thou shouldest keep all His commandments; and to make thee high above all nations which He hath made, in praise, and in name, and in honor; and that thou mayest be an holy people unto the Lord thy God, as He hath spoken." Deuteronomy 7:6; 26:18, 19.

It was God's purpose that by the revelation of His character through Israel men should be drawn to Him. To all the world the gospel invitation was to be given. Through the teaching of the sacrificial service, Christ was to be uplifted, and all who would look to Him should unite themselves with His chosen people. As the numbers of Israel increased, they were to enlarge their borders until their kingdom should embrace the world.

But ancient Israel did not fulfill God's purpose. The Lord declared, "I had planted thee a noble vine, wholly a right seed: how then art thou turned into the degenerate plant of a strange vine unto Me?" "Wherefore, when I looked that it should bring forth grapes, brought it forth wild grapes? And now go to; I will tell you what I will do to My vineyard: I will take away the hedge thereof, and it shall be eaten up; and break down the wall thereof, and it shall be trodden down: and I will lay it waste. . . . He looked for judgment, but behold oppression; for righteousness, but behold a cry." Jeremiah 2:21; Isaiah 5:4-7.

By refusing to keep His covenant, God's people would cut themselves off from His blessings. Often in their history they forgot God, robbed Him of the service He required of them, and robbed their fellowmen of religious guidance and a holy example. Their covetousness and greed caused them to be despised even by the heathen. Thus the world was given occasion to misinterpret the character of God and the laws of His kingdom.

With a father's heart, God patiently set before His people their sins and waited for their acknowledgment. Prophets and messengers were sent to urge His claim, but, instead of being welcomed, these men of discernment and spiritual power were treated as enemies. God sent still other messengers, but they received still more determined hatred.

The withdrawal of divine favor during the Exile led many to repentance, yet after their return to the Land of Promise the Jewish people repeated the mistakes of former generations and brought themselves into political conflict with surrounding nations. The prophets whom God sent to correct evils were received with suspicion and scorn. Thus, from century to century, the keepers of the vineyard added to their guilt.

The goodly vine planted by the divine Husbandman on the hills of Palestine was despised by Israel and was finally cast over the vineyard wall. The Husbandman removed it, and again planted it, but on the other side of the wall and in such a manner that the stock was no longer visible. The branches hung over the wall, and grafts might be joined to it; but the stem itself was placed beyond the power of men to harm.

Of special value to God's church today—the keepers of His vineyard—are the messages given through the prophets. In them His love for the lost race and His plan for their salvation are clearly revealed. The story of Israel's call, their successes and failures, their restoration to divine favor, their rejection of the Master of the vineyard, and the carrying out of the plan of the ages by a remnant—this has been the theme of God's messengers to His church throughout the centuries that have passed.

The Master of the vineyard is now gathering from among men of all nations and peoples the precious fruits for which He has long been waiting. Soon He will come unto His own, and in that glad day His eternal purpose will finally be fulfilled. "Israel shall blossom and bud, and fill the face of the world with fruit." Isaiah 27:6.

Contents

1 / Solomon's Spectacular Beginning

In the reign of David and Solomon, Israel had many opportunities to wield a mighty influence in behalf of truth and right. The name of Jehovah was exalted and held in honor. Seekers after truth from the lands of the heathen were not turned away unsatisfied. Conversions took place, and the church of God on earth prospered.

Solomon was anointed king in the closing years of his father David. His early life was bright with promise, and it was God's purpose that he should ever approach nearer the similitude of the character of God, and thus inspire His people to fulfill their sacred trust as the depositaries of divine truth. David knew that in order for Solomon to fulfill the trust with which God honored him, the youthful ruler must be not merely a warrior and statesman, but a good man, a teacher of righteousness, an example of fidelity. With earnestness David entreated Solomon to be noble, to show mercy to his subjects, and in all his dealings with the nations to honor the name of God and to manifest the beauty of holiness. "He that ruleth over men must be just, ruling in the fear of God." 2 Samuel 23:3.

In his youth Solomon made David's choice his own, and for many years his life was marked with strict obedience to God's commands. Early in his reign he went to Gibeon, where the tabernacle built in the wilderness still was, and united with his chosen advisers and "all the leaders in all Israel, the heads of fathers' houses," in offering sacrifices to God and in consecrating themselves fully to the Lord's service. 2 Chronicles 1:2, RSV. Solomon knew that those bearing heavy burdens must seek the Source of wisdom for guidance. This led him to encourage his counselors to unite with him in making sure of their acceptance with God.

Solomon's Dream From God

Above every earthly good, the king desired wisdom and understanding, largeness of heart and tenderness of spirit. That night the Lord appeared to Solomon in a dream and said, "Ask what I shall give thee." In his answer the young ruler gave utterance to his feeling of helplessness and desire for aid. "Thou hast made Thy servant king instead of David my father: and I am but a little child: I know not how to go out or come in. . . . Give therefore Thy servant an understanding heart to judge Thy people, that I may discern between good and bad: for who is able to judge this Thy so great a people?

"And the speech pleased the Lord, that Solomon had asked this thing."

"Because thou hast asked this," God said to Solomon, "and hast not asked for thyself long life; neither hast asked riches for thyself, nor hast asked the life of thine enemies; but hast asked for thyself understanding to discern judgment; behold, I have done according to thy words: lo, I have given thee a wise and an understanding heart; so that there was none like thee before thee, neither after thee shall any arise like unto thee. And I have also given thee that which thou hast not asked, both riches, and honor: so that there shall not be any among the kings like unto thee all thy days.

"And if thou wilt walk in My ways, to keep My statutes and My commandments, as thy father David did walk, then I will lengthen thy days." 1 Kings 3:5-14; see also 2 Chronicles 1:7-12.

The language used by Solomon before the altar at Gibeon reveals his humility and his strong desire to honor God. In his heart there was no selfish aspiration for a knowledge that would exalt him above others. He chose the gift that would be the means of causing his reign to bring glory to God. Solomon was never so rich or so wise or so truly great as when he confessed, "I am but a little child: I know not how to go out or come in."

The higher the position a man occupies, the wider will be the influence he exerts and the greater his need of dependence on God. He is to stand before God in the attitude of a learner. Position does not give holiness of character. It is by honoring God and obeying His commands that a man is made truly great.

The God who gave to Solomon the spirit of wise discernment is willing to impart the same blessing to His children today. "If any of you lack wisdom, let him ask of God, that giveth to all men liberally, and upbraideth not; and it shall be given him." James 1:5. When a burden bearer desires wisdom more than wealth, power, or fame, he will not be disappointed.

How to Succeed as a Leader

So long as he remains consecrated, the man whom God has endowed with discernment and ability will not be eager for high position, nor seek to rule or control. Instead of striving for supremacy, a true leader will pray for an understanding heart, to discern between good and evil. The path of leaders is not an easy one. But they are to see in every difficulty a call to prayer. Strengthened and enlightened by the Master, they will stand firm against unholy influences and discern right from wrong.

The wisdom that Solomon desired above riches, honor, or long life, God gave him. "God gave Solomon wisdom and understanding exceeding much, and largeness of heart, even as the sand that is on the seashore. . . . For he was wiser than all men; . . . and his fame was in all nations round about." 1 Kings 4:29-31.

"And all Israel . . . stood in awe of the king, because they perceived that the wisdom of God was in him, to render justice." 1 Kings 3:28, RSV. The hearts of the people were turned toward Solomon. "Solomon . . . was strengthened in his kingdom, and the Lord his God was with him, and magnified him exceedingly." 2 Chronicles 1:1.

Solomon's Brilliant Success

For many years Solomon's life was marked with devotion to God and strict obedience to His commands. He managed wisely the business matters connected with the kingdom. The magnificent buildings and public works that he constructed during the early years of his reign, the piety, justice, and magnanimity that he revealed in word and deed won the loyalty of his subjects and the admiration of the rulers of many lands. For a time Israel was as the light of the world, showing forth the greatness of Jehovah.

As the years went by and Solomon's fame increased, he sought to honor God by adding to his mental and spiritual strength and by continuing to impart to others the blessings he received. None understood better than he that these gifts were bestowed that he might give to the world a knowledge of the King of kings.

Solomon took a special interest in natural history. Through a diligent study of all created things, both animate and inanimate, he gained a clear concept of the Creator. In the forces of nature, in the mineral and animal world, and in every tree, shrub, and flower, he saw a revelation of God's wisdom; and his knowledge of God and his love for Him constantly increased.

Solomon's inspired wisdom found expression in songs and in many proverbs. "He spake three thousand proverbs: and his songs were a thousand and five. And he spake of trees, from the cedar tree that is in Lebanon even unto the hyssop that springeth out of the wall: he spake also of beasts, and of fowl, and of creeping things, and of fishes." 1 Kings 4:32, 33.

In the proverbs are outlined principles of holy living and high endeavor. It was the wide dissemination of these principles and the recognition of God as the One to whom all praise and honor belong that made Solomon's early reign a time of moral uplift as well as of material prosperity.

"Happy is the man that findeth wisdom," he wrote, "and the man that getteth understanding. For the merchandise of it is better than the merchandise of silver, and the gain thereof than fine gold. She is more precious than rubies: and all the things thou canst desire are not to be compared unto her. Length of days is in her right hand; in her left hand riches and honor." Proverbs 3:13-16. "The fear of the Lord is to hate evil: pride, and arrogancy, and the evil way, and the froward mouth, do I hate." Proverbs 8:13.

O that in later years Solomon had heeded these wonderful words of wisdom. He who had taught the kings of the earth to render praise to the King of kings, in "pride and arrogancy" took to himself the glory due to God alone!

2 / Solomon's Magnificent Temple

For seven years Jerusalem was filled with busy workers leveling the chosen site of the temple, building vast retaining walls, laying broad foundations, shaping timbers brought from the Lebanon forests, and erecting the magnificent sanctuary. See 1 Kings 5:17. Simultaneously the manufacture of the furnishings was progressing under the leadership of Hiram of Tyre, "a cunning man, . . . skillful to work in gold and in silver, in brass, in iron, in stone, and in timber, in purple, in blue, and in fine linen, and in crimson." 2 Chronicles 2:13, 14.

The building on Mount Moriah was noiselessly upreared with "stone prepared at the quarry; so that neither hammer nor ax nor any tool of iron was heard in the temple, while it was being built." 1 Kings 6:7, RSV. The beautiful fittings included the altar of incense, the table of showbread, the candlestick and lamps, with the vessels and instruments connected with the holy place, all of "perfect gold." 2 Chronicles 4:21. The brazen altar of burnt offering, the laver supported by twelve oxen, with many other vessels—"in the plain of Jordan did the king cast them, in the clay ground." 2 Chronicles 4:17.

The Surpassing Beauty of the Temple

Of unrivaled splendor was the palatial building Solomon erected for God and His worship. Garnished with precious stones and lined with carved cedar and burnished gold, the temple with its rich furnishings was a fit emblem of the living church of God on earth, which through the ages has been building with materials that have been likened to "gold, silver, [and] precious stones," "polished after the similitude of a palace." 1 Corinthians 3:12; Psalm 144:12. Christ is "the chief Cornerstone; in whom all the building fitly framed together groweth unto an holy temple in the Lord." Ephesians 2:20, 21.

At last the temple was completed. "All that came into Solomon's heart to make in the house of the Lord," he had "prosperously effected." 2 Chronicles 7:11. Now, in order that the palace crowning Mount Moriah might indeed be a dwelling place "not for man, but for the Lord God" (1 Chronicles 29:1), there remained the solemn ceremony of dedicating it.

The spot on which the temple was built had long been regarded as consecrated. Here Abraham had revealed his willingness to sacrifice his only son in obedience to the command of Jehovah, who renewed the glorious Messianic promise of deliverance through the sacrifice of the Son of the Most High. See Genesis 22:9, 16-18. Here, when David offered offerings to stay the avenging sword of the destroying angel, God had answered him by fire. See 1 Chronicles 21:26. And now once more worshipers were here to meet their God and renew their vows of allegiance to Him.

God's Glory Fills the Temple at Its Dedication

The time chosen for the dedication was the Feast of Tabernacles. This feast was preeminently an occasion of rejoicing. The labors of the harvest being ended, the people were free from care and could give themselves up to the joyous influences of the hour.

The hosts of Israel, with richly clad representatives from many foreign nations, assembled in the temple courts. The scene was one of unusual splendor. Solomon, with the elders and influential men, had brought the ark of the testament from another part of the city. From Gibeon had been transferred the ancient "tabernacle of the congregation, and all the holy vessels" in it. 2 Chronicles 5:5. These cherished reminders of Israel's wanderings in the wilderness now found a permanent home in the splendid building.

With singing, music, and great ceremony "the priests brought in the ark of the covenant of the Lord unto his place, to the oracle of the house, into the most holy place." Verse 7. The singers, arrayed in white linen, having cymbals and harps, stood at the east end of the altar with 120 priests sounding with trumpets. See verse 12.

As "the trumpeters and singers" made "themselves heard in unison in praise and thanksgiving to the Lord, and when the song was raised, with trumpets and cymbals and other musical instruments, in praise to the Lord, . . . the house of the Lord was filled with a cloud, so that the priests could not stand to minister because of the cloud; for the glory of the Lord filled the house of God." Verses 13, 14, RSV.

Solomon's Prayer

In the midst of the court of the temple had been erected a brass platform. On this Solomon stood and with uplifted hands blessed the vast multitude before him. "Blessed be the Lord God of Israel, who hath with His hands fulfilled that which He spake with His mouth to my father David, saying, . . . I have chosen Jerusalem, that My name might be there." 2 Chronicles 6:4-6.

Solomon then knelt upon the platform and lifting his hands toward heaven, prayed: "Heaven and the highest heaven cannot contain Thee; how much less this house which I have built! . . . Hearken Thou to the supplications of Thy servant and of Thy people Israel, when they pray toward this place; yea, hear Thou from heaven Thy dwelling place; and when Thou hearest, forgive. . . .

"If Thy people Israel . . . have sinned against Thee, when they turn again and acknowledge Thy name, and pray and make supplication to Thee in this house, then hear Thou from heaven, and forgive the sin of Thy people Israel. . . .

"When heaven is shut up and there is no rain because they have sinned against Thee, if they pray toward this place, and acknowledge Thy name, and turn from their sin, when Thou dost afflict them, then hear Thou in heaven, and forgive the sin of Thy servants. . . .

"If their enemies besiege them in any of their cities; whatever plague, whatever sickness there is; whatever prayer, whatever supplication is made by any man or by all Thy people Israel, each knowing his own affliction, and his own sorrow and stretching out his hands toward this house; then hear Thou from heaven Thy dwelling place, and forgive, . . . that they may fear Thee and walk in Thy ways all the days that they live in the land which Thou gavest to our fathers.

"Likewise when a foreigner, who . . . comes from a far country for the sake of Thy great name, . . . when he comes and prays toward this house, hear Thou from heaven Thy dwelling place, and do according to all for which the foreigner calls to Thee; in order that all the peoples of the earth may know Thy name and fear Thee. . . .

"If Thy people . . . sin against Thee—for there is no man who does not sin—and Thou art angry with them, and dost give them to an enemy, so that they are carried away captive to a land far or near; yet if they lay it to heart in the land to which they have been carried captive, and repent, and make supplication to Thee in the land of their captivity, saying, 'We have sinned, and have acted perversely and wickedly'; if they repent with all their mind and with all their heart in the land of their captivity, . . . then hear Thou from heaven Thy dwelling place their prayer and their supplications, and maintain their cause and forgive Thy people who have sinned against Thee. Now, O my God, let Thy eyes be open and Thy ears attentive to a prayer of this place.''

And now arise, O Lord God, and go
to Thy resting place,
Thou and the ark of Thy might.
Let Thy priests, O Lord God, be
clothed with salvation,
and let Thy saints rejoice in Thy
goodness. Verses 18-41, RSV

As Solomon ended his prayer, "fire came down
from heaven, and consumed the burnt offering and the
sacrifices." The priests could not enter the temple because "the glory of the Lord had filled" it. 2 Chronicles 7:1, 2. Then king and people offered sacrifices.
"So the king and all the people dedicated the house of
God." Verse 5. For seven days the multitudes kept a
joyous feast. The week following was spent in observ-
ing the Feast of Tabernacles. At the close of the season
the people returned to their homes "glad and merry in
heart for the goodness that the Lord had showed unto
David, and to Solomon, and to Israel His people."
Verse 10.

The Lord Warns the King Against Backsliding

Now once more, as at Gibeon early in his reign, Israel's ruler was given evidence of divine acceptance. In a
night vision the Lord appeared to him with the message: "I have heard thy prayer, and have chosen this
place to Myself for an house of sacrifice. If I shut up
heaven that there be no rain, or if I command the locusts to devour the land, or if I send pestilence among
My people; if My people, which are called by My
name, shall humble themselves, and pray, and seek
My face, and turn from their wicked ways; then will I
hear from heaven, and will forgive their sin, and will
heal their land. . . . For now have I chosen and sanctified this house, that My name may be there forever:
and Mine eyes and Mine heart shall be there perpet-
ually." Verses 12-16.

Had Israel remained true to God, this glorious building would have stood forever, a perpetual sign of God's special favor. "The sons of the stranger, that join themselves to the Lord, to serve Him, and to love the name of the Lord, to be His servants, every one that keepeth the Sabbath, from polluting it, . . . them will I bring to My holy mountain, and make them joyful in My house of prayer: . . . for Mine house shall be called an house of prayer for all people." Isaiah 56:6, 7.

The Lord made very plain the path of duty before the king: "If thou wilt walk before Me, as David thy father walked, and do according to all that I have commanded thee, and shalt observe My statutes and My judgments; then will I establish the throne of thy kingdom, according as I have covenanted with David thy father, saying, There shall not fail thee a man to be ruler in Israel." 2 Chronicles 7:17, 18.

Had Solomon continued to serve the Lord, his entire reign would have exerted a powerful influence over the surrounding nations. Foreseeing the terrible temptations that attend prosperity and worldly honor, God warned Solomon against apostasy. The beautiful temple that had just been dedicated, He declared, would become "a proverb and a byword among all nations" should the Israelites forsake "the Lord God of their fathers" and persist in idolatry. Verses 20, 22.

Israel's Greatest Glory

Strengthened and cheered by the message from heaven, Solomon now entered the most glorious period of his reign. "All the kings of the earth" began to seek his presence, "to hear his wisdom, that God had put in his heart." 2 Chronicles 9:23. Solomon taught them of God as the Creator, and they returned with clearer conceptions of the God of Israel and of His love for the human race. In nature they now beheld a revelation of His character, and many were led to worship Him as their God.

The humility of Solomon when he acknowledged before God, "I am but a little child" (1 Kings 3:7), his reverence for things divine, his distrust of self, and his exaltation of the infinite Creator—all these traits of character were revealed when during his dedicatory prayer he knelt as a humble petitioner. Christ's followers today should guard against the tendency to lose the spirit of reverence and godly fear. They should approach their Maker with awe, through a divine Mediator. The psalmist has declared:

> O come, let us worship and bow down:
> Let us kneel before the Lord, our Maker.
>   Psalm 95:6

Both in public and in private worship it is our privilege to bow on our knees when we offer our petitions to God. Jesus, our example, "kneeled down, and prayed." Luke 22:41. His disciples, too, "kneeled down, and prayed." Acts 9:40. Paul declared, "I bow my knees unto the Father." Ephesians 3:14. Daniel "kneeled upon his knees three times a day, and prayed, and gave thanks before his God." Daniel 6:10.

True reverence for God is inspired by a sense of His infinite greatness and a realization of His presence. The hour and place of prayer are sacred, because God is there. "Holy and reverend is His name." Psalm 111:9. Angels, when they speak that name, veil their faces. With what reverence, then, should we take it upon our lips!

Jacob, after beholding the vision of the angel, exclaimed, "The Lord is in this place; and I knew it not. . . . This is none other but the house of God, and this is the gate of heaven." Genesis 28:16, 17.

In that which was said during the dedicatory services, Solomon sought to remove the superstition in regard to the Creator that had beclouded the minds of the heathen. The God of heaven is not confined to temples made with hands, yet He would meet with His people by His Spirit when they assembled at the house dedicated to His worship.

Blessed is the nation whose God is the Lord,
The people whom He hath chosen for His own inheritance.

Thy way, O God, is in the sanctuary: . . .
Thou art the God that doest wonders:
Thou hast declared Thy strength among the
  people.
                Psalm 33:12; 77:13, 14

God honors with His presence the assemblies of His people. He has promised that when they come together to acknowledge their sins and to pray for one another, He will meet with them by His Spirit. But unless those who assemble to worship put away every evil thing, their coming together will be of no avail. Those who worship God must worship Him "in spirit and in truth: for the Father seeketh such to worship Him." John 4:23.

3 / Prosperity and Pride Bring Disaster

At first, as wealth and worldly honor came to him, Solomon remained humble. He "reigned over all kingdoms from the river [Euphrates] unto the land of the Philistines, and unto the border of Egypt." "He had peace on all sides round about him." 1 Kings 4:21, 24.

But after a morning of great promise Solomon's life was darkened by apostasy. He who had been honored with tokens of divine favor so remarkable that his wisdom gained him worldwide fame, he who had led others to ascribe honor to the God of Israel, turned from Jehovah to bow before the idols of the heathen.

The Lord, foreseeing the perils that would beset those chosen as rulers of Israel, gave Moses instruction for their guidance. "He shall read it all the days of his life, that he may learn to fear the Lord his God, by keeping all the words of this law and these statutes, and doing them; that his heart may not be lifted up above his brethren, and that he may not turn aside from the commandment, either to the right hand or to the left; so that he may continue long in his kingdom." Deuteronomy 17:19, 20, RSV.

The Warning and Solomon's First Wrong Step

The Lord particularly cautioned the one who might be anointed king not to "multiply wives to himself, that his heart turn not away: neither shall he greatly multiply to himself silver and gold." Verse 17.

For a time Solomon heeded these warnings. His greatest desire was to live and rule in accordance with

26

the statutes given at Sinai. His manner of conducting the affairs of the kingdom was in striking contrast with the customs of the nations of his time whose rulers trampled underfoot God's holy law.

In seeking to strengthen his relations with the powerful kingdom south of Israel, Solomon ventured on forbidden ground. Satan knew the results that would attend obedience; and he sought to undermine Solomon's loyalty to principle and to cause him to separate from God. "Solomon made a marriage alliance with Pharaoh king of Egypt; he took Pharaoh's daughter, and brought her into the city of David." 1 Kings 3:1, RSV.

From a human point of view, this marriage seemed to prove a blessing, for Solomon's heathen wife united with him in the worship of the true God. Furthermore, Solomon apparently strengthened his kingdom along the Mediterranean seacoast. But in forming an alliance with a heathen nation and sealing the compact by marriage with an idolatrous princess, Solomon rashly disregarded the provision God had made for maintaining the purity of His people. The hope that his Egyptian wife might be converted was a feeble excuse for the sin.

For a time in His mercy God overruled this terrible mistake, and the king, by a wise course, could have checked in a measure the evil forces that his imprudence had set in operation. But Solomon had begun to lose sight of the Source of his power and glory. Self-confidence increased, and he reasoned that political and commercial alliances with surrounding nations would bring these nations to a knowledge of the true God. Often these alliances were sealed by marriages with heathen princesses.

Solomon flattered himself that his wisdom and example would lead his wives to worship the true God and that the alliances would draw the nations into close touch with Israel. Vain hope! Solomon's mistake in regarding himself strong enough to resist the influence of heathen associates was fatal.

The king's relations with heathen nations brought him renown, honor, and riches. "The king made silver and gold at Jerusalem as plenteous as stone, and cedar trees made he as the sycamore trees that are in the vale for abundance." 2 Chronicles 1:15. Wealth came in Solomon's day to an increasingly large number of people; but the fine gold of character was marred.

Wealth and Fame Bring a Curse

Before Solomon was aware of it, he had wandered far from God. He began to trust less in divine guidance. Little by little he withheld from God unswerving obedience and conformed more closely to the customs of the surrounding nations. Yielding to temptations incident to his honored position, he forgot the Source of his prosperity. Money that should have been held in sacred trust for the worthy poor and for the extension of principles of holy living throughout the world was selfishly absorbed in ambitious projects.

To glorify himself before the world, he sold his honor and integrity. The enormous revenues acquired through commerce were supplemented by heavy taxes. Pride, ambition, and indulgence bore fruit in cruelty and exaction. From the wisest and most merciful of rulers, he degenerated into a tyrant. Once the God-fearing guardian of the people, he became oppressive and despotic. Tax after tax was levied to support the luxurious court. The respect and admiration the people had cherished for their king was changed into abhorrence.

Attractive Women Prove a Snare

More and more the king came to regard luxury, self-indulgence, and the favor of the world as indications of greatness. Hundreds of beautiful women were brought from Egypt, Phoenicia, Edom, Moab, and other places. Their religion was idol worship, and they had been taught cruel and degrading rites. Infatuated with their beauty, the king neglected his duties.

His wives gradually prevailed on him to unite with them in their worship of false gods. "It came to pass, when Solomon was old, that his wives turned away his heart after other gods: and his heart was not perfect with the Lord his God, as was the heart of David his father. For Solomon went after Ashtoreth the goddess of the Zidonians, and after Milcom the abomination of the Ammonites." 1 Kings 11:4, 5.

Opposite Mount Moriah, Solomon erected imposing buildings as idolatrous shrines. To please his wives, he placed huge idols amidst the groves. There before the altars of heathen deities were practiced the most degrading rites of heathenism. See verse 7.

Solomon's separation from God was his ruin. He lost the mastery of himself. His moral efficiency was gone. His fine sensibilities became blunted, his conscience seared. He who in his early reign had displayed so much wisdom and sympathy in restoring a helpless babe to its unfortunate mother (see 1 Kings 3:16-28), fell so low as to erect an idol to whom living children were offered as sacrifices! He in later years departed so far from purity as to countenance licentious, revolting rites connected with the worship of Chemosh and Ashtoreth. He mistook license for liberty. He tried—but at what cost!—to unite light with darkness, good with evil, purity with impurity, Christ with Belial.

Solomon became a profligate, the tool and slave of others. His character became effeminate. His faith in God was supplanted by atheistic doubts. Unbelief weakened his principles and degraded his life. The justice and magnanimity of his early reign were changed to despotism and tyranny. God can do little for men who lose their sense of dependence on Him.

During these years of apostasy the enemy worked to confuse the Israelites in regard to true and false worship. Their keen sense of the holy character of God was deadened. They transferred their allegiance to the enemy of righteousness. It came to be a common practice to intermarry with idolaters. Polygamy was countenanced. In the lives of some, the pure religious service instituted by God was replaced by idolatry of the darkest hue.

God is fully able to keep us in the world, but we are not to be of the world. He watches over His children with a care that is measureless, but He requires undivided allegiance. "No man can serve two masters. . . . Ye cannot serve God and mammon." Matthew 6:24.

Men today are no stronger than Solomon; they are as prone to yield to the influences that caused his downfall. God today warns His children not to imperil their souls by affinity with the world. "Come out from among them," He pleads, "and be ye separate, . . . and touch not the unclean thing; and I will receive you, and will be a Father unto you, and ye shall be My sons and daughters, saith the Lord Almighty." 2 Corinthians 6:17, 18.

None of Us Is Wiser Than Solomon

Throughout the ages, riches and honor have been attended with peril to humility and spirituality. It is not the empty cup that we have difficulty in carrying; it is the cup full to the brim. Adversity may cause sorrow, but it is prosperity that is most dangerous to spiritual life. In the valley of humiliation, where men depend on God to guide their every step, there is comparative safety. But men who stand, as it were, on a lofty pinnacle and who are supposed to possess great wisdom—these are in gravest peril.

Pride, feeling no need, closes the heart against the infinite blessings of Heaven. He who makes self-glorification his aim will find himself destitute of the grace of God, through whose efficiency the truest riches and the most satisfying joys are won. But he who gives all and does all for Christ will know the fulfillment of the promise, "The blessing of the Lord, it maketh rich, and He addeth no sorrow with it." Proverbs 10:22. The Saviour banishes from the soul unrest and unholy ambition, changing enmity to love and unbelief to confidence. When He speaks to the soul, saying, "Follow Me," the spell of the world's enchantment is broken. At the sound of His voice, greed and ambition flee from the heart, and men arise, emancipated, to follow Him.

4 / How Solomon Missed His Chance

Among the causes that led Solomon into oppression was his failure to maintain the spirit of self-sacrifice. When Moses at Sinai told the people of the divine command, "Let them make Me a sanctuary; that I may dwell among them," the Israelites "came, everyone whose heart stirred him up, and everyone whom his spirit made willing," and brought offerings. For building the sanctuary a large amount of precious and costly material was required, but the Lord accepted only freewill offerings. "Of every man that giveth it willingly with his heart ye shall take My offering" was the command to the congregation. Exodus 25:8; 35:21; 25:2.

A similar call to self-sacrifice was made when David asked, "Who then is willing to consecrate his service this day unto the Lord?" 1 Chronicles 29:5. This call to consecration should ever have been kept in mind by those who erected the temple.

For the construction of the wilderness tabernacle, chosen men were endowed by God with special skill. "The Lord hath called by name Bezaleel . . . , of the tribe of Judah; and He hath filled him with the Spirit of God, in wisdom, in understanding, and in knowledge, and in all manner of workmanship . . . to work all manner of work, of the engraver, and of the cunning workman, and of the embroiderer, . . . and of the weaver. . . . Bezaleel and Aholiab, and every wise-hearted man, in whom the Lord put wisdom and understanding." Exodus 35:30 to 36:1. Heavenly intelligences cooperated with the workmen whom God Himself had chosen.

The descendants of these workmen inherited to a large degree the talents conferred on their forefathers. But gradually, almost imperceptibly, they lost their hold on God and their desire to serve Him unselfishly. They asked higher wages because of their superior skill as workmen in the finer arts. Often they found employment in the surrounding nations. In place of the noble spirit of their illustrious ancestors, they indulged a spirit of covetousness, of grasping for more and more. That their selfish desires might be gratified, they used their God-given skill in the service of heathen kings and lent their talent to perfecting works which were a dishonor to their Maker.

Among these men Solomon looked for a master workman to superintend the construction of the temple. Minute specifications regarding every portion of the sacred structure had been entrusted to the king, and he could have looked to God in faith for consecrated helpers who would have been granted special skill for doing the work required. But Solomon lost sight of this opportunity to exercise faith. He sent to the king of Tyre for a man "cunning to work in gold, and in silver, and in brass, and in iron, and in purple, and crimson, and blue, and that can skill to grave with the cunning men . . . in Judah and in Jerusalem." 2 Chronicles 2:7.

The Phoenician king sent Huram, "the son of a woman of the daughters of Dan, and his father was a man of Tyre." Verse 14. Huram was a descendant, on his mother's side, of Aholiab, to whom, hundreds of years before, God had given special wisdom for the construction of the tabernacle. Thus at the head of Solomon's workmen was placed a man who was not prompted by an unselfish desire to serve God. The fibers of his being were inwrought with the principles of selfishness.

Because of his unusual skill, Huram demanded large

wages. Gradually as his associates labored with him day after day, they compared his wages with their own, and they began to lose sight of the holy character of their work. The spirit of self-denial left them. The result was a demand for higher wages, which was granted.

Steps That Led to Apostasy

The baleful influences thus set in operation extended throughout the kingdom. High wages gave many the opportunity to indulge in luxury and extravagance. The poor were oppressed by the rich; the spirit of self-sacrifice was well-nigh lost. In the far-reaching effects of these influences may be traced one of the principal causes of the terrible apostasy of Solomon.

The sharp contrast between the spirit and motives of the people building the wilderness tabernacle and of those erecting Solomon's temple has a lesson of deep significance. Today selfishness rules the world. Seeking the highest position and the highest wage is rife. The joyous self-denial of the tabernacle workers is seldom met with. But this is the only spirit that should actuate the followers of Jesus. To those to whom He said, "Follow Me, and I will make you fishers of men" (Matthew 4:19) He offered no stated sum as a reward for their services. They were to share His self-denial and sacrifice.

Not for wages are we to labor. Unselfish devotion and a spirit of sacrifice always will be the first requisite of acceptable service. Our Lord designs that not one thread of selfishness shall be woven into His work. Into our efforts we are to bring the tact and skill, exactitude and wisdom that God required of the builders of the earthly tabernacle; yet we are to remember that the greatest talents or most splendid services are acceptable only when self is laid on the altar, a living, consuming sacrifice.

Another of the deviations from principle that led to Solomon's downfall was taking to himself the glory that belongs to God alone. From the day that Solomon was entrusted with building the temple to its completion, his avowed purpose was "to build an house for the name of the Lord God of Israel." 2 Chronicles 6:7. This purpose was recognized before the assembled hosts of Israel at the time of the dedication of the temple. One of the most touching portions of Solomon's prayer was his plea to God for the strangers that should come from countries afar to learn more of Him. In behalf of these strangers Solomon had petitioned: "Hear Thou, . . . and do according to all that the stranger calleth to Thee for: that all people of the earth may know . . . that this house, which I have builded, is called by Thy name." 1 Kings 8:43.

A Greater than Solomon was the designer of the temple. Those unacquainted with this fact naturally admired and praised Solomon as the architect and builder, but the king disclaimed any honor for its conception or erection.

Visit of the Queen of Sheba

Thus it was when the Queen of Sheba came to visit Solomon. Hearing of his wisdom and the magnificent temple he had built, she determined to "prove him with hard questions" and to see for herself his famous works. Attended by a retinue of servants she made the long journey to Jerusalem. "And when she was come to Solomon, she communed with him of all that was in her heart." Solomon taught her of the God of nature, of the great Creator, who dwells in heaven and rules over all. And "Solomon told her all her questions: there was not anything hid from the king, which he told her not." 1 Kings 10:1-3; see 2 Chronicles 9:1, 2.

"When the Queen of Sheba had seen all Solomon's wisdom, and the house that he had built, . . . there was no more spirit in her." She acknowledged, "It was a true report that I heard in mine own land of thy acts and of thy wisdom. Howbeit I believed not the words, until I came, and mine eyes had seen it: and, behold, the half was not told me: thy wisdom and prosperity exceedeth the fame which I heard." 1 Kings 10:4-7; see 2 Chronicles 9:3-6.

The queen had been so fully taught by Solomon as to the source of his wisdom and prosperity that she was constrained not to extol the human agent, but to exclaim, "Blessed be the Lord thy God, which delighteth in thee, to set thee on the throne of Israel: because the Lord loved Israel forever, therefore made He thee king, to do judgment and justice." 1 Kings 10:9. This is the impression that God designed should be made upon all peoples.

Had Solomon continued to turn attention from himself to the One who had given him wisdom, riches, and honor, what a history might have been his! But, raised to a pinnacle of greatness, Solomon became dizzy, lost his balance, and fell. Constantly extolled he finally permitted men to speak of him as the one most worthy of praise for the matchless splendor of the building planned and erected for the honor of the name of the Lord God of Israel.

Thus the temple of Jehovah came to be known throughout the nations as "Solomon's temple." The human agent had taken to himself the glory that belonged to the One "higher than the highest." Ecclesiastes 5:8. Even to this day the temple of which Solomon declared, "This house which I have built is called by Thy name" (2 Chronicles 6:33) is spoken of as "Solomon's temple."

Man cannot show greater weakness than by allowing men to ascribe to him the honor for gifts that are Heaven-bestowed. When we are faithful in exalting the name of God, our impulses are under divine supervision, and we are enabled to develop spiritual and intellectual power.

Jesus, the divine Master, taught His disciples to pray, "Our Father who art in heaven, hallowed be *Thy* name." Matthew 6:9, RSV, emphasis supplied. And they were to acknowledge, "*Thine* is . . . the glory."

So careful was the great Healer to direct attention from Himself to the Source of His power, that the multitude, "when they saw the dumb speaking, the maimed whole, the lame walking, and the blind seeing," did not glorify Him, but "glorified the God of Israel." Matthew 15:31, RSV.

"Let not the wise man glory in his wisdom, neither let the mighty man glory in his might, let not the rich man glory in his riches: but let him that glorieth glory in this, that he understandeth and knoweth Me, that I am the Lord which exercise loving-kindness, judgment, and righteousness, in the earth: for in these things I delight, saith the Lord." Jeremiah 9:23, 24.

Another Gross Perversion of God's Plan

The introduction of principles leading toward self-glorification was accompanied by another perversion of the divine plan. God had designed that from His people was to shine forth the glory of His law. For carrying out this design, He had caused the chosen nation to occupy a strategic position among the nations of earth. In the days of Solomon the kingdom extended from Hamath on the north to Egypt on the south, and from the Mediterranean Sea to the river Euphrates. Through this territory ran many natural highways of the world's commerce, and caravans from distant lands were constantly passing to and fro. Thus there was given to Solomon and his people opportunity to reveal to all nations the character of the King of kings and to teach them to reverence and obey Him. Through the sacrificial offerings, Christ was to be uplifted, that all who would might live.

Solomon should have used his God-given wisdom and influence in directing a great movement for the enlightenment of those who were ignorant of God and His truth. Multitudes would have been won, Israel would have been shielded from the evils practiced by the heathen, and the Lord would have been honored. But Solomon lost sight of this high purpose. He failed of enlightening those who were continually passing through his territory.

The missionary spirit that God had implanted in the hearts of all true Israelites was supplanted by a spirit of commercialism. The opportunities afforded by contact with many nations were used for personal aggrandizement. Solomon sought to strengthen his position politically by building fortified cities at the gateways of commerce. The commercial advantages of an outlet at the head of the Red Sea were developed by the construction of "a navy of ships . . . on the shore of the Red Sea, in the land of Edom." "The servants of Solomon" manned these vessels on voyages "to Ophir, and fetched from thence gold" and "great plenty of almug trees, and precious stones." 1 Kings 9:26-28; 10:11.

Revenue was greatly increased, but at what a cost! Through the cupidity of those to whom had been entrusted the oracles of God, the countless multitudes who thronged the highways of travel were allowed to remain in ignorance of Jehovah.

Christ and Solomon Contrasted

In striking contrast to Solomon, the Saviour, though possessing "all power," never used this power for self-aggrandizement. No dream of worldly greatness marred the perfection of His service for mankind. Those who enter the service of the Master Worker may well study His methods. He took advantage of the opportunities to be found along the great thoroughfares of travel.

In His journeys to and fro, Jesus dwelt at Capernaum. Situated on the highway from Damascus to Jerusalem and Egypt and to the Mediterranean Sea, it was well adapted to be the center of the Saviour's work. People from many lands passed through the city. There Jesus met with those of all nations and all ranks, and thus His lessons were carried to other countries. Interest was aroused in the prophecies pointing to the

Messiah, and His mission was brought before the world.

In our day, such opportunities are much greater than in the days of Israel. The thoroughfares of travel have multiplied a thousandfold. Like Christ, messengers of the Most High should take their position in these great thoroughfares, where they can meet the passing multitudes from all parts of the world. Hiding self in God, they are to present before others the precious truths of Holy Scripture that will take root and spring up unto life eternal.

Solemn are the lessons of Israel's failure when ruler and people turned from the high purpose they had been called to fulfill. Wherein they were weak, the representatives of heaven today must be strong; for on them devolves the finishing of the work committed to man, and of ushering in the day of final awards. Yet the same influences that prevailed against Israel when Solomon reigned are to be met with still. Only by the power of God can the victory be gained. The conflict calls for a spirit of self-denial, distrust of self, and dependence on God alone for the wise use of every opportunity for the saving of souls.

The Lord's blessing will attend His church as they advance unitedly, revealing to a world in the darkness of error the beauty of holiness as manifested in a Christlike spirit of self-sacrifice, in an exaltation of the divine rather than the human, and in loving service for those in need of the gospel.

5 / Solomon's Deep Repentance

Plain were the admonitions, wonderful the promises given to Solomon; yet of him it is recorded: "He kept not that which the Lord commanded." "His heart was turned from the Lord God of Israel, which had appeared unto him twice, and had commanded him concerning this thing, that he should not go after other gods." 1 Kings 11:10, 9. So hardened was his heart in transgression, that his case seemed well-nigh hopeless.

From the joy of divine communion, Solomon turned to the pleasures of sense. He says: "I made great works; I built houses and planted vineyards for myself; I made myself gardens and parks, and planted in them all kinds of fruit trees. . . . I bought male and female slaves. . . . I also gathered for myself silver and gold. . . . So I became great and surpassed all who were before me in Jerusalem. . . .

"And whatever my eyes desired I did not keep from them; I kept my heart from no pleasure. . . . Then I considered all that my hands had done and the toil I had spent in doing it, and behold, all was vanity and a striving after wind, and there was nothing to be gained under the sun." "So I hated life. . . . I hated all my toil in which I had toiled under the sun." Ecclesiastes 2:4-11, 17, 18, RSV.

By bitter experience, Solomon learned the emptiness of a life that seeks in earthly things its highest good. Gloomy and harassing thoughts troubled him night and day. There was no longer any joy or peace of mind, and the future was dark with despair.

Yet the Lord forsook him not. By reproof and severe judgments He sought to arouse the king to realize the sinfulness of his course. He permitted adversaries to harass and weaken the kingdom. "The Lord stirred up an adversary unto Solomon, Hadad the Edomite." And "Jeroboam . . . , Solomon's servant," "a mighty man of valor," "even he lifted up his hand against the king." 1 Kings 11:14, 26-28.

A Prophetic Warning Arouses Solomon

At last a prophet delivered to Solomon the startling message: "I will surely rend the kingdom from thee, and will give it to thy servant. Notwithstanding in thy days I will not do it for David thy father's sake: but I will rend it out of the hand of thy son." Verses 11, 12.

Awakened as from a dream by this sentence of judgment, Solomon began to see his folly. With mind and body enfeebled, he turned from earth's broken cisterns to drink once more at the fountain of life. Long had he been harassed by the fear of utter ruin because of inability to turn from folly; but now he discerned in the message given him a ray of hope. God stood ready to deliver him from a bondage more cruel than the grave, and from which he had no power to free himself.

Solomon Acknowledges His Sin

In penitence Solomon began to retrace his steps toward the exalted plane of purity and holiness from whence he had fallen. He could never hope to escape the blasting results of sin, but he would humbly confess the error of his ways and warn others lest they be lost irretrievably because of the evil influences he had set in operation. The true penitent thinks of those who have been led into evil by his course and tries to lead them back to the true path. He does not gloss over his wayward course, but lifts the danger signal that others may take warning.

Solomon acknowledged that "the heart of the sons of men is full of evil, and madness is in their heart."

"Though a sinner do evil an hundred times, and his days be prolonged, yet surely I know that it shall be well with them that fear God, . . . but it shall not be well with the wicked, neither shall he prolong his days." Ecclesiastes 9:3; 8:12, 13.

By inspiration the king recorded the history of his wasted years with their lessons of warning. And thus his lifework was not wholly lost. With lowliness Solomon in his later years "taught the people knowledge, weighing and studying and arranging proverbs with great care." He "sought to find pleasing words, and uprightly he wrote words of truth." Ecclesiastes 12:9, 10, RSV.

"Fear God, and keep His commandments," he wrote, "for this is the whole duty of man. For God shall bring every work into judgment, with every secret thing, whether it be good, or whether it be evil." Verses 13, 14.

Counsel to Youths

Solomon's later writings reveal that as he realized more and more the wickedness of his course, he gave special attention to warning the youth against the errors that had led him to squander Heaven's choicest gifts. With sorrow and shame he confessed that in the prime of manhood, when he should have found God his comfort, his support, his life, he put idolatry in the place of the worship of God. And now his yearning desire was to save others from the bitter experience through which he had passed.

With touching pathos he wrote concerning the privileges before the youth: "Rejoice, O young man, in thy youth; and let thy heart cheer thee in the days of thy youth, walk in the ways of thine heart, and in the sight of thine eyes: but know thou, that for all these things God will bring thee into judgment. Therefore remove sorrow from thy heart, and put away evil from thy flesh: for childhood and youth are vanity." Ecclesiastes 11:9, 10.

Remember now thy Creator in the days of
  thy youth,
While the evil days come not,
Nor the years draw nigh,
When thou shalt say, I have no pleasure in them.
              Ecclesiastes 12:1

The life of Solomon is full of warning. When he should have been in character as a sturdy oak, he fell under the power of temptation. When his strength should have been the firmest, he was found to be the weakest. In watchfulness and prayer is the only safety for both young and old. In the battle with inward sin and outward temptation, even the wise and powerful Solomon was vanquished. His failure teaches that whatever a man's intellectual qualities may be and however faithfully he may have served God in the past, he can never trust his own wisdom and integrity.

It is as true now as when the words were spoken to Israel of obedience to God's commandments: "This is your wisdom and your understanding in the sight of the nations." Deuteronomy 4:6. Here is the only safeguard for individual integrity, the purity of the home, or the stability of the nation. "The statutes of the Lord are right," and "he that doeth these things shall never be moved." Psalm 19:8; 15:5.

Only Obedience Keeps From Apostasy

Those who heed the warnings of Solomon's apostasy will shun the first approach of those sins that overcame him. Only obedience to the requirements of Heaven will keep man from apostasy. So long as life shall last, there will be need of guarding the affections and passions with a firm purpose. Not one moment can we be secure except as we rely upon God, the life hidden with Christ. Watchfulness and prayer are the safeguards of purity.

All who enter the City of God will enter through the strait gate, for "there shall in no wise enter into it anything that defileth." Revelation 21:27. But none who have fallen need give up to despair. Aged men, once honored of God, may have defiled their souls, sacrificing virtue on the altar of lust; but if they repent, forsake sin, and turn to God, there is hope for them. "Let the wicked forsake his way, and the unrighteous man his thoughts: and let him return unto the Lord, and He will have mercy upon him; and to our God, for He will abundantly pardon." Isaiah 55:7. God hates sin, but He loves the sinner.

The Effects of Solomon's Apostasy

Solomon's repentance was sincere; but the harm that his example had wrought could not be undone. During his apostasy there were in the kingdom men who maintained their purity and loyalty, but the forces of evil set in operation by idolatry and worldly practices could not easily be stayed by the penitent king. His influence was greatly weakened. Many hesitated to place full confidence in his leadership. The king could never hope entirely to destroy the baleful influence of his wrong deeds. Emboldened by his apostasy, many continued to do evil. And in the downward course of many of the rulers who followed him may be traced the sad influence of the prostitution of his God-given powers.

In the anguish of bitter reflection on his course Solomon declared, "Wisdom is better than weapons of war: but one sinner destroyeth much good." "Dead flies cause the ointment of the apothecary to send forth a stinking savor: so doth a little folly him that is in reputation for wisdom and honor." Ecclesiastes 9:18; 10:1.

Beyond our knowledge or control, our influence tells on others in blessing or cursing. It may be heavy with the gloom of discontent and selfishness, or poisonous with the deadly taint of cherished sin; or it may be charged with the life-giving power of faith, courage, and hope, and sweet with the fragrance of love. But potent for good or for ill it will be.

One soul misled—who can estimate the loss! And yet one rash act, one thoughtless word on our part, may exert so deep an influence on the life of another that it will prove the ruin of the soul. One blemish on the soul may turn many away from Christ.

Every act, every word, will bear fruit. Every deed of kindness, of obedience, of self-denial, will reproduce itself in others, and through them in still others. So every act of envy, malice, or dissension will spring up in a "root of bitterness" whereby many shall be defiled. Hebrews 12:15. Thus the sowing of good and evil goes on for time and for eternity.

6 / Rehoboam's Arrogance: The Rending of the Kingdom

"Solomon slept with his fathers, . . . and Rehoboam his son reigned in his stead." 1 Kings 11:43.

Soon after his accession to the throne, Rehoboam went to Shechem, where he expected to receive formal recognition from all the tribes. "To Shechem were all Israel come to make him king." 2 Chronicles 10:1. Among those present was Jeroboam, who during Solomon's reign had been known as "a mighty man of valor," and to whom the prophet Ahijah had delivered the startling message, "Thus saith the Lord, . . . I will rend the kingdom out of the hand of Solomon, and will give ten tribes to thee." 1 Kings 11:28, 31.

The Lord through His messenger had spoken plainly to Jeroboam. This division must take place, He had declared, because Solomon "has forsaken Me, . . . and has not walked in My ways, doing what is right in My sight and keeping My statutes and My ordinances, as David his father did." Verse 33, RSV. Yet Jeroboam had also been instructed that the kingdom was not to be divided before the close of Solomon's reign: "I will make him prince all the days of his life for David My servant's sake, whom I chose, because he kept My commandments and My statutes: but I will take the kingdom out of his son's hand, and will give it unto thee, even ten tribes." Verses 34, 35.

Although Solomon had longed to prepare Rehoboam to meet with wisdom the crisis foretold by the prophet of God, he had never been able to exert a strong influence for good over his son, whose early training had been grossly neglected. Rehoboam had received from his mother, an Ammonitess, the stamp of a vacillating character. At times he endeavored to serve God, but at last he yielded to the evil influences that had surrounded him from infancy. In the mistakes of Rehoboam's life and in his final apostasy is revealed the fearful result of Solomon's union with idolatrous women.

The tribes had long suffered under the oppressive measures of their former ruler. Extravagance had led Solomon to tax the people heavily and to require much menial service. Before the coronation of a new ruler, the leading men determined to ascertain whether it was the purpose of Solomon's son to lessen these burdens. "Jeroboam and all Israel came and spake to Rehoboam, saying, Thy father made our yoke grievous: now therefore ease thou somewhat the grievous servitude of thy father, and his heavy yoke that he put upon us, and we will serve thee."

Desirous of taking counsel with his advisers before outlining his policy, Rehoboam answered, "Come again unto me after three days. And the people departed. And King Rehoboam took counsel with the old men that had stood before Solomon his father while he yet lived, saying, What counsel give ye me to return answer to this people? And they spake unto him, saying, If thou be kind to this people, and please them, and speak good words to them they will be thy servants forever." 2 Chronicles 10:3-7.

The Mistake That Could Never Be Undone

Dissatisfied, Rehoboam turned to younger men with whom he had associated during his youth: "What counsel give ye that we may answer this people, who have spoken to me, saying, Make the yoke which thy father did put upon us lighter?" 1 Kings 12:9. The young men suggested that he deal sternly with his subjects and make plain to them that he would brook no interference with his personal wishes.

Thus it came to pass that on the day appointed for Rehoboam to make a statement concerning his policy, he "answered the people roughly, . . . saying, My father made your yoke heavy, and I will add to your yoke: my father also chastised you with whips, but I will chastise you with scorpions." Verses 13, 14. Rehoboam's expressed determination to add to the oppression of Solomon's reign was in direct conflict with God's plan for Israel. In this unfeeling attempt to exercise power, the king and his counselors revealed pride of position and authority.

There were many who had become thoroughly aroused over the oppressive measures of Solomon's reign, and these now felt that they could not do otherwise than rebel against the house of David. "When all Israel saw that the king hearkened not unto them, the people answered the king, saying, What portion have we in David? . . . to your tents, O Israel: now see to thine own house, David. So Israel departed unto their tents." Verse 16.

The breach created by the rash speech of Rehoboam proved irreparable. The twelve tribes of Israel were divided, Judah and Benjamin composing the southern kingdom of Judah, under Rehoboam; while the ten northern tribes formed a separate government, the kingdom of Israel, with Jeroboam as ruler. Thus was fulfilled the prediction of the prophet concerning the rending of the kingdom. "It was a turn of affairs brought about by the Lord." Verse 15, RSV.

When Rehoboam saw the ten tribes withdrawing allegiance from him, he was aroused to action. Through Adoram, one of the influential men of his kingdom, he made an effort to conciliate them. But "all Israel stoned him with stones, that he died." Startled, "King Rehoboam made speed to get him up into his chariot, to flee to Jerusalem." Verse 18.

At Jerusalem "he assembled all the house of Judah, with the tribe of Benjamin, an hundred and fourscore thousand chosen men, which were warriors, to fight against the house of Israel, to bring the kingdom again to Rehoboam. . . . But the word of God came unto Shemaiah, . . . Thus saith the Lord, Ye shall not go up, nor fight against your brethren the children of Israel: return every man to his house; for this thing is from Me. They hearkened therefore to the word of the Lord.'' Verses 21-24.

For three years Rehoboam tried to profit by his sad experience, and in this effort he was prospered. He built fortified cities ''and made them exceeding strong.'' 2 Chronicles 11:12. But the secret of Judah's prosperity during the first years of Rehoboam's reign lay in recognition of God as the supreme Ruler. It was this that placed the tribes of Judah and Benjamin on vantage ground. ''From all the tribes of Israel,'' the record reads, ''those who had set their hearts to seek the Lord God of Israel came . . . to Jerusalem to sacrifice to the Lord, the God of their fathers. They strengthened the kingdom of Judah, and for three years they made Rehoboam the son of Solomon secure, for they walked for three years in the way of David and Solomon.'' 2 Chronicles 11:16, 17, RSV.

Rehoboam Fails

But Solomon's successor failed to exert a strong influence for loyalty to Jehovah. He was naturally headstrong, confident, self-willed, and inclined to idolatry; nevertheless, had he placed his trust wholly in God, he would have developed steadfast faith and submission to the divine requirements. But as time passed, the king put his trust in the power of position and in the strongholds he had fortified. Little by little he gave way to inherited weaknesses until he threw his influence wholly on the side of idolatry. ''When Rehoboam had established the kingdom, and had strengthened himself, he forsook the law of the Lord, and all Israel with him.'' 2 Chronicles 12:1.

The people whom God had chosen to stand as a light to the surrounding nations were seeking to become like the nations about them. As with Solomon, so with Rehoboam—the influence of wrong example led many astray.

God did not allow the apostasy of Judah's ruler to remain unpunished. "In the fifth year of King Rehoboam, because they had been unfaithful to the Lord, Shishak king of Egypt came up against Jerusalem with twelve hundred chariots and sixty thousand horsemen. And the people were without number who came with him from Egypt. . . . And he took the fortified cities of Judah, and came as far as Jerusalem.

"Then Shemaiah the prophet came to Rehoboam and to the princes of Judah, who had gathered at Jerusalem because of Shishak, and said to them, 'Thus says the Lord, "You abandoned Me, so I have abandoned you to the hand of Shishak." ' " Verses 2-5, RSV. In the losses sustained by the invasion of Shishak, the people recognized the hand of God and for a time humbled themselves. "So Shishak king of Egypt came up against Jerusalem; he took away the treasures of the house of the Lord and the treasures of the king's house; he took away everything. He also took away the shields of gold which Solomon had made; and King Rehoboam made in their stead shields of bronze. . . . And when he humbled himself the wrath of the Lord turned from him, so as not to make a complete destruction; moreover, conditions were good in Judah." Verses 9-12, RSV.

The Aftereffects of Rehoboam's Apostasy

But as the nation prospered once more, many turned again to idolatry. Among these was King Rehoboam himself. Forgetting the lesson that God had endeavored to teach him, he relapsed into the sins that had brought judgments on the nation. After a few inglorious years, "Rehoboam slept with his fathers, and was buried in the City of David: and Abijah his son reigned in his stead." Verse 16.

At times during the centuries that followed, the

throne of David was occupied by men of moral worth, and under the rulership of these sovereigns the blessings resting on Judah were extended to the surrounding nations. But the seeds of evil already springing up when Rehoboam ascended the throne were never to be wholly uprooted, and at times the once-favored people of God were to fall so low as to become a byword among the heathen.

Notwithstanding these idolatrous practices, God in mercy would do everything in His power to save the divided kingdom from utter ruin. And as the years rolled on and His purpose concerning Israel seemed utterly thwarted by men inspired by satanic agencies, He still manifested His beneficent designs through the captivity and restoration of the chosen nation.

The rending of the kingdom was but the beginning of a wonderful history, wherein are revealed the long-sufferance and tender mercy of God. And the worshipers of idols were at last to learn the lesson that false gods are powerless to uplift and save. Only in allegiance to the living God can man find rest and peace.

7 / Jeroboam Leads Israel Back to Idol Worship

Under the rulership of Solomon, Jeroboam had shown aptitude and sound judgment; the years of faithful service fitted him to rule with discretion. But Jeroboam failed to make God his trust.

His greatest fear was that his subjects might be won over by the ruler occupying the throne of David. He reasoned that if the ten tribes should often visit the ancient seat of the monarchy, where the temple services were still conducted as in Solomon's reign, many might renew their allegiance to the government at Jerusalem. He determined by one bold stroke to lessen this probability. He would create within his newly formed kingdom two centers of worship, one at Bethel, the other at Dan. In these places the ten tribes should be invited to worship God, instead of at Jerusalem.

In arranging this transfer, Jeroboam thought to appeal to the imagination of the Israelites by some visible representation to symbolize the presence of the invisible God. Accordingly he placed two calves of gold within shrines at the centers of worship. In this, he violated the plain command: "Thou shalt not make unto thee any graven image. . . . Thou shalt not bow down thyself to them, nor serve them." Exodus 20:4, 5. He failed to consider the great peril to which he was exposing the Israelites by setting before them the symbol with which their ancestors had been familiar during centuries of Egyptian bondage. His purpose of inducing the northern tribes to discontinue annual visits to the Holy City led him to adopt the most imprudent of measures. "It is too much for you to go up to Jerusalem," he urged; "behold thy gods, O Israel, which brought thee up out of the land of Egypt." 1 Kings 12:28.

The king tried to persuade the Levites within his realm to serve as priests in the new shrines at Bethel and Dan, but in this he failed. He therefore elevated to the priesthood men from "the lowest of the people." Verse 31. Alarmed, many of the faithful fled to Jerusalem, where they might worship in harmony with the divine requirements.

The King's Defiance Rebuked

The king's bold defiance of God in setting aside divinely appointed institutions was not allowed to pass unrebuked. During the dedication of the strange altar at Bethel, there appeared before him a man of God from Judah, sent to denounce him for presuming to introduce new forms of worship. The prophet "cried against the altar . . . , and said, . . . Behold, a child shall be born unto the house of David, Josiah by name; and upon thee shall he offer the priests of the high places that burn incense upon thee, and men's bones shall be burnt upon thee.

"And he gave a sign the same day, saying, This is the sign which the Lord hath spoken; Behold, the altar shall be rent, and the ashes that are upon it shall be poured out." Immediately the altar "was rent, and the ashes poured out from the altar, according to the sign which the man of God had given by the word of the Lord." 1 Kings 13:2, 3, 5.

On seeing this, Jeroboam attempted to restrain the one who had delivered the message. In wrath he cried out, "Lay hold on him." His impetuous act met with swift rebuke. The hand outstretched against the messenger of Jehovah suddenly became withered and could not be withdrawn. Terror-stricken, the king appealed to the prophet: "Entreat now the face of the Lord thy God," he pleaded, "and pray for me, that my hand may be restored me again. And the man of God besought the Lord, and the king's hand was restored him again, and became as it was before." Verses 4, 6. The king of Israel should have been led to renounce his wicked purposes, which were turning people away from the true worship of God. But he hardened his heart and determined to follow a way of his own choosing.

The Lord seeks to save, not to destroy. He gives His chosen messengers a holy boldness, that those who hear may be brought to repentance. How firmly the man of God rebuked the king! In no other way could the evils have been rebuked. The messengers of the Lord are to stand unflinchingly for the right. So long as they put their trust in God, they need not fear, for He who gives them their commission gives them also the assurance of His protecting care.

How a Prophet Was Tricked Into Disobeying

The prophet was about to return to Judea, when Jeroboam said to him, "Come home with me, and refresh thyself, and I will give thee a reward."

"If thou wilt give me half thine house," the prophet replied, "I will not go in with thee, neither will I eat bread nor drink water in this place: for so was it charged me by the word of the Lord, saying, Eat no bread, nor drink water, nor turn again by the same way that thou camest." 1 Kings 13:7-9.

While traveling home by another route, the prophet was overtaken by an aged man who claimed to be a prophet and who falsely declared, "I am a prophet also as thou art; and an angel spake unto me by the word of the Lord, saying, Bring him back with thee into thine house, that he may eat bread and drink water." Again and again the lie was repeated until the man of God was persuaded to return.

God permitted the prophet to suffer the penalty of transgression. While he and the one who had invited him were sitting together at the table, the false prophet "cried unto the man of God that came from Judah, saying, Thus saith the Lord, Forasmuch as thou hast disobeyed the mouth of the Lord, and hast not kept the commandment which the Lord thy God commanded thee, . . . thy carcass shall not come unto the sepulcher of thy fathers." Verses 18, 21, 22.

This prophecy of doom was soon fulfilled. "After he had eaten bread, and after he had drunk, that he saddled for him the ass. . . . And when he was gone, a lion met him by the way, and slew him: and his carcass was cast in the way, and the ass stood by it, the lion also stood by the carcass. And behold, men passed by, and saw the carcass cast in the way, . . . and they came and told it in the city where the old prophet dwelt. And when the prophet that brought him back from the way heard thereof, he said, It is the man of God, who was disobedient unto the word of the Lord." Verses 23-26.

If, after disobeying, the prophet had been permitted to go on in safety, the king would have used this to vindicate his own disobedience. The rent altar, the palsied arm, and the terrible fate of the one who dared disobey an express command of the Lord—these judgments should have warned Jeroboam not to persist in wrongdoing. But, far from repenting, Jeroboam not only sinned greatly himself, but "made Israel to sin"; and "this thing became sin unto the house of Jeroboam, even to cut it off, and to destroy it." 1 Kings 14:16; 13:34.

God's Judgment on Jeroboam

Toward the close of a troubled reign of twenty-two years, Jeroboam met with disastrous defeat in a war with Abijah, the successor of Rehoboam. "Neither did Jeroboam recover strength again in the days of Abijah: and the Lord struck him, and he died." 2 Chronicles 13:20.

The apostasy introduced during Jeroboam's reign finally resulted in the utter ruin of the kingdom of Israel. Even before the death of Jeroboam, Ahijah, the aged prophet who many years before had predicted the elevation of Jeroboam to the throne, declared: "The Lord shall . . . root up Israel out of this good land. . . . And shall give Israel up because of the sins of Jeroboam, who did sin, and who made Israel to sin." 1 Kings 14:15, 16.

Yet the Lord did all He could to lead Israel back to allegiance to Him. Through long, dark years when ruler after ruler stood up in bold defiance of Heaven, God sent message after message to His backslidden people. Through His prophets He gave them every opportunity to return to Him. Elijah and Elisha were to live and labor, and the tender appeals of Hosea, Amos, and Obadiah were to be heard in the land. Never was the kingdom of Israel left without noble witnesses to the mighty power of God to save from sin. Through these faithful ones the eternal purpose of Jehovah was finally to be fulfilled.

8 / National Apostasy Brings National Ruin

From Jeroboam's death to Elijah's appearance before Ahab Israel suffered a steady spiritual decline. The larger number of the people rapidly lost sight of their duty to serve the living God and adopted practices of idolatry.

Nadab, the son of Jeroboam, who occupied the throne of Israel a few months, was suddenly slain with all his kindred in the line of succession, "according unto the saying of the Lord, which He spake by His servant Ahijah the Shilonite: because of the sins of Jeroboam which he sinned, and which he made Israel sin." 1 Kings 15:29, 30.

The idolatrous worship introduced by Jeroboam had brought the retributive judgments of Heaven, and yet the rulers who followed—Baasha, Elah, Zimri, and Omri—continued the same fatal course of evildoing.

King Asa's Good Rule

During the greater part of this time, Asa was ruling in Judah. He "did that which was good and right in the eyes of the Lord his God: for he took away the altars of the strange gods, . . . and commanded Judah to seek the Lord God of their fathers, and to do the law and the commandment. . . . And the kingdom was quiet before him." 2 Chronicles 14:2-5.

The faith of Asa was put to a severe test when "Zerah the Ethiopian with an host of a thousand thousand, and three hundred chariots" invaded his kingdom. Verse 9. In this crisis Asa did not put his trust in the "fenced cities in Judah" that he had built, with "walls, and towers, gates, and bars," nor in the "mighty men of valor" in his army. Verses 6-8. The king's trust was in Jehovah. Setting his forces in battle array, he sought the help of God.

A Signal Victory Gained by Trusting God

The opposing armies now stood face to face. Had every sin been confessed? Had Judah full confidence in God's power to deliver? From every human viewpoint the vast host from Egypt would sweep everything before it. But in time of peace Asa had not been giving himself to amusement and pleasure; he had been preparing for any emergency. He had an army trained for conflict; he had endeavored to lead his people to make peace with God. Now his faith did not weaken.

Having sought the Lord in prosperity, the king could now rely on Him in adversity. "It is nothing with Thee to help," he pleaded, "whether with many, or with them that have no power: help us, O Lord our God; for we rest on Thee, and in Thy name we go against this multitude." Verse 11.

King Asa's faith was signally rewarded. "The Lord smote the Ethiopians before Asa, and before Judah; and the Ethiopians fled. . . . They were destroyed before the Lord, and before His host." Verses 12, 13.

As the victorious armies were returning to Jerusalem, "Azariah the son of Oded . . . went out to meet Asa, and said unto him, . . . The Lord is with you, while ye be with Him; and if ye seek Him, He will be found of you; but if ye forsake Him, He will forsake you." "Be ye strong therefore, and let not your hands be weak: for your work shall be rewarded." 2 Chronicles 15:1, 2, 7.

Greatly encouraged, Asa soon led out in a second reformation. He "put away the abominable idols out of all the land of Judah and Benjamin." "And they entered into a covenant to seek the Lord God of their fathers with all their heart and with all their soul." "And

He was found of them: and the Lord gave them rest round about." Verses 8, 12, 15.

Asa's long record of faithful service was marred by some mistakes. When, on one occasion, the king of Israel entered Judah and seized Ramah, a city only five miles from Jerusalem, Asa sought deliverance by an alliance with Benhadad, king of Syria. This failure to trust God was sternly rebuked by Hanani the prophet, who appeared before Asa with the message: "Were not the Ethiopians and the Lubims a huge host, with very many chariots and horsemen? yet, because thou didst rely on the Lord, He delivered them into thine hand. . . . Thou hast done foolishly: therefore from henceforth thou shalt have wars." 2 Chronicles 16:8, 9.

Instead of humbling himself before God, "Asa was wroth with the seer, and put him in a prison house. . . . And Asa oppressed some of the people at the same time." Verse 10.

"In the thirty and ninth year of his reign" Asa was "diseased in his feet, until his disease was exceeding great: yet in his disease he sought not to the Lord, but to the physicians." Verse 12. The king died in the forty-first year of his reign and was succeeded by Jehoshaphat, his son.

Ahab's Wicked Reign Begins

Two years before the death of Asa, Ahab began to rule in Israel. From the beginning his reign was marked by a strange, terrible apostasy. He "did more to provoke the Lord God of Israel to anger than all the kings of Israel that were before him," acting "as if it had been a light thing for him to walk in the sins of Jeroboam the son of Nebat." 1 Kings 16:33, 31. He boldly led the people into the grossest heathenism.

Taking to wife Jezebel, "the daughter of Ethbaal king of the Zidonians" and high priest of Baal, Ahab "served Baal, and worshiped him. And reared up an altar for Baal in the house of Baal, which he had built in Samaria." Verses 31, 32.

Under the leadership of Jezebel, Ahab erected heathen altars in many "high places," until well-nigh all Israel were following after Baal. "There was none like unto Ahab," who "did sell himself to work wickedness in the sight of the Lord, whom Jezebel his wife stirred up." 1 Kings 21:25. Ahab's marriage with an idolatrous woman resulted disastrously both to himself and to the nation. His character was easily molded by the determined spirit of Jezebel. His selfish nature was incapable of appreciating the mercies of God to Israel and his own obligations as guardian and leader of the chosen people.

Under Ahab's rule Israel wandered far from the living God. The dark shadow of apostasy covered the whole land. Images of Baalim and Ashtoreth were everywhere. Idolatrous temples were multiplied. The air was polluted with the smoke of sacrifices offered to false gods. Hill and vale resounded with the drunken cries of a heathen priesthood who sacrificed to the sun, moon, and stars.

The people were taught that these idol gods were deities, ruling by their mystic power the elements of earth, fire, and water. The running brooks, the streams of living water, the gentle dew, the showers of rain which caused the fields to bring forth abundantly—all were ascribed to the favor of Baal and Ashtoreth, instead of to the Giver of every good and perfect gift. The people forgot that the living God controlled the sun, the clouds of heaven, and all the powers of nature.

Through faithful messengers the Lord sent repeated warnings to the apostate king and the people, but in vain were these words of reproof. Captivated by the gorgeous display and the fascinating rites of idol worship, the people gave themselves up to the intoxicating, degrading pleasures of sensual worship. The light so graciously given them had become darkness.

Never before had the chosen people of God fallen so low in apostasy. Of the "prophets of Baal" there were four hundred and fifty, besides four hundred "prophets of the groves." 1 Kings 18:19. Nothing short of the miracle-working power of God could preserve the nation from utter destruction. Israel had voluntarily separated from Jehovah, yet the Lord in compassion still yearned after those who had been led into sin, and He was about to send them one of the mightiest of His prophets.

9 / Elijah Confronts King Ahab

Among the mountains east of Jordan there dwelt a man of faith and prayer whose fearless ministry was to check the rapid spread of apostasy. Occupying no high station in life, Elijah nevertheless entered on his mission confident in God's purpose to give him abundant success. His was the voice of one crying in the wilderness to rebuke sin and press back the tide of evil. And, while he came as a reprover of sin, his message offered balm to sin-sick souls.

As Elijah saw Israel going deeper into idolatry, his indignation was aroused. God had done great things for His people "that they might observe His statutes, and keep His laws." Psalm 105:45. But unbelief was fast separating the chosen nation from the Source of their strength. Viewing this apostasy from his mountain retreat, in anguish of soul Elijah besought God to arrest the people in their wicked course, to visit them with judgments if need be, that they might be brought to repentance.

Elijah's prayer was answered. The time had come when God must speak by means of judgments. The worshipers of Baal claimed that dew and rain came from the ruling forces of nature, and that through the creative energy of the sun the earth was made to bring forth abundantly. The apostate tribes of Israel were to be shown the folly of trusting to Baal for temporal blessings. Until they should turn to God with repen-

This chapter is based on 1 Kings 17:1-7.

tance, there should fall upon the land neither dew nor rain.

To Elijah was entrusted the mission of delivering to Ahab Heaven's message of judgment. He did not seek to be the Lord's messenger; the word of the Lord came to him. To obey the divine summons seemed to invite swift destruction at the hand of the wicked king, but the prophet set out at once and traveled night and day until he reached the palace. Clad in the coarse garments usually worn by the prophets, he passed the guards apparently unnoticed and stood for a moment before the astonished king.

Elijah made no apology for his abrupt appearance. A Greater than the ruler of Israel had commissioned him to speak. "As the Lord God of Israel liveth, before whom I stand," he declared, "there shall not be dew nor rain these years, but according to my word."

On his way to Samaria, Elijah had passed by ever-flowing streams and stately forests that seemed beyond the reach of drought. The prophet might have wondered how streams that had never ceased their flow could become dry, or how those hills and valleys could be burned with drought. But he gave no place to doubt. God's word could not fail. Like a thunderbolt from a clear sky, the message of judgment fell on the ears of the wicked king; but before Ahab could recover from his astonishment, Elijah disappeared. And the Lord went before him, making plain the way. "Turn thee eastward, and hide thyself by the brook Cherith, that is before Jordan. And it shall be, that thou shalt drink of the brook; and I have commanded the ravens to feed thee."

The king made diligent inquiry, but the prophet was not to be found. Queen Jezebel, angered over the message that had locked up the treasures of heaven, lost no time in conferring with the priests of Baal, who united in cursing the prophet and defying Jehovah. Tidings of Elijah's denunciation of the sins of Israel and his prophecy of swift-coming punishment quickly spread throughout the land. The fears of some were aroused, but in general the heavenly message was received with scorn and ridicule.

The prophet's words went into immediate effect. The earth, unrefreshed by dew or rain, became dry, and vegetation withered. Streams never known to fail began to decrease, and brooks to dry up. Yet people were urged by their leaders to have confidence in Baal and to set aside as idle words the prophecy of Elijah. Fear not the God of Elijah, they urged. It is Baal that brings the harvest and provides for man and beast.

Priests of Baal Keep the People Deceived

Against the assurances of hundreds of idolatrous priests, the prophecy of Elijah stood alone: If Baal could still give dew and rain, then let the king of Israel worship him and the people say that he is God. Determined to keep the people in deception, the priests of Baal continued to call on their gods night and day to refresh the earth. With a zeal and perseverance worthy of a better cause they lingered round their pagan altars and night after night prayed earnestly for rain. But no clouds appeared in the heavens, no dew or rain refreshed the thirsty earth.

A year passed. The scorching heat of the sun destroyed what little vegetation had survived. Streams dried up, and lowing herds and bleating flocks wandered in distress. Once-flourishing fields became like desert sands. The forest trees, gaunt skeletons of nature, afforded no shade. Dust storms blinded the eyes and nearly stopped the breath. Hunger and thirst told on man and beast with fearful mortality. Famine, with all its horrors, came closer and still closer.

Yet Israel repented not nor learned the lesson that God would have them learn. Proudhearted, enamored of their false worship, they began to cast about for some other cause to which to attribute their sufferings.

Unyielding in her determination to defy the God of heaven, Jezebel with nearly the whole of Israel united in denouncing Elijah as the cause of their misery. If only he could be put out of the way, their troubles would end. Urged on by the queen, Ahab instituted a diligent search for the prophet. To surrounding nations he sent messengers to seek for the man whom he hated, yet feared; and in his anxiety he required of these kingdoms an oath that they knew nothing of the whereabouts of the prophet. But the search was in vain. The prophet was safe from the malice of the king.

Failing in her efforts against Elijah, Jezebel determined to slay all the prophets of Jehovah. The infuriated woman massacred many; but not all perished. Obadiah, the governor of Ahab's house, "took an hundred prophets," and at the risk of his own life, "hid them by fifty in a cave, and fed them with bread and water." 1 Kings 18:4.

Drought and Famine for Two Years

The second year passed, and still the pitiless heavens gave no sign of rain. Fathers and mothers were forced to see their children die. Yet apostate Israel seemed unable to discern in their suffering a call to repentance, a divine interposition to save them from taking the fatal step beyond the boundary of Heaven's forgiveness.

The apostasy of Israel was an evil more dreadful than all the horrors of famine. God was trying to help His people recover their lost faith, and He must needs bring on them great affliction. "Have I any pleasure at all that the wicked should die? saith the Lord God: and not that he should return from his ways, and live?" "I have no pleasure in the death of him that dieth, saith the Lord God: wherefore turn yourselves, and live ye." Ezekiel 18:23, 32.

God had sent messengers to Israel, with appeals to return to their allegiance. But their anger had been aroused against the messengers, and now they regarded with intense hatred the prophet Elijah. If only he should fall into their hands, gladly they would deliver him to Jezebel—as if by silencing his voice they could stay the fulfillment of his words!

For stricken Israel there was but one remedy—turning away from the sins that had brought upon them the chastening hand of the Almighty. To them had been given the assurance, "If I shut up heaven that there be no rain, or if I command the locusts to devour the land, or if I send pestilence among My people; if My people, which are called by My name, shall humble themselves, and pray, and seek My face, and turn from their wicked ways; then will I hear from heaven, and will forgive their sin, and will heal their land." 2 Chronicles 7:13, 14. To bring to pass this blessed result, God continued to withhold the dew and the rain until a decided reformation should take place.

10 / The Voice of Stern Rebuke

Hidden in the mountains by the brook Cherith, for many months Elijah was miraculously provided with food. When, because of the continued drought, the brook became dry, God told His servant: "Arise, get thee to Zarephath [known in New Testament times as Sarepta]. . . : behold, I have commanded a widow woman there to sustain thee."

This woman was not an Israelite. She had never had the privileges that the chosen people of God had enjoyed, but she was a believer in the true God and had walked in all the light shining on her pathway. And now, when there was no safety for Elijah in Israel, God sent him to this woman to find asylum in her home.

"So he arose and went to Zarephath, and when he came to the gate of the city, behold, the widow woman was there gathering of sticks: and he called to her, and said, Fetch me, I pray thee, a little water in a vessel, that I may drink. And . . . bring me, I pray thee, a morsel of bread."

In this poverty-stricken home the famine pressed sore, and the widow feared that she must give up the struggle to sustain life. But in her dire extremity she bore witness to her faith. In response to Elijah's request she said, "As the Lord thy God liveth, I have not a cake, but an handful of meal in a barrel, and a little oil in a cruse: and, behold, I am gathering two sticks, that

This chapter is based on 1 Kings 17:8-24; 18:1-18.

I may go in and dress it for me and my son, that we may eat it, and die. And Elijah said unto her, Fear not; go and do as thou hast said: but make me thereof a little cake first, and bring it unto me, and after make for thee and for thy son. For thus saith the Lord God of Israel, The barrel of meal shall not waste, neither shall the cruse of oil fail, until the day that the Lord sendeth rain upon the earth."

No greater test of faith could have been required. Regardless of the suffering that might result to herself and child and trusting in the God of Israel to supply her need, the widow met this supreme test of hospitality by doing "according to the saying of Elijah."

Hospitality Rewarded

Wonderfully were her faith and generosity rewarded. "She, and he, and her house did eat many days. And the barrel of meal wasted not, neither did the cruse of oil fail, according to the word of the Lord, which He spake by Elijah."

"After these things . . . the son of the woman, the mistress of the house, fell sick; and his sickness was so sore, that there was no breath left in him. And she said unto Elijah, . . . Art thou come to me to call my sin to remembrance, and to slay my son?

"And he said unto her, Give me thy son. And he . . . carried him up into a loft, where he abode, and laid him upon his own bed. . . . And he stretched himself upon the child three times, and cried unto the Lord. . . . And the Lord heard the voice of Elijah; and the soul of the child came into him again, and he revived.

"And Elijah took the child, and brought him down out of the chamber into the house, and delivered him unto his mother: and Elijah said, See, thy son liveth. And the woman said to Elijah, Now by this I know that thou art a man of God, and that the word of the Lord in thy mouth is truth."

The widow of Zarephath shared her morsel with Elijah, and in return her life and that of her son were preserved. And to all who give sympathy and assistance to others more needy, God has promised great blessing. His power is no less now than in the days of Elijah. "He that receiveth a prophet in the name of a prophet shall receive a prophet's reward." Matthew 10:41.

"Be not forgetful to entertain strangers: for thereby some have entertained angels unawares." Hebrews 13:2. Our heavenly Father still places in the pathway of His children opportunities that are blessings in disguise; and those who improve these opportunities find great joy. "If you pour yourself out for the hungry and satisfy the desire of the afflicted, then . . . you shall be like a watered garden, like a spring of water, whose waters fail not." Isaiah 58:10, 11, RSV.

Today Christ says, "He that receiveth you receiveth Me." No act of kindness shown in Christ's name will fail to be rewarded. And Christ includes even the lowliest of the family of God: "Whosoever shall give to drink unto one of these little ones"—those who are as children in faith and knowledge—"a cup of cold water only in the name of a disciple, verily I say unto you, he shall in no wise lose his reward." Matthew 10:40-42.

Three Years of Drought

Through the long years of famine, Elijah prayed earnestly and waited patiently while the hand of the Lord rested heavily on the stricken land. As he saw suffering and want on every side, his heart was wrung with sorrow, and he longed to bring about a reformation quickly. But God was working out His plan, and His servant was to pray on and await the time for action.

The apostasy in Ahab's day was the result of many years of evildoing. Step by step Israel had been departing from the right way, and at last the great majority had yielded themselves to the powers of darkness.

About a century had passed since, under King David, Israel had united in hymns of praise to the Most High in recognition of their entire dependence on Him for daily mercies. Then they sang:

O God of our salvation, . . .
> Thou makest the outgoings of the morning and
> evening to rejoice.
Thou visitest the earth, and waterest it:
> Thou greatly enrichest it with the river of God,
> which is full of water:
> Thou preparest them corn, when Thou hast so
> provided for it.
Thou crownest the year with Thy goodness;
> And Thy paths drop fatness.
>> Psalm 65:5, 8, 9, 11

He causeth the grass to grow for the cattle,
> And herb for the service of man:
That He may bring forth food out of the earth;
> And wine that maketh glad the heart of man.

O Lord, how manifold are Thy works!
In wisdom hast Thou made them all:
> The earth is full of Thy riches.
>> Psalm 104:14, 15, 24

The land to which the Lord had brought Israel was flowing with milk and honey, a country where they need never suffer for lack of rain. "The land, whither thou goest in to possess it," He had told them, "is not as the land of Egypt, from whence ye came out, where thou sowedst thy seed, and wateredst it with thy foot, as a garden of herbs: but the land, whither ye go to possess it, is a land of hills and valleys, and drinketh water of the rain of heaven: a land which the Lord thy God careth for."

The promise of abundance of rain had been given on condition of obedience: "If ye shall hearken diligently unto My commandments which I command you this day, to love the Lord your God, and to serve Him with all your heart and with all your soul, that I will give you the rain of your land in his due season, the first rain and the latter rain."

"Take heed to yourselves, that your heart be not deceived, and ye turn aside, and serve other gods, and worship them; and then . . . He [the Lord] shut up the heaven, that there be no rain, and that the land yield not her fruit; and lest ye perish quickly from off the good land which the Lord giveth you." Deuteronomy 11:10-14, 16, 17.

"If thou wilt not hearken unto the voice of the Lord thy God, to observe to do all His commandments and His statutes," "thy heaven that is over thy head shall be brass, and the earth that is under thee shall be iron. The Lord shall make the rain of thy land powder and dust." Deuteronomy 28:15, 23, 24.

Plain were these commands, yet as the centuries passed, apostasy threatened to sweep aside every barrier of divine grace. Now the prediction of Elijah was meeting terrible fulfillment. For three years the messenger of woe was sought for. Many rulers had given their oath of honor that the strange prophet could not be found in their dominions. Jezebel and the prophets of Baal hated Elijah and spared no effort to bring him within reach of their power. And still there was no rain.

The People Are Finally Ready for Reformation

At last "the word of the Lord came to Elijah . . . , saying, Go, show thyself unto Ahab; and I will send rain upon the earth." In obedience to the command, Elijah set forth on his journey.

About this time Ahab proposed to Obadiah, the governor of his household, that they search for springs and brooks in the hope of finding pasture for their starving flocks. The king, deeply concerned over the outlook for his household, decided to unite personally with his servant in a search for some favored spots where pasture might be had. "Ahab went one way by himself, and Obadiah went another way by himself." "As Obadiah was in the way, behold, Elijah met him: and he knew him, and fell on his face, and said, Art thou that my lord Elijah?"

During the apostasy of Israel, Obadiah had remained faithful. The king had been unable to turn him from his allegiance to the living God. Now he was honored with a commission from Elijah: "Go, tell thy lord, Behold, Elijah is here."

Terrified, Obadiah exclaimed, "What have I sinned, that thou wouldest deliver thy servant into the hand of Ahab, to slay me?" This was to court certain death! "As the Lord thy God liveth," he explained to the prophet, "there is no nation or kingdom, whither my lord hath not sent to seek thee: and when they said, He is not there; he took an oath of the kingdom and nation, that they found thee not. And now thou sayest, Go, tell thy lord, Behold, Elijah is here. And it shall come to pass, as soon as I am gone from thee, that the Spirit of the Lord shall carry thee whither I know not; and so when I come and tell Ahab, and he cannot find thee, he shall slay me."

With a solemn oath Elijah promised Obadiah that the errand should not be in vain. "As the Lord of hosts liveth, before whom I stand, I will surely show myself unto him today." Thus assured, "Obadiah went to meet Ahab, and told him."

In astonishment mingled with terror the king listened to the message from the man whom he feared and hated, and for whom he had sought untiringly. Could it be possible that the prophet was about to utter another woe against Israel? The king's heart was seized with dread. He remembered the withered arm of Jeroboam. Ahab could not avoid obeying the summons, neither dared he lift up his hand against the messenger of God. Accompanied by a bodyguard of soldiers, the trembling monarch went to meet the prophet.

Brave Prophet, Guilty King

The king and the prophet stood face to face. In the presence of Elijah, Ahab seemed unmanned, powerless. In his first faltering words, "Art thou he that troubleth Israel?" he unconsciously revealed the inmost feelings of his heart and sought to cast on the prophet the blame for the heavy judgments resting on the land.

It is natural for the wrongdoer to hold the messengers of God responsible for the calamities that come as the result of departure from the way of righteousness. When the mirror of truth is held up before those in Satan's power, they become indignant at receiving reproof. Blinded by sin, they feel that God's servants have turned against them and are worthy of severest censure.

Standing in conscious innocence, Elijah made no attempt to excuse himself or to flatter the king. Nor did he seek to evade the king's wrath by the good news that the drought was almost over. Indignant, and jealous for the honor of God, he fearlessly declared to the king that it was *his* sins, and the sins of *his* fathers, that had brought this terrible calamity. "I have not troubled Israel," Elijah boldly asserted, "but thou, and thy father's house, in that ye have forsaken the commandments of the Lord, and thou hast followed Baalim."

Need of Reform Today

Today there is need of the voice of stern rebuke, for grievous sins have separated the people from God. Infidelity is fashionable. "We will not have this Man to reign over us" (Luke 19:14) is the language of thousands. The smooth sermons often preached make no lasting impression; the trumpet does not give a certain sound. Men are not cut to the heart by the plain, sharp truths of God's Word.

Many say, What need is there of speaking so plainly? They might as well ask, Why need John the Baptist have provoked the anger of Herodias by telling Herod that it was unlawful for him to live with his brother's wife? The forerunner of Christ lost his life by his plain speaking.

So men who should be guardians of God's law have argued, till policy has taken the place of faithfulness and sin is allowed to go unreproved. When will the voice of faithful rebuke be heard once more in the church?

"Thou art the man." 2 Samuel 12:7. Words as plain as these spoken by Nathan to David are seldom heard in pulpits today, seldom seen in the public press. The Lord's messengers should not complain that their efforts are without fruit until they repent of their desire to please men, which leads them to suppress truth.

It is not from love for their neighbor that ministers smooth down the message entrusted to them, but because they are self-indulgent and ease-loving. True love seeks first the honor of God and the salvation of souls. Those who have this love will not evade the truth to save themselves from the unpleasant results of plain speaking. When souls are in peril, God's ministers will speak the word given them, refusing to excuse evil.

Would that every minister might show the courage that Elijah showed! Ministers are to "convince, rebuke, and exhort, be unfailing in patience and in teaching." 2 Timothy 4:2, RSV. In Christ's stead they are to encourage the obedient and warn the disobedient. With them worldly policy is to have no weight. They are to go forward in faith. They are not to speak their own words, but their message is to be, "Thus saith the Lord." God calls for men like Elijah, Nathan, and John the Baptist—men who will bear His message regardless of consequences; men who will speak the truth though it call for the sacrifice of all they have.

God calls for men who will do faithful battle against wrong, warring against spiritual wickedness in high places. To such He will speak the words: "Well done, good and faithful servant; . . . enter thou into the joy of thy Lord." Matthew 25:23.

11 / God Vindicated on Mount Carmel

Standing before Ahab, Elijah commanded, "Send, and gather to me all Israel unto Mount Carmel, and the prophets of Baal four hundred and fifty, and the prophets of the groves four hundred, which eat at Jezebel's table."

Ahab obeyed at once, as if the prophet were monarch, and the king a subject. Swift messengers were sent with the summons. In every town and village the people prepared to assemble at the appointed time. As they journeyed toward the place, the hearts of many were filled with strange forebodings. Why this summons to gather at Carmel? What new calamity was about to fall?

Mount Carmel had been a place of beauty, its streams fed from never-failing springs and its fertile slopes covered with flowers and flourishing groves. But now its beauty languished under a withering curse. The altars erected to Baal and Ashtoreth stood in leafless groves. On the summit of one of the highest ridges was the broken-down altar of Jehovah.

Carmel's heights were visible from many parts of the kingdom. At the foot of the mount were vantage points from which could be seen much of what took place above. Elijah chose this elevation as the most conspicuous place for the display of God's power and the vindication of His name.

Early on the morning of the day appointed, the hosts of Israel gathered near the top of the mountain. Jezebel's prophets marched in imposing array. In regal

This chapter is based on 1 Kings 18:19-40.

pomp the king appeared at the head of the priests, and the idolaters shouted his welcome. But the priests remembered that at the word of the prophet the land of Israel for three years and a half had been destitute of dew and rain. Some fearful crisis was at hand, they felt sure. The gods in whom they had trusted had been unable to prove Elijah a false prophet. To their frantic cries, their prayers, their revolting ceremonies, their costly sacrifices, the objects of their worship had been strangely indifferent.

Facing King Ahab and the false prophets, and surrounded by the assembled host of Israel, Elijah stood, the only one who had appeared to vindicate the honor of Jehovah. He was apparently defenseless in the presence of the monarch, the prophets of Baal, the men of war, and the surrounding thousands. But around him were angels that excel in strength.

Unashamed, unterrified, the prophet was fully aware of his commission to execute the divine command. In anxious expectancy the people waited for him to speak. Looking first on the broken-down altar of Jehovah and then on the multitude, Elijah cried out in trumpet tones, "How long halt ye between two opinions? if the Lord be God, follow Him: but if Baal, then follow him."

No One Has the Courage to Stand With Elijah

The people answered not a word. Not one in that vast assembly dared reveal loyalty to Jehovah. Deception and blindness had overspread Israel. Not all at once but gradually. Each departure from rightdoing, each refusal to repent had deepened their guilt and driven them farther from Heaven. And now, in this crisis, they persisted in refusing to take their stand for God.

The Lord abhors indifference in a time of crisis. The whole universe is watching with inexpressible interest the closing scenes of the great controversy between good and evil. What can be of more importance to the people of God than to be loyal to the God of heaven? All through the ages, God has had moral heroes, and He has them now—those who, like Joseph, Elijah, and Daniel, are not ashamed to acknowledge themselves His peculiar people. His special blessing accompanies men of action, men who will not be swerved from duty, but who will inquire, "Who is on the Lord's side?" (Exodus 32:26)—men who will demand that those who choose to identify with the people of God shall step forward and reveal their allegiance to the King of kings. Such men make their wills subordinate to the law of God. For love of Him they count not their lives dear unto themselves. Fidelity to God is their motto.

While Israel on Carmel hesitated, the voice of Elijah again broke the silence: "I, even I only, remain a prophet of the Lord; but Baal's prophets are four hundred and fifty men. Let them therefore give us two bullocks; and let them choose one bullock for themselves, and cut it in pieces, and lay it on wood, and put no fire under: and I will dress the other bullock, and lay it on wood, and put no fire under: and call ye on the name of your gods, and I will call on the name of the Lord: and the God that answereth by fire, let Him be God."

The proposal of Elijah was so reasonable that the people answered, "It is well spoken." The prophets of Baal dared not dissent; and, addressing them, Elijah directed, "Choose you one bullock for yourselves, and dress it first; for ye are many."

With terror in their guilty hearts, the false priests laid on the wood and the victim. Then they began their incantations. Their shrill cries echoed through the forests and the surrounding heights: "O Baal, hear us!" Leaping, writhing, and screaming, with tearing of hair and cutting of flesh, the priests pleaded with their god to help them. Morning passed, noon came, and yet there was no reply to their frantic prayers. The sacrifice remained unconsumed.

As they continued their frenzied devotions, the

crafty priests continually tried to devise some means to kindle a fire on the altar. But Elijah watched every movement; and the priests, hoping against hope for some opportunity to deceive, continued their senseless ceremonies.

"It came to pass at noon, that Elijah mocked them, and said, Cry aloud: for he is a god; either he is talking, or he is pursuing, or he is in a journey, or peradventure he sleepeth, and must be awaked. And they cried aloud, and cut themselves after their manner with knives and lancets, till the blood gushed out upon them. And it came to pass, when midday was past, . . . that there was neither voice, nor any to answer, nor any that regarded."

Gladly would Satan have helped those who were devoted to his service. Gladly would he have sent lightning to kindle their sacrifice. But Jehovah had set Satan's bounds, and he could not convey one spark to Baal's altar.

At last, their voices hoarse with shouting, the priests became desperate. With unabated frenzy they mingled with their pleading terrible cursings of their sun-god. Elijah continued to watch intently. He knew that if by any device the priests should succeed in kindling their altar fire, he would instantly be torn to pieces.

The Prophets of Baal Give Up

Evening drew on. The prophets of Baal were weary, faint, confused. One suggested one thing, and another something else, until finally in despair they retired from the contest.

All day long the people had witnessed the baffled priests' wild leaping around the altar, as if they would grasp the burning rays of the sun to serve their purpose. The people had looked with horror on their self-inflicted mutilations and had reflected on the follies of idol worship. Many were weary of the exhibitions of demonism and now awaited with deep interest the movements of Elijah.

At the hour of the evening sacrifice, Elijah bade the people, "Come near unto me." He turned to the broken-down altar where once men worshiped the God of heaven and repaired it. To him this heap of ruins was more precious than all the magnificent altars of heathendom. Choosing "twelve stones, according to the number of the tribes of the sons of Jacob, . . . he built an altar in the name of the Lord."

The disappointed, exhausted priests of Baal waited to see what Elijah would do. They hated the prophet for proposing a test that had exposed their gods; yet they feared his power. Almost breathless with expectancy, the people watched. The calm demeanor of the prophet stood in sharp contrast with the senseless frenzy of the followers of Baal.

The altar completed, the prophet made a trench about it. Having put the wood in order and prepared the bullock, he laid the victim on the altar. "Fill four barrels with water," he directed, "and pour it on the burnt sacrifice, and on the wood. And he said, Do it the second time. And they did it the second time. And he said, Do it the third time. And they did it the third time. And the water ran round about the altar; and he filled the trench also with water."

Reminding the people of their long apostasy, Elijah called on the people to humble their hearts and turn to the God of their fathers, that the curse on the land might be removed. Then, bowing reverently before the unseen God, he raised his hands toward heaven and offered a simple prayer. Baal's priests had screamed and leaped, from early morning until late in the afternoon. But as Elijah prayed, no senseless shrieks resounded over Carmel's height. He prayed simply and fervently, asking God to show His superiority over Baal that Israel might be led to turn to Him:

"Lord God of Abraham, Isaac, and of Israel, let it be known this day that Thou art God in Israel, and that I am Thy servant, and that I have done all these things at Thy word. Hear me, O Lord, hear me, that this people may know that Thou art the Lord God, and that Thou hast turned their heart back again.''

A silence, oppressive in its solemnity, rested upon all. The priests of Baal trembled with terror, conscious of their guilt.

Fire From Heaven Answers Elijah's Simple Prayer

No sooner was the prayer of Elijah ended than flames of fire, like flashes of lightning, descended from heaven on the altar, consuming the sacrifice, licking up the water in the trench, and consuming even the stones of the altar. The brilliance of the blaze illumined the mountain and dazzled the eyes of the multitude. In the valleys below, where many were watching, the descent of fire was clearly seen, and all were amazed at the sight.

The people on the mount prostrated themselves. They dared not continue to look on the Heaven-sent fire. Convicted of their duty to acknowledge the God of Elijah as the God of their fathers, they cried out with one voice, "The Lord, He is the God; the Lord, He is the God." The cry resounded over the mountain and echoed in the plain below. At last Israel was aroused, undeceived, penitent. At last the people saw how greatly they had dishonored God. The character of Baal worship in contrast with the reasonable service required by the true God, stood fully revealed. The people recognized God's justice and mercy in withholding the dew and rain until they had been brought to confess His name.

The Priests of Baal Unrepentant

But the priests of Baal, even in their discomfiture and in the presence of divine glory, refused to repent. They would still remain the prophets of Baal. Thus they showed themselves ripe for destruction.

That repentant Israel might be protected from those who taught them to worship Baal, Elijah was directed by the Lord to destroy these false teachers. The anger of the people had already been aroused, and when Elijah gave the command, "Take the prophets of Baal; let not one of them escape," they were ready to obey. They took them to the brook Kishon, and there, before the close of the day that marked the beginning of decided reform, the ministers of Baal were slain.

12 / The Prophet Loses Faith, and Panics

With the slaying of the prophets of Baal, the way was opened for carrying forward a mighty spiritual reformation. The judgments of Heaven had been executed; the people had confessed their sins and acknowledged the God of their fathers. Now the curse was to be withdrawn, and the land was to be refreshed with rain. "Get thee up, eat and drink," Elijah said to Ahab, "for there is a sound of abundance of rain." Then the prophet went to the top of the mount to pray.

He saw no clouds in the heavens; he heard no thunder. Throughout the day he had revealed his implicit confidence in God's word; and now he knew that Heaven would bestow the blessings foretold. The same God who had sent the drought had promised rain as the reward of rightdoing. In an attitude of humility, Elijah interceded with God in behalf of penitent Israel.

Again and again he sent his servant to a point overlooking the Mediterranean, to learn whether there was any visible token that God had heard his prayer. Each time the servant returned with the word, "There is nothing." The prophet did not lose faith, but continued pleading. Six times the servant returned with the word that there was no sign of rain in the brassy heavens. Undaunted, Elijah sent him forth once more. This time the servant returned with the word, "Behold, there ariseth a little cloud out of the sea, like a man's hand."

This was enough! In that small cloud Elijah beheld

This chapter is based on 1 Kings 18:41-46; 19:1-8.

THE PROPHET LOSES FAITH, AND PANICS / 83

by faith an abundance of rain; and he acted in harmony
with his faith, sending his servant quickly to Ahab with
the message, "Prepare thy chariot, get thee down, that
the rain stop thee not."

Because Elijah was a man of large faith, God could
use him. His faith grasped the promises of Heaven, and
he persevered in prayer. He did not wait for the full
evidence that God had heard him but was willing to
venture all on the slightest token of divine favor. And
what he was enabled to do under God, all may do in
their sphere in God's service. "Elijah was a man of like
nature with ourselves and he prayed fervently that it
might not rain, and for three years and six months it did
not rain on the earth." James 5:17, RSV.

Faith such as this is needed today—faith that will lay
hold of the promises of God's Word, faith that brings
strength for coping with the powers of darkness.
Through faith God's children have "conquered kingdoms, enforced justice, received promises, . . . won
strength out of weakness, became mighty in war, put
foreign armies to flight." Hebrews 11:33, 34, RSV.

Faith is an essential element of prevailing prayer.
"He that cometh to God must believe that He is, and
that He is a rewarder of them that diligently seek
Him." Hebrews 11:6. With the persistence of Elijah,
we may present our petitions to the Father. The honor
of His throne is staked for the fulfillment of His word.

The shades of night were gathering about Mount
Carmel as Ahab prepared for the descent. "It came to
pass in the meanwhile, that the heaven was black with
clouds and wind, and there was a great rain. And Ahab
rode, and went to Jezreel." As he journeyed toward
the royal city through the darkness and blinding rain,
he was unable to see before him. Elijah had that day
humiliated him before his subjects and slain his idolatrous priests, but he still acknowledged him as Israel's
king. Now, as an act of homage, he ran before the royal
chariot, guiding the king to the city.

In this gracious act shown to a wicked king is a lesson for all who claim to be servants of God. There are those who hesitate to perform menial duties, fearing that they will be doing the work of a servant. Elijah had been signally honored of God as fire had flashed from heaven and consumed the sacrifice; his petition for rain had been granted. And yet, after God had been pleased to honor his public ministry, he was willing to perform the service of a menial.

Jezebel Threatens Elijah's Life

At the gate of Jezreel, Elijah and Ahab separated. The prophet, choosing to remain outside the walls, wrapped himself in his mantle and lay down on the bare earth to sleep. The king soon reached the shelter of his palace and related to his wife the events of the day. As Ahab told of the slaying of the idolatrous prophets, Jezebel, hardened and impenitent, became infuriated. She refused to recognize the overruling providence of God, and still defiant, boldly declared that Elijah should die.

That night a messenger aroused the weary prophet and delivered the word of Jezebel: "So let the gods do to me, and more also, if I make not thy life as the life of one of them by tomorrow about this time."

It would seem that after showing courage so undaunted, and after triumphing so completely over king and priests and people, Elijah could never afterward have given way to despondency nor been awed into timidity. But in this dark hour his faith and courage forsook him. Bewildered, he started from his slumber. The rain was pouring from the heavens, and darkness was on every side. Forgetting that three years before, God had directed his course to a place of refuge, the prophet now fled for his life.

Elijah's Lack of Faith

Elijah should not have fled. He should have met the threat of Jezebel with an appeal for protection to the One who had commissioned him. He should have told the messenger that the God in whom he trusted would protect him against the hatred of the queen. Had he made God his refuge and strength, he would have been shielded from harm. The Lord would have sent His judgments on Jezebel, and the impression made on king and people would have wrought a great reformation.

Elijah had hoped that after the miracle on Carmel Jezebel would no longer have influence over Ahab and that there would be a speedy reform throughout all Israel. All day on Carmel he had toiled without food. Yet when he guided the chariot of Ahab to Jezreel, his courage was strong despite the physical strain. But a reaction frequently follows high faith and glorious success. Elijah feared that the reformation begun might not be lasting, and depression seized him. In this time of discouragement, with Jezebel's threat sounding in his ears and Satan still apparently prevailing, he lost his hold on God.

Elijah's Utter Despondency

Forgetting God, Elijah fled on and on, until he found himself in a dreary waste, alone. Utterly wearied, he sat down to rest under a juniper tree, and requested that he might die: "It is enough; now, O Lord, take away my life; for I am not better than my fathers." His spirit crushed by bitter disappointment, he desired never again to look on the face of man. At last, exhausted, he fell asleep.

To all there come times of keen disappointment and discouragement—days when it is hard to believe that God is still kind, days when troubles harass till death seems preferable to life. Then many lose their hold on God and are brought into the slavery of doubt and unbelief. Could we at such times discern the meaning of God's providences, we should see angels seeking to save us from ourselves, striving to plant our feet on a firm foundation, and new faith, new life, would spring into being.

The faithful Job in his affliction and darkness declared:

> Let the day perish wherein I was born.
> O that I might have my request, . . .
> I would choose . . . death. . . . I loathe my life.
> Job 3:3; 6:8; 7:15, 16, RSV

But though weary of life, Job was not allowed to die. To him was given the message of hope:

> You will forget your misery;
> You will remember it as waters that have passed away.
>   And your life will be brighter than the noonday;
>   Its darkness will be like the morning.
> Job 11:16, 17, RSV

From the depths of despondency Job rose to the heights of trust in God. Triumphantly he declared:

> For I know that my Redeemer lives,
> And He will stand at last on the earth;
> And after my skin is destroyed, this I *know*,
> That in my flesh I shall see God.
> Job 19:25, NKJV

When Job caught a glimpse of his Creator, he abhorred himself and repented in dust and ashes. Then the Lord was able to bless him and make his last years the best of his life.

Despondency is sinful and unreasonable. God is willing "more abundantly" (Hebrews 6:17) to bestow on His servants the strength they need. The plans of the enemies of His work may seem firmly established, but God can overthrow the strongest of these. For the disheartened there is a sure remedy—faith, prayer, work. Are you tempted to give way to anxious foreboding or despondency? In the darkest days, when appearances seem most forbidding, fear not. God knows your need. His infinite love and compassion never weary. Never will He change the covenant He has made with those who love Him. And He will bestow on His faithful servants the efficiency that their need demands. Paul has testified: "He said to me, 'My grace is sufficient for you, for My power is made perfect in weakness.' . . . For the sake of Christ, then, I am content with weakness . . . ; for when I am weak, then I am strong." 2 Corinthians 12:9, 10, RSV.

Did God forsake Elijah in his trial? No! He loved His servant no less when he felt forsaken of God and man. And now a soft touch and pleasant voice awoke him. The pitying face bending over him was not the face of an enemy, but of a friend. God had sent an angel with food. "Arise and eat," the angel said. "And he looked, and, behold, there was a cake baken on the coals, and a cruse of water at his head."

After Elijah had partaken of the refreshment, he slept again. A second time the angel touched the exhausted man, and said with pitying tenderness, "Arise and eat; because the journey is too great for thee." In the strength of that food he was able to journey "forty days and forty nights unto Horeb the mount of God," where he found refuge in a cave.

13 / "What Doest Thou Here?"

Elijah's retreat on Mount Horeb was known to God, and the discouraged prophet was not left to struggle alone with the powers of darkness. At the cave where Elijah had taken refuge, God met with him through a mighty angel to inquire into his needs and to make plain the divine purpose for Israel.

Not until Elijah learned to trust wholly in God could he complete his work. The triumph on Carmel had opened the way for still greater victories, yet from the wonderful opportunities opening before him, Elijah had been turned away by the threat of Jezebel. The man of God must be made to understand the vantage ground the Lord would have him occupy.

"What doest thou here, Elijah?" I sent you to the brook Cherith and to the widow of Sarepta. I commissioned you to stand before the idolatrous priests on Carmel and to guide the chariot of the king to Jezreel. But who sent you into the wilderness? What errand have you here?

In bitterness Elijah complained: "I have been very jealous for the Lord God of hosts: for the children of Israel have forsaken Thy covenant, thrown down Thine altars, and slain Thy prophets with the sword; and I, even I only, am left; and they seek my life."

The angel told the prophet to stand and listen to the Lord's word. "And, behold, the Lord passed by, and a great and strong wind rent the mountains, and brake in

This chapter is based on 1 Kings 19:9-18.

pieces the rocks before the Lord; but the Lord was not in the wind: and after the wind an earthquake; but the Lord was not in the earthquake: and after the earthquake a fire; but the Lord was not in the fire: and after the fire a still small voice.''

By "a still small voice" God chose to teach Elijah that it is not always the work that makes the greatest demonstration that is most successful. Elijah's petulance was silenced, his spirit subdued. He now knew that a firm reliance on God would ever find for him help in time of need.

Not by eloquence or logic are men's hearts reached, but by the Holy Spirit. The still, small voice of the Spirit of God has power to change the heart.

"What doest thou here, Elijah?" the voice inquired; and again the prophet answered, "The children of Israel have forsaken Thy covenant, thrown down Thine altars, and slain Thy prophets with the sword; and I, even I only, am left; and they seek my life."

The Lord answered Elijah that the wrongdoers should not go unpunished. Men were to be chosen to punish the idolatrous kingdom. There was stern work to be done. Elijah was to return to Israel and share with others the burden of bringing about a reformation.

"Go," the Lord commanded Elijah, "anoint Hazael to be king over Syria: and Jehu . . . shalt thou anoint to be king over Israel: and Elisha . . . shalt thou anoint to be a prophet in thy room. . . . Him that escapeth the sword of Hazael shall Jehu slay: and him that escapeth from the sword of Jehu shall Elisha slay."

He who reads the hearts of all revealed to the prophet that there were many others who had remained true to Him through the long years of apostasy. "I have left Me seven thousand in Israel, . . . which have not bowed unto Baal."

The apostasy today is similar to that which overspread Israel in Elijah's day. In exalting the human above the divine, in the praise of popular leaders, in the worship of mammon, and in the placing of science above the truths of revelation, multitudes today are following Baal. Many are substituting for the oracles of God the theories of men. It is taught that human reason should be exalted above the teachings of the Word. The law of God is declared to be of no effect. The enemy is working to cause men and women to forget that which was ordained for the happiness and salvation of mankind.

Many Today Have Not Bowed to Baal

Yet this widespread apostasy is not universal. Not all are lawless and sinful. God has many who long to understand more fully in regard to Christ and the law, many who are hoping that Jesus will come soon to end the reign of sin and death, many with whom the Spirit of God is still striving.

These need the personal help of those who know God and His Word. As those who understand Bible truth seek out the men and women who are longing for light, angels will attend them. As a result, many will cease to pay homage to man-made institutions and will take their stand fearlessly on the side of God and His law.

Satan puts forth every possible effort to cause the obedient to lose sight of their mission and become satisfied with the pleasures of this life. He leads them to settle down at ease, or, for the sake of worldly advantages, to move from places where they might be a power for good. Others he causes to flee in discouragement from duty, because of persecution. To every child of God whose voice the enemy of souls has succeeded in silencing, the question is addressed, "What doest thou here?" I commissioned you to go into all the world and preach the gospel, to prepare a people for the day of God. Who sent you here?

The joy that sustained Christ through sacrifice and suffering was the joy of seeing sinners saved. This should be the joy of every follower of His. Those who realize what redemption means will be moved to compassion as they see the moral and spiritual destitution of thousands who are under the shadow of a terrible doom, in comparison with which physical suffering fades into nothingness.

In many churches there are families who might move to places in need of the ministry they are capable of giving. God calls for families to go to the dark places of earth and work wisely for those who are enshrouded in spiritual gloom. This requires self-sacrifice. While many wait to have every obstacle removed, souls are dying, without hope and without God. For worldly advantage, or to acquire scientific knowledge, men endure hardship and privation. Where are those willing to do as much for the sake of telling others of the Saviour?

In Times of Weakness, Trust in God

If, under trying circumstances, men of spiritual power, pressed beyond measure, become discouraged, this is nothing strange or new. One of the mightiest of the prophets fled for his life before the rage of an infuriated woman. A weary fugitive, bitter disappointment crushing his spirits, he asked that he might die. But when hope was gone and his lifework seemed threatened with defeat, he learned the possibility of trusting God under circumstances the most forbidding.

Those who, while spending their life energies in self-sacrificing labor, are tempted to give way to despondency, may gather courage from the experience of Elijah. God's watchful care, His love, His power, are especially manifest in behalf of His servants whose counsels and reproofs are slighted and whose efforts toward reform are repaid with hatred and opposition.

At the time of greatest weakness Satan assails the soul with the fiercest temptations. It was thus that he hoped to prevail over the Son of God; for by this policy he had gained many victories over man. When will-power weakened and faith failed, then those who had stood long and valiantly for the right yielded to temptation. Moses, wearied with forty years of wandering and unbelief, failed just on the borders of the Promised Land. Elijah, who had maintained his trust in Jehovah during the years of drought, in a moment of weariness allowed the fear of death to overcome his faith in God.

So it is today, when we are encompassed with doubt or afflicted by poverty or distress, Satan seeks to shake our confidence in Jehovah. He tempts us to distrust God, to question His love. He hopes to discourage the soul and break our hold on God.

Those who stand in the forefront of the conflict will frequently feel a reaction when the pressure is removed. Despondency may shake the faith and weaken the will. But God understands. He still pities and loves. He reads the motives of the heart. To wait patiently, to trust when everything looks dark, is the lesson that leaders in God's work need to learn. Heaven will not fail them in adversity. Nothing is apparently more helpless, yet really more invincible, than the soul that feels its nothingness and relies wholly on God.

He who was Elijah's strength is strong to uphold every struggling child of His, no matter how weak. To everyone He grants power according to the need. In the might of God man may overcome evil and help others to overcome. Satan can never gain advantage of him who makes God his defense.

Satan knows your weakness; therefore cling to Jesus. The righteousness of Christ can give you power to stem the tide of evil sweeping over the world. Bring faith into your experience. Faith lightens every burden, relieves every weariness. Providences that are now mysterious you may solve by continued trust in God. The records of sacred history are written that the same faith which wrought in God's servants of old may work in us. In no less marked manner will the Lord work now wherever there are hearts of faith to be channels of His power.

Christ will never abandon those for whom He died. We may leave Him and be overwhelmed with temptation, but Christ can never turn from one for whom He has paid the ransom of His own life. Could our spiritual vision be quickened, we should see souls bowed under oppression, burdened with grief, and ready to die in discouragement. We should see angels flying quickly to the aid of these tempted ones, forcing back the hosts of evil. The battles between the two armies are real, and on the issue of the spiritual conflict eternal destinies depend.

God's messengers are not to feel that His work is dependent on them. He who slumbers not will carry forward His work. He will thwart the purposes of wicked men and bring to confusion the counsels of those who plot mischief against His people. He who is the King, the Lord of hosts, sitteth between the cherubim, and amidst the strife and tumult of nations He guards His children still. When the arrows of wrath shall strike through the hearts of His enemies, His people will be safe in His hands.

14 / God's Call to Modern Apostates

Through long centuries the record of Elijah's life-work has brought inspiration and courage to those who have been called to stand for the right in the midst of apostasy. For us it has special significance. History is being repeated. The present age is one of idolatry, as verily as was that in which Elijah lived. No outward shrine may be visible, yet thousands are following after the gods of this world—riches, fame, pleasure, and the fables that permit man to follow the inclinations of the unregenerate heart. Multitudes have a wrong conception of God and are as truly serving a false god as were the worshipers of Baal. Many even of those who claim to be Christians have allied themselves with influences that are unalterably opposed to God and His truth.

The prevailing spirit of our time is one of infidelity and apostasy. Human theories are exalted and placed where God and His law should be. Satan tempts men and women with the promise that in disobedience they will find freedom that will make them as gods. There is seen a spirit of idolatrous exaltation of human wisdom above divine revelation. Men seem to have lost all power to discriminate between light and darkness, truth and error. They hold the opinions of a few philosophers, so-called, to be more trustworthy than the truths of the Bible. A faith such as actuated Paul, Peter, and John they regard as old-fashioned and unworthy of the intelligence of modern thinkers.

In the beginning, God gave His law to mankind as a means of attaining happiness and eternal life. Satan's hope is to lead men and women to disobey this law; his constant effort is to misrepresent it and belittle its importance. His master stroke has been an attempt to change the law itself, so as to lead men to violate its precepts while professing to obey it. One writer has likened the attempt to change the law of God to an ancient mischievous practice of turning in a wrong direction a signpost where two roads met. The perplexity and hardship which this often caused was great.

A signpost was erected by God for those journeying through this world. One arm pointed out willing obedience to the Creator as the road to life, while the other indicated disobedience as the path to death. But in an evil hour for our race, the great enemy of all good turned the signpost around, and multitudes have mistaken the way.

Through Moses the Lord instructed the Israelites: "Verily My Sabbaths ye shall keep: for it is a sign between Me and you throughout your generations; that ye may know that I am the Lord that doth sanctify you." "It is a sign between Me and the children of Israel forever: for in six days the Lord made heaven and earth, and on the seventh day He rested, and was refreshed." Exodus 31:13, 17.

The Lord clearly defined obedience as the way to the City of God, but the "man of sin" has changed the signpost. He has set up a false sabbath and has caused men and women to think that by resting on it they were obeying the command of the Creator. When "the heavens and the earth were finished," God exalted the seventh-day Sabbath as a memorial of His creative work. "God blessed the seventh day, and sanctified it." Genesis 2:1, 3.

At the time of the Exodus the Sabbath was brought prominently before the people of God. While in Egypt their taskmasters had attempted to force them to labor on the Sabbath by increasing the amount of work required each week. But the Israelites were delivered from bondage and brought to a place where they might observe unmolested all the precepts of the Lord. At Sinai the law was spoken, and a copy of it, on two tables of stone, "written with the finger of God," was delivered to Moses. Exodus 31:18. And through forty years of wandering the Israelites were constantly reminded of God's appointed rest day by the withholding of the manna every seventh day and the miraculous preservation of the double portion that fell on the preparation day.

The Lord designed that by observance of the Sabbath command, Israel should continually be reminded of Him as their Creator and Redeemer. While they should keep the Sabbath in the proper spirit, idolatry could not exist; but should the claims of this precept be set aside, the Creator would be forgotten. Yet "they rejected My ordinances and did not walk in My statutes, and profaned My Sabbaths; for their heart went after their idols." Ezekiel 20:16, RSV.

In calling the attention of Judah to the sins that finally brought upon them the Babylonian Captivity, the Lord declared: "Thou hast profaned My Sabbaths." "Therefore have I poured out Mine indignation upon them; I have consumed them with the fire of My wrath: their own way have I recompensed upon their heads." Ezekiel 22:8, 31.

At the restoration of Jerusalem, in the days of Nehemiah, Sabbathbreaking was met with the inquiry, "Did not your fathers thus, and did not our God bring all this evil upon us, and upon this city? yet ye bring more wrath upon Israel by profaning the Sabbath." Nehemiah 13:18.

How Christ Upheld the Sabbath

Christ, during His earthly ministry, emphasized the binding claims of the Sabbath. He showed reverence for the institution He Himself had given. In His days the Sabbath had become so perverted that its observance reflected the character of selfish men rather than the character of God. Christ set aside the false teaching which had misrepresented Him. Although followed with merciless hostility by the rabbis, He went straight forward, keeping the Sabbath according to the law of God.

In unmistakable language He testified to His regard for the law. "Think not that I have come to abolish the law and the prophets," He said; "I have come not to abolish them but to fulfill them. For truly, I say to you, till heaven and earth pass away, not an iota, not a dot, will pass from the law until all is accomplished. Whoever then relaxes one of the least of these commandments and teaches men so, shall be called least in the kingdom of heaven; but he who does them and teaches them shall be called great in the kingdom of heaven." Matthew 5:17-19, RSV.

The great enemy of man's happiness has made the Sabbath of the fourth commandment an object of special attack. Satan says, "I will work at cross purposes with God. I will set aside God's memorial, the seventh-day Sabbath. I will show the world that the day sanctified by God has been changed. I will obliterate the memory of it. I will place in its stead a day that does not bear the credentials of God, a day that cannot be a sign between God and His people. Through my vicegerent, I will exalt myself. The first day will be extolled, and the Protestant world will receive this spurious sabbath as genuine. I will be the prince of this world. I will so control minds that God's Sabbath shall be a special object of contempt. A sign? I will make the observance of the seventh day a sign of disloyalty to the authorities of earth. Human laws will be made so stringent that men and women will not dare to observe the seventh-day Sabbath. For fear of being without food and clothing, they will join the world in transgressing God's law. The earth will be wholly under my dominion." Through setting up a false sabbath, the enemy thought "to change times and laws." But has he really succeeded in changing God's law? He who is the same yesterday, today, and forever, has declared of the seventh-day Sabbath: "It is a sign between Me and you throughout your generations." "It is a sign . . . forever." Exodus 31:13, 17. The changed signpost is pointing the wrong way, but God has not changed. He is just as jealous for His law now as in the days of Ahab and Elijah.

Elijah Is Needed Today!

But how is that law disregarded! Behold the world today in open rebellion against God. Men neglect the Bible and hate truth. Jesus sees His law rejected, His love despised, His ambassadors treated with indifference. His mercies have been unacknowledged, His warnings unheeded. The temple courts of the human soul have been turned into places of unholy traffic. Selfishness, envy, pride, malice—all are cherished.

Many do not hesitate to sneer at the Word of God. Those who believe it just as it reads are ridiculed. There is a growing contempt for law and order, directly traceable to a violation of the plain commands of Jehovah. Violence and crime are the result of turning aside from the path of obedience.

Behold the well-nigh universal disregard of the Sabbath commandment. Behold also the daring impiety of those who, while enacting laws to safeguard the supposed sanctity of the first day of the week, at the same time are making laws legalizing the liquor traffic. They attempt to coerce the consciences of men while lending their sanction to an evil that destroys the beings created in the image of God. Satan inspires such legislation.

Almost the whole world is following after idols. But the Lord will not always suffer His law to be broken and despised with impunity. Skepticism may treat the claims of God's law with jest and denial, the cause of God may hold its ground only by great exertion and continual sacrifice; yet in the end truth will triumph gloriously.

In the closing work of God on earth, the standard of

His law will be again exalted. False religion may prevail, the cross of Calvary may be lost sight of, darkness may spread over the world, and the popular current may be turned against the truth; but in the hour of greatest peril the God of Elijah will raise up human instruments to bear a message that will not be silenced. In the places where men have gone to the greatest lengths in speaking against the Most High, the voice of stern rebuke will be heard. Boldly will men of God's appointment denounce the union of the church with the world. Earnestly will they call on men and women to turn from a man-made institution to the observance of the true Sabbath. "Fear God, and give glory to Him," they will proclaim to every nation, "for the hour of His judgment is come: and worship Him that made heaven, and earth. . . . If any man worship the beast and his image, and receive his mark in his forehead, or in his hand, the same shall drink of the wine of the wrath of God, which is poured out without mixture into the cup of His indignation." Revelation 14:7-10. The world will be arraigned before the bar of Infinite Justice to receive sentence.

Today, as in the days of Elijah, the line between God's commandment-keeping people and the worshipers of false gods is clearly drawn. "How long halt ye between two opinions?" Elijah cried; "if the Lord be God, follow Him: but if Baal, then follow him." 1 Kings 18:21. And the message for today is: "Babylon the great is fallen, is fallen." "Come out of her, My people, that ye be not partakers of her sins, and that ye receive not of her plagues. For her sins have reached unto heaven, and God hath remembered her iniquities." Revelation 18:2, 4, 5.

The Test That Will Come to All

The test will come to every soul. The observance of the false sabbath will be urged. The contest will be between the commandments of God and the commandments of men. Those who have yielded step by step to worldly demands and customs will then yield to the powers that be, rather than subject themselves to derision, insult, threatened imprisonment, and death. At that time the gold will be separated from the dross. True godliness will be clearly distinguished from the appearance and tinsel of it. Many a star that we have admired for its brilliance will then go out in darkness. Those who are not clothed with Christ's righteousness will appear in the shame of their nakedness.

Scattered in every land, there are those who have not bowed the knee to Baal. Like the stars of heaven, which appear only at night, these faithful ones will shine forth when darkness covers the earth. In Africa, in Europe, in South America, in China, in India, in the islands of the sea, and in all the corners of the earth, God has in reserve a firmament of chosen ones that will yet shine forth amidst the darkness, revealing clearly to an apostate world the transforming power of obedience to His law. In the hour of deepest apostasy, when Satan's supreme effort is made to cause "all" to receive, under penalty of death, the sign of allegiance to a false day, these faithful ones, "blameless and innocent, children of God without blemish," will "shine as lights in the world." Revelation 13:16; Philippians 2:15, RSV. The darker the night, the more brilliantly will they shine.

Elijah could count only one on the Lord's side when he said: "I, even I only, am left; and they seek my life." But the word of the Lord surprised him: "Yet I have left Me seven thousand in Israel, . . . which have not bowed unto Baal." 1 Kings 19:14, 18.

Then let no man attempt to number Israel today, but let everyone have a heart like the heart of Christ, a heart that reaches out for the salvation of a lost world.

15 / Jehoshaphat, the King Who Believed God

Called to the throne at the age of thirty-five, Jehoshaphat had before him the example of good King Asa, who in nearly every crisis had done "that which was right in the eyes of the Lord." 1 Kings 15:11. During a reign of twenty-five years, Jehoshaphat sought to walk "in all the ways of Asa his father; he turned not aside." 1 Kings 22:43. He endeavored to persuade his subjects to take a firm stand against idolatry. Many in his realm "sacrificed and burned incense on the high places." 1 Kings 22:43, RSV. From the beginning the king tried to safeguard Judah from the sins characterizing the northern kingdom under Ahab. Jehoshaphat "sought not unto Baalim, but sought to the Lord God of his father, and walked in His commandments, and not after the doings of Israel." The Lord was with him, and "stablished the kingdom in his hand." 2 Chronicles 17:3-5.

Jehoshaphat "had riches and honor in abundance." As time passed, the king "took away the high places and groves out of Judah." Verses 5, 6. "And the remnant of the sodomites, which remained in the days of his father Asa, he took out of the land." 1 Kings 22:46. Thus gradually the inhabitants of Judah were freed from perils that had threatened to retard seriously their spiritual development.

Throughout the kingdom the people were in need of instruction in the law of God. By conforming their lives to its requirements they would become loyal both to God and to man. Knowing this, Jehoshaphat took steps

101

to ensure to his people thorough instruction in the Holy Scriptures. By royal appointment instructors "went about throughout all the cities of Judah, and taught the people." 2 Chronicles 17:9. And, as many put away sin, a revival was effected.

In obedience to God's law there is great gain. If the teachings of God's Word were made the controlling influence in the life of every man and woman, the evils that now exist in national and social life would find no place. From every home would go forth an influence that would make men and women strong in spiritual insight and in moral power.

For many years Jehoshaphat was unmolested by surrounding nations. "The fear of the Lord fell upon all the kingdoms of the lands that were round about Judah." "Jehoshaphat waxed great exceedingly; and he built in Judah castles, and cities of store. . . . Men of war . . . waited on the king." 2 Chronicles 17:10, 12-19. Blessed with "riches and honor" (2 Chronicles 18:1), he was enabled to wield a mighty influence for truth and righteousness. In the height of his prosperity Jehoshaphat consented to the marriage of his son Jehoram to Athaliah, daughter of Ahab and Jezebel. This union formed between Judah and Israel an alliance which in time of crisis brought disaster to the king and to many of his subjects.

On one occasion Jehoshaphat visited the king of Israel at Samaria. Special honor was shown the royal guest from Jerusalem, and he was persuaded to unite with Israel in war against the Syrians. Ahab hoped that by joining with Judah he might regain Ramoth, one of the old cities of refuge, which, he contended, rightfully belonged to Israel.

Jehoshaphat in a moment of weakness rashly promised to join him against the Syrians; yet his better judgment led him to seek the will of God concerning the undertaking. "Inquire, I pray thee, at the word of the Lord," he suggested to Ahab. In response, Ahab called four hundred false prophets, and asked, "Shall we go to Ramothgilead to battle, or shall I forbear?" They answered, "Go up; for God will deliver it into the king's hand." Verses 4, 5.

Unsatisfied, Jehoshaphat asked, "Is there not here a prophet of the Lord besides, that we might inquire of him?" Verse 6. "There is yet one man, Micaiah the son of Imlah, by whom we may inquire of the Lord," Ahab answered, "but I hate him; for he doth not prophesy good concerning me." 1 Kings 22:8. Jehoshaphat was firm in his request that the man of God be called. Micaiah said: "I saw all Israel scattered upon the hills, as sheep that have not a shepherd: and the Lord said, These have no master: let them return every man to his house in peace." Verse 17.

Jehoshaphat Makes a Mistake

Neither ruler felt inclined to heed the warning. Ahab had marked out his course and was determined to follow it. Jehoshaphat had given his word, "We will be with thee in the war" (2 Chronicles 18:3), and after making such a promise he was reluctant to withdraw his forces. "So the king of Israel and Jehoshaphat the king of Judah went up to Ramothgilead." 1 Kings 22:29. During the battle that followed, Ahab was shot by an arrow and died.

From this disastrous battle Jehoshaphat returned to Jerusalem. The prophet Jehu met him with the reproof: "Shouldest thou help the ungodly, and love them that hate the Lord? therefore is wrath upon thee from before the Lord. Nevertheless there are good things found in thee, in that thou hast taken away the groves out of the land, and hast prepared thine heart to seek God." 2 Chronicles 19:2, 3. Jehoshaphat's later years were largely spent in strengthening the national and spiritual defenses of Judah. He "went out again through the people from Beersheba to Mount Ephraim, and brought them back unto the Lord God of their fathers." Verse 4.

One important step taken by the king was the establishment of efficient courts of justice. He "set judges in the land," and in the charge given them he urged: "Take heed what ye do: for ye judge not for man, but for the Lord, who is with you in the judgment. . . . With the Lord our God . . . [there is no] respect of persons, nor taking of gifts." Verses 5-7.

The king exhorted the judges of the court of appeal at Jerusalem to be faithful. "Amariah the chief priest is over you in all matters of the Lord. . . . The Levites shall be officers before you. Deal courageously, and the Lord shall be with the good." Verse 11. In safeguarding the rights and liberties of his subjects, Jehoshaphat emphasized the consideration that every member of the human family receives from God, who rules over all. Those who are appointed to act as judges under Him are to "defend the poor and fatherless," and "do justice to the afflicted and needy." Psalm 82:3.

Armies That Threaten to Destroy Judah

Toward the close of Jehoshaphat's reign Judah was invaded. "The children of Moab, and the children of Ammon . . . came against Jehoshaphat to battle." Tidings of this invasion reached the king through a messenger, who appeared with the startling word, "There cometh a great multitude against thee from beyond the sea on this side Syria." 2 Chronicles 20:1, 2.

Jehoshaphat was a man of courage. For years he had been strengthening his armies and fortified cities. He was well prepared to meet almost any foe; yet in this crisis he put not his trust in the arm of flesh. Only by a living faith in God could he hope to gain the victory over these heathen who boasted of their power to humble Judah in the eyes of the nations.

"Jehoshaphat feared, and set himself to seek the Lord, and proclaimed a fast throughout all Judah. And Judah gathered themselves together to ask help of the Lord." Standing in the temple court before his people, Jehoshaphat poured out his soul in prayer: "O Lord

God of our Fathers, . . . rulest not Thou over all the kingdoms of the heathen? and in Thine hand is there not power and might, so that none is able to withstand Thee? Art not Thou our God, who didst drive out the inhabitants of this land before Thy people Israel . . . ?

"And now, behold, the children of Ammon and Moab and Mount Seir, whom Thou wouldest not let Israel invade, when they came out of the land of Egypt, . . . and destroyed them not; behold, I say, how they reward us, to come to cast us out of Thy possession, which Thou hast given us to inherit. . . . We have no might against this great company that cometh against us; neither know we what to do: but our eyes are upon Thee." Verses 3, 4, 6, 7, 10-12.

For years Jehoshaphat had taught the people to trust in the One who had so often saved His chosen ones from destruction; and now he did not stand alone: "All Judah stood before the Lord, with their little ones, their wives, and their children." Verse 13. Unitedly they besought the Lord to put their enemies to confusion:

> O God, do not keep silence;
> Do not hold Thy peace or be still, O God!
> For lo, Thy enemies are in tumult; . . .
> They say, "Come, let us wipe them out as a nation; . . ."
> Against Thee they make a covenant. . . .
> Let them be put to shame and dismayed forever;
> Let them perish in disgrace.
> Let them know that Thou alone,
>   whose name is the Lord,
> Art the Most High over all the earth.
>   Psalm 83, RSV

As the people joined with their king in humbling themselves before God, the Spirit of the Lord came upon Jahaziel, a Levite, and he said: "Thus saith the Lord unto you, Be not afraid nor dismayed by reason of this great multitude; for the battle is not yours, but God's. . . . Ye shall not need to fight in this battle: set yourselves, stand ye still, and see the salvation of the Lord with you, O Judah and Jerusalem: fear not, nor be dismayed; tomorrow go out against them: for the Lord will be with you." 2 Chronicles 20:15-17.

A Battle Won by a Choir Singing

Early in the morning as they advanced into the wilderness of Tekoa to battle, Jehoshaphat said, "Believe in the Lord your God, so shall ye be established; believe His prophets, so shall ye prosper. And . . . he appointed singers unto the Lord, and that should praise the beauty of holiness." Verses 20, 21. These singers went before the army, lifting their voices in praise to God for the promise of victory.

It was a singular way of going to battle—singing and exalting the God of Israel! This was their battle song. They possessed the beauty of holiness. Would not more praising of God strengthen the hands of the valiant soldiers who today are standing in defense of truth?

"The Lord set ambushments against the children of Ammon, Moab, and Mount Seir, which were come against Judah; and they were smitten. For the children of Ammon and Moab stood up against the inhabitants of Mount Seir, utterly to slay and destroy them: and when they had made an end of the inhabitants of Seir, everyone helped to destroy another." Verses 22, 23.

God was the strength of Judah in this crisis, and He is the strength of His people today. We are not to trust in princes, or to set men in the place of God. In every emergency we are to feel that the battle is God's. His resources are limitless, and apparent impossibilities will make the victory all the greater.

Laden with spoil, the armies of Judah returned "with joy; for the Lord had made them to rejoice over their enemies. And they came to Jerusalem with psalteries and harps and trumpets unto the house of the

Lord." Verses 27, 28. They had put their trust wholly in God, and He had proved to be their fortress and deliverer. Now they could sing with understanding the inspired hymn of David:

> God is our refuge and strength,
>   A very present help in trouble.
>
> He breaks the bow, and shatters the spear,
> He burns the chariots with fire!
> Be still, and know that I am God.
>   I am exalted among the nations,
>   I am exalted in the earth!
> The Lord of hosts is with us;
>   The God of Jacob is our refuge.
>   Psalm 46:1, 9-11, RSV

Through the faith of Judah's ruler and of his armies "the fear of God was on all the kingdoms of those countries, when they had heard that the Lord fought against the enemies of Israel. So the realm of Jehoshaphat was quiet: for his God gave him rest." 2 Chronicles 20:29, 30.

16 / The Fall of the House of Ahab

The evil influence that Jezebel exercised over Ahab bore fruit in deeds of shame and violence. "There was none like unto Ahab, which did sell himself to work wickedness in the sight of the Lord, whom Jezebel his wife stirred up." Strengthened in wrongdoing by Jezebel, Ahab had followed the dictates of his evil heart until he was fully controlled by selfishness. The things he desired, he felt should by right be his.

This dominant trait is revealed in an incident which took place while Elijah was still a prophet in Israel. By the palace was a vineyard belonging to Naboth. Ahab set his heart on possessing it. "Give me thy vineyard," he said to Naboth, "that I may have it for a garden of herbs, because it is near unto my house: and I will give thee for it a better vineyard than it; or, if it seem good to thee, I will give thee the worth of it in money."

Naboth's vineyard had belonged to his fathers, and he refused to part with it. "The Lord forbid it me, that I should give the inheritance of my fathers unto thee."

Naboth's refusal made the selfish monarch ill. "Ahab came into his house heavy and displeased. . . . And he laid him down upon his bed, and turned away his face, and would eat no bread." Jezebel soon learned the particulars, and, indignant that anyone should refuse the request of the king, she assured Ahab that he need no longer be sad. "Dost thou now govern Israel?" she said. "Arise, and eat bread, and let thine heart be merry: I will give thee the vineyard of Naboth."

This chapter is based on 1 Kings 21; 2 Kings 1.

Jezebel immediately proceeded to carry out her wicked purpose. She wrote letters in the name of the king and sent them to the elders of the city where Naboth dwelt, saying: "Set Naboth on high among the people: and set two men, sons of Belial, before him, to bear witness against him, saying, Thou didst blaspheme God and the king. And then carry him out, and stone him, that he may die."

The command was obeyed. "The men of his city, even the elders and the nobles. . . , did as Jezebel had . . . written in the letters which she had sent unto them." Then Jezebel went to the king and bade him take the vineyard. And Ahab went down to take possession of the coveted property.

The king was not allowed to enjoy unrebuked that which he had gained by fraud and bloodshed. "The word of the Lord came to Elijah the Tishbite, saying, Arise, go down to meet Ahab king of Israel, . . . behold, he is in the vineyard of Naboth, whither he is gone down to possess it. And thou shalt speak unto him, saying, Thus saith the Lord, Hast thou killed, and also taken possession?" The Lord further instructed Elijah to pronounce on Ahab a terrible judgment.

The guilty ruler, meeting the stern prophet face to face in the vineyard, gave voice to his startled fear: "Hast thou found me, O mine enemy?"

Without hesitation the messenger of the Lord replied, "I have found thee: because thou hast sold thyself to work evil in the sight of the Lord. Behold, I will bring evil upon thee, and will take away thy posterity." The house of Ahab was to be utterly destroyed. And of Jezebel the Lord declared, "The dogs shall eat Jezebel by the wall of Jezreel. Him that dieth of Ahab in the city the dogs shall eat; and him that dieth in the field shall the fowls of the air eat."

When the king heard this fearful message, "he rent his clothes, and put sackcloth upon his flesh, and fasted, and lay in sackcloth, and went softly.

"And the word of the Lord came to Elijah the

Tishbite, saying, Seest thou how Ahab humbleth himself before Me? because he humbleth himself before Me, I will not bring the evil in his days: but in his son's days will I bring the evil upon his house.''

Ahaziah Follows the Ways of His Father and Mother

Less than three years later King Ahab met his death at the hands of the Syrians. Ahaziah, his successor, "did evil in the sight of the Lord. . . . He served Baal, and worshiped him, and provoked to anger the Lord God of Israel," as his father Ahab had done. Judgments followed. A disastrous war with Moab, and then an accident by which his own life was threatened, attested to God's wrath against him. Having fallen "through a lattice in his upper chamber," Ahaziah, seriously injured, sent his servants to make inquiry of Baal-zebub whether he should recover. The god of Ekron, through priests, was supposed to give information concerning future events. But the predictions proceeded from the prince of darkness.

Ahaziah's servants were met by a man of God, who directed them to return to the king with the message: "Is it not because there is not a God in Israel, that ye go to inquire of Baal-zebub, the god of Ekron? Now therefore thus saith the Lord, Thou shalt not come down from the bed on which thou art gone up, but shalt surely die.''

The astonished servants hastened back to the king and repeated to him the words of the man of God. The king inquired, "What kind of man was he?" They answered, "He wore a garment of haircloth, with a girdle of leather above his loins." "It is Elijah the Tishbite," Ahaziah exclaimed. RSV. He knew that if it was indeed Elijah, the words of doom would surely come to pass.

Anxious to avert the judgment, he determined to send for the prophet. Twice Ahaziah sent soldiers to intimidate the prophet, and twice the wrath of God fell on them in judgment. The third company of soldiers humbled themselves before God, and their captain "fell on his knees before Elijah, and besought him, . . . O man of God, I pray thee, let my life, and the life of these fifty thy servants, be precious in thy sight."

"The angel of the Lord said unto Elijah, Go down with him: be not afraid of him. And he arose, and went down with him unto the king. And he said unto him, Thus saith the Lord, Forasmuch as thou hast sent messengers to inquire of Baal-zebub the god of Ekron, is it because there is no God in Israel to inquire of His word? therefore thou shalt not come down from the bed whither thou art gone up, but shalt surely die."

During his father's reign, Ahaziah had seen the terrible evidences God had given apostate Israel of the way in which He regards those who set aside the claims of His law. Ahaziah had acted as if these awful realities were but idle tales. He had followed Baal, and at last had ventured upon this, his most daring act of impiety. Rebellious and unwilling to repent, Ahaziah died "according to the word of the Lord which Elijah had spoken."

Modern Satanic Forms of Worship

Men today may not pay homage to heathen gods, yet thousands are worshiping at Satan's shrine as verily as did the king of Israel. The spirit of idolatry is rife, although it has assumed forms more refined and attractive than when Ahaziah sought to the god of Ekron. Faith in the sure word of prophecy is decreasing, and in its stead superstition and satanic witchery are captivating the minds of many. The mysteries of heathen worship are replaced by the obscurities and wonders of spiritistic mediums. The disclosures of these mediums are received by thousands who refuse to accept light from God's Word. Many who shrink from the thought of consulting spirit mediums are attracted by more pleasing forms of spiritism. Others are led astray by Christian Science and by the mysticism of Theosophy and other Oriental religions.

The apostles of nearly all forms of spiritism claim to have power to heal. And there are not a few who go to these healers instead of trusting in the living God and the skill of well-qualified physicians. The mother, watching by the sickbed of her child, exclaims, "Is there no physician who has power to restore my child?" She is told of the cures performed by some clairvoyant and trusts her dear one to his charge, placing it as verily in the hand of Satan as if he were standing by her side. In many instances the future life of the child is controlled by a satanic power.

God had cause for displeasure at Ahaziah's impiety. What had He not done to inspire Israel with confidence in Himself? Yet now the king of Israel, turning to ask help of the worst enemy of his people, proclaimed to the heathen that he had more confidence in their idols than in the God of heaven. Men and women dishonor Him when they turn from the Source of strength and wisdom to ask help or counsel from the powers of darkness.

Those who give themselves up to the sorcery of Satan may boast of great benefit received, but does this prove their course wise or safe? What if life should be prolonged? What if temporal gain should be secured? Will it pay in the end to disregard the will of God? All such apparent gain will prove at last an irrecoverable loss.

Ahaziah was succeeded by Jehoram, his brother, who reigned for twelve years. Throughout these years Jezebel was still living and continued to exercise her evil influence over the nation. Jehoram "wrought evil in the sight of the Lord; but not like his father, and like his mother: for he put away the image of Baal that his father had made. Nevertheless he cleaved unto the sin of Jeroboam the son of Nebat, which made Israel to sin; he departed not therefrom." 2 Kings 3:2, 3.

During Jehoram's reign over Israel Jehoshapat died, and his son, also named Jehoram, ascended the throne of Judah. By his marriage with the daughter of Ahab and Jezebel, Jehoram of Judah was closely connected with the king of Israel and followed after Baal "like as did the house of Ahab." "Moreover he . . . caused the inhabitants of Jerusalem to commit fornication, and compelled Judah thereto." 2 Chronicles 21:6, 11.

The king of Judah was not permitted to continue his terrible apostasy unreproved. The prophet Elijah could not remain silent while Judah was pursuing the same course that had brought the northern kingdom to the verge of ruin. The prophet sent Jehoram of Judah a written communication, in which the wicked king read the awful words:

"Thus saith the Lord God of David thy father, Because thou hast not walked in the ways of Jehoshaphat thy father, . . . but has walked in the way of the kings of Israel, and hast made Judah and the inhabitants of Jerusalem to go a whoring, . . . and also hast slain thy brethren of thy father's house, which were better than thyself: behold, with a great plague will the Lord smite thy people, and thy children, and thy wives, and all thy goods: and thou shalt have great sickness."

In fulfillment of this prophecy "the Lord stirred up against Jehoram the spirit of the Philistines, and of the Arabians . . . : and they . . . carried away all the substance that was found in the king's house, and his sons also, and his wives; so that there was never a son left him, save Jehoahaz [Ahaziah, Azariah], the youngest of his sons.

"And after all this the Lord smote him in his bowels with an incurable disease. And . . . in process of time, after the end of two years, . . . he died of sore diseases." "And Ahaziah [Jehoahaz] his son reigned in his stead." Verses 12-19; 2 Kings 8:24.

Ahaziah ruled only one year, and during this time, influenced by his mother Athaliah, "his counselor to do wickedly," "he did evil in the sight of the Lord." 2 Chronicles 22:3, 4. Jezebel, his grandmother, was still living, and he allied himself boldly with Jehoram of Israel, his uncle.

The surviving members of the house of Ahab were indeed "his counselors, to his undoing." 2 Chronicles 22:4, RSV. While Ahaziah was visiting his uncle at Jezreel, the prophet Elisha was divinely directed to send one of the sons of the prophets to Ramothgilead to anoint Jehu king of Israel. The combined forces of Judah and Israel were at the time engaged in a military campaign against the Syrians. Jehoram had been wounded in battle and had returned to Jezreel, leaving Jehu in charge of the armies. The messenger of Elisha solemnly charged Jehu with a special commission from heaven: "Thou shalt smite the house of Ahab thy master, that I may avenge the blood of My servants the prophets, and the blood of all the servants of the Lord. . . . For the whole house of Ahab shall perish." 2 Kings 9:6-8.

Jehu Takes the Kingship

After he had been proclaimed king by the army, Jehu hastened to Jezreel, where he began his work of execution. Jehoram of Israel, Ahaziah of Judah, and Jezebel the queen mother, with "all that remained of the house of Ahab in Jezreel," were slain. "All his great men, and his kinsfolks, and his priests" were put to the sword. The temple of Baal was laid in ruins, the idolatrous images burned. "Thus Jehu destroyed Baal out of Israel." 2 Kings 10:11, 28.

Tidings of this general execution reached Athaliah, Jezebel's daughter, who still occupied a commanding position in the kingdom of Judah. When she saw that her son, the king of Judah, was dead, "she arose and destroyed all the seed royal of the house of Judah." 2 Chronicles 22:10. In this massacre all the descendants of David who were eligible to the throne were destroyed, save one, a babe named Joash, whom the wife of Jehoiada the high priest hid within the temple. For six years the child remained hidden, while "Athaliah reigned over the land." Verse 12.

At the end of this time, "the Levites and all Judah"

(2 Chronicles 23:8) united with Jehoiada the high priest in crowning the child Joash and acclaiming him their king. "And they clapped their hands, and said, God save the king." 2 Kings 11:12.

"When Athaliah heard the noise of the people running and praising the king, she came to the people into the house of the Lord." 2 Chronicles 23:12.

"And when she looked, behold, the king stood by a pillar, as the manner was, and the princes and the trumpeters by the king, and all the people of the land rejoiced, and blew with trumpets."

"Athaliah rent her clothes, and cried, Treason! Treason!" 2 Kings 11:14. But Jehoiada commanded the officers to lay hold of Athaliah and her followers and lead them out of the temple to be slain.

Thus perished the last member of the house of Ahab. The terrible evil that had been wrought through his alliance with Jezebel continued till the last of his descendants was destroyed. Immediately after the execution of impenitent Queen Athaliah, "all the people of the land went into the house of Baal, and brake it down; . . . and his images brake they in pieces thoroughly, and slew Mattan the priest of Baal." 2 Kings 11:18.

Reformation followed. Those who took part in acclaiming Joash king had covenanted "that they should be the Lord's people." And now that the daughter of Jezebel had been removed from Judah and the priests of Baal had been slain and their temple destroyed, "all the people of the land rejoiced: and the city was quiet." 2 Chronicles 23:16, 21.

17 / Elisha Called to Succeed Elijah

God had told Elijah to anoint another to be prophet in his stead—"Elisha the son of Shaphat." 1 Kings 19:16. In obedience to the command, Elijah went to find Elisha. As he journeyed northward, how changed was the scene from what it had been only a short time before! On every hand vegetation was springing up as if to redeem the time of drought and famine.

Elisha's father was a wealthy farmer whose household had not bowed the knee to Baal. Theirs was a home where God was honored. In the quietude of country life, under the teaching of God and nature and the discipline of useful work, Elisha received training in habits of simplicity and of obedience to his parents and to God that helped to fit him for the high position he was afterward to occupy.

The prophetic call came while he was plowing in the field. He had taken up the work that lay nearest. Of a quiet and gentle spirit, he was nevertheless energetic and steadfast. In humble toil he gained strength of character, constantly increasing in grace and knowledge. While cooperating with his father in homelife duties, he was learning to cooperate with God. By faithfulness in little things, he was preparing for weightier trusts. Day by day he gained a fitness for a higher work. In learning to serve he learned also how to instruct and lead. None can know God's purpose in His discipline; but all may be certain that faithfulness in little things is the evidence of fitness for greater responsibilities. Only he who in small duties proves himself "a workman that needeth not to be ashamed'' (2 Timothy 2:15) can be honored by God with higher service.

Many feel that their lives are useless, that they are doing nothing for the advancement of God's kingdom. Because they can serve only in little things, they think themselves justified in doing nothing. In this they err. One may be in the active service of God while engaged in ordinary, everyday duties—felling trees, clearing the ground, or following the plow. The mother who trains her children for Christ is as truly working for God as is the minister in the pulpit.

Many long for special talent with which to do a wonderful work, while duties close at hand are lost sight of. Let such ones take up the duties lying directly in their pathway. It is not splendid talents that enable us to render acceptable service, but the conscientious performance of daily duties, the contented spirit, the sincere interest in others. The commonest tasks, wrought with loving faithfulness, are beautiful in God's sight.

As Elijah passed the field in which Elisha was plowing, he cast upon the young man's shoulders the mantle of consecration. During the famine the family of Shaphat had become familiar with the work and mission of Elijah, and now the Spirit of God impressed Elisha that God had called him to be the successor of Elijah.

"And he left the oxen, and ran after Elijah, and said, Let me, I pray thee, kiss my father and my mother, and then I will follow thee." "Go back again," was Elijah's answer, "for what have I done to thee?" 1 Kings 19:20. This was not a repulse, but a test of faith. Elisha must count the cost—to accept or reject the call. If his desires clung to his home and its advantages, he was at liberty to remain there.

But Elisha understood the meaning of the call, and he did not hesitate to obey. Not for any worldly advantage would he forgo the opportunity of becoming God's messenger or sacrifice the privilege of association with His servant. He "took a yoke of oxen, and slew them, and boiled their flesh with the instruments of the oxen, and gave unto the people, and they did eat. Then he arose, and went after Elijah, and ministered unto him." 1 Kings 19:21. Without hesitation he left a home where he was beloved, to attend the prophet in his uncertain life.

A Young Man Who Rejected Christ's Call to Service

Similar to the call that came to Elisha was the answer given by Christ to the young ruler who asked Him, "What good thing must I do, that I may have eternal life?" "If thou wilt be perfect," Christ replied, "go and sell that thou hast, and give to the poor, and thou shalt have treasure in heaven: and come and follow Me." Matthew 19:16, 21.

Elisha accepted the call, casting no backward glance at the pleasures and comforts he was leaving. The young ruler "went away sorrowful: for he had great possessions." Verse 22. His love for his possessions was greater than his love for God. He proved himself unworthy of a place in the Master's service.

We are not all asked to serve as Elisha served, nor to sell everything we have; but God asks us to give His service first place in our lives, to allow no day to pass without doing something to advance His work. One may be called to a foreign land, another to give means to support gospel work. God accepts the offering of each. It is the consecration of the life and all its interests that is necessary.

To everyone who partakes of His grace the Lord appoints a work for others. We are to say, "Here am I; send me." See Isaiah 6:8. Whether one is a minister of the Word, a physician, a merchant, farmer, professional man, or mechanic, it is his work to reveal to others the gospel.

No great work was at first required of Elisha; he is spoken of as pouring water on the hands of Elijah. He was willing to do anything the Lord directed, and at every step he continued to prove faithful in little things. With daily strengthening purpose he devoted himself to the mission appointed him by God.

After uniting with Elijah, Elisha was tempted to think of the home that he had left. But he was resolved not to turn back, and through test and trial he proved true to his trust.

Ministry comprehends far more than preaching. It means training young men as Elijah trained Elisha, giving them responsibilities in God's work—small at first, larger as they gain strength and experience. Ministers of faith and prayer can say, "That which was from the beginning, which we have heard, which we have seen with our eyes, which we have looked upon, and our hands have handled, of the Word of life; . . . declare we unto you." 1 John 1:1-3. Young, inexperienced workers should be trained in connection with experienced servants of God.

God has honored young men by choosing them for His service, and they should be faithful, obedient, and willing to sacrifice. If they submit to God's discipline, choosing His servants as their counselors, they will develop into high-principled, steadfast men whom God can entrust with responsibilities.

The Great Results of Elijah's Work

As the gospel is proclaimed in its purity, men will be called from the plow and from common commercial business vocations and will be educated in connection with men of experience. As they learn to labor effectively, they will proclaim the truth with power. Through wonderful workings of providence, mountains of difficulty will be cast into the sea. The message that means so much to the dwellers on earth will be heard and understood. Onward and still onward the work will advance until the whole earth shall have been warned, and then shall the end come.

For several years Elijah and Elisha labored together. Elijah had been God's instrument for the overthrow of gigantic evils. The idolatry by which Ahab and the heathen Jezebel had seduced the nation had been given a decided check. Baal's prophets had been slain. Israel had been deeply stirred, and many were returning to the worship of God. Elisha, by careful, patient instruction, must guide Israel in safe paths. His association with Elijah, the greatest prophet since Moses, prepared him for the work he was soon to take up alone.

During these years Elijah from time to time was called to meet flagrant evils with stern rebuke. When Ahab seized Naboth's vineyard, the voice of Elijah prophesied his doom and the doom of all his house. And when Ahaziah turned from the living God to Baal-zebub, Elijah's voice was heard in earnest protest.

The schools of the prophets, established by Samuel, had fallen into decay during Israel's apostasy. Elijah reestablished them, making provision for young men to gain an education that would lead them to magnify the law and make it honorable. Three schools are mentioned in the record—Gilgal, Bethel, and Jericho. Just before Elijah was taken to heaven, he and Elisha visited these centers of training. The lessons that the prophet of God had given on former visits, he now repeated. Especially did he instruct them concerning maintaining their allegiance to the God of heaven. He also impressed on their minds the importance of letting simplicity mark every feature of their education. Only in this way could they receive the mold of heaven and work in the ways of the Lord.

Elijah was cheered as he saw what was being accomplished by these schools. The reformation was not complete, but he could see a verification of the word of the Lord, "Yet I have left Me seven thousand in Israel, . . . all the knees which have not bowed unto Baal." 1 Kings 19:18.

As Elisha accompanied the prophet from school to school, his faith and resolution were once more tested. He was invited by the prophet to turn back: "Tarry here, I pray thee," Elijah said, "for the Lord hath sent me to Bethel." 2 Kings 2:2. But Elisha had learned not to become discouraged, and now he would not be parted from his master, so long as opportunity remained for gaining a further fitting up for service.

Unknown to Elijah, the revelation that he was to be translated had been made known to his disciples in the schools of the prophets and to Elisha. And now the servant of the man of God kept close beside him. As often as the invitation to turn back was given, his answer was, "I will not leave thee." Verse 2.

"And the two of them went on. . . . And Elijah took his mantle, and wrapped it together, and smote the waters [of the Jordan River], and they were divided hither and thither, so that the two went over on dry ground. And it came to pass, when they were gone over, that Elijah said unto Elisha, Ask what I shall do for thee, before I be taken away from thee." Verses 6-9.

That which Elisha craved was a large measure of the Spirit that God had bestowed on the one about to be honored with translation. He knew that nothing but the Spirit which had rested on Elijah could fit him to fill the place in Israel to which God had called him, and so he asked, "Let a double portion of thy Spirit be upon me." Verse 9.

In response Elijah said, "Thou hast asked a hard thing: nevertheless, if thou see me when I am taken from thee, it shall be so unto thee; but if not, it shall not be so. And it came to pass, as they still went on, and talked, that, behold, there appeared a chariot of fire, and horses of fire, and parted them both asunder; and Elijah went up by a whirlwind into heaven." 2 Kings 2:10, 11.

Many Will Be Translated Without Tasting Death

Elijah was a type of the saints who will be living at the time of the second advent of Christ and who will be "changed, in a moment, in the twinkling of an eye, at the last trump," without tasting death. 1 Corinthians 15:51, 52. As a representative of those who shall be thus translated, Elijah was permitted to stand with

Moses by the side of the Saviour on the mount of trans-figuration. The disciples saw Jesus clothed with the light of heaven; they heard the "voice out of the cloud" (Luke 9:35), acknowledging Him as the Son of God. They saw Moses, representing those who will be raised from the dead at the second advent. And there also stood Elijah, representing those who at the close of earth's history will be changed from mortal to immortal, translated to heaven without seeing death.

In the desert, in loneliness and discouragement, Elijah had prayed that he might die. But there was yet a great work for Elijah to do; and when his work was done, he was not to perish in discouragement and solitude. Not for him the descent into the tomb, but the ascent with God's angels to the presence of His glory.

"And Elisha . . . saw him no more: and . . . he took up also the mantle of Elijah that fell from him, and went back, and stood by the bank of Jordan; and he took the mantle . . . and smote the waters, and said, Where is the Lord God of Elijah? and when he also had smitten the waters, they parted hither and thither: and Elisha went over.

"And when the sons of the prophets which were to view at Jericho saw him, they said, The spirit of Elijah doth rest on Elisha." 2 Kings 2:12-15.

When the Lord sees fit to remove from His work those to whom He has given wisdom, He strengthens their successors, if they will look to Him for aid and will walk in His ways. They may be even wiser than their predecessors, for they may profit by their experience.

Henceforth Elisha stood in Elijah's place. Faithful in that which was least, he was to prove himself faithful also in much.

18 / The Healing of the Waters

In the Jordan Valley, rich with fields of grain and forests of fruit-bearing trees, the hosts of Israel had encamped after crossing the Jordan. Before them had stood Jericho, the center of the worship of Ashtoreth, vilest of all Canaanitish forms of idolatry. Soon its walls were thrown down, and at the time of its fall the solemn declaration was made: "Cursed be the man before the Lord that riseth up and buildeth this city Jericho: he shall lay the foundation thereof in his firstborn, and in his youngest son shall he set up the gates of it." Joshua 6:26.

Five centuries passed. The spot lay desolate, accursed of God. Even the springs suffered the blighting effects of the curse. But when through Jezebel's influence the worship of Ashtoreth was revived, Jericho, the ancient seat of this worship, was rebuilt, though at a fearful cost to the builder. Hiel the Bethelite "laid the foundation thereof in Abiram his first-born, and set up the gates thereof in his youngest son Segub, according to the word of the Lord." 1 Kings 16:34.

Not far from Jericho was one of the schools of the prophets, and thither Elisha went after the ascension of Elijah. During his sojourn among them the men of the city came to him and said, "The situation of this city is pleasant, as my lord seeth: but the water is nought, and the ground barren." The spring that had been pure and life-giving was now unfit for use. In response Elisha said, "Bring me a new cruse, and put salt therein." Having received this, "he went forth unto the spring of the waters, and cast the salt in there, and said, Thus saith the Lord, I have healed these waters; there shall not be from thence any more death or barren land." 2 Kings 2:19-21.

The healing of the waters of Jericho was accomplished by the miraculous interposition of God. He who "maketh His sun to rise on the evil and on the good, and sendeth rain on the just and on the unjust," saw fit to reveal, through this token of compassion, His willingness to heal Israel of their spiritual maladies. Matthew 5:45.

The restoration was permanent. From age to age the waters have flowed on, making that portion of the valley an oasis of beauty.

The Lord Still Heals the Bitter Springs

In casting salt into the bitter spring, Elisha taught the same spiritual lesson imparted centuries later by the Saviour when He declared, "Ye are the salt of the earth." Matthew 5:13. Salt mingling with the polluted spring purified its waters. When God compares His children to salt, He would teach them that His purpose is that they may become agents in saving others, that through them the world might receive the grace that brings salvation.

The world needs evidences of sincere Christianity. The poison of sin is at work at the heart of society. Cities and towns are steeped in moral corruption, suffering, and iniquity. Souls in poverty and distress are weighed down with guilt and perishing for want of a saving influence. The gospel of truth is kept before them, yet they perish because those who should be a savor of life to them are a savor of death. Their souls drink in bitterness because the springs are poisoned.

Salt must be mingled with the substance to which it is added; it must penetrate, infuse it, that it may be preserved. So through personal association men are reached by the saving power of the gospel. Personal influence is a power to work with the influence of

Christ, to lift where Christ lifts, to impart correct principles, and to stay the progress of the world's corruption. It is to uplift, to sweeten the lives of others by a pure example united with faith and love.

The polluted stream at Jericho represents the soul that is separate from God. Sin destroys in the human soul both the desire and the capacity for knowing Him. The whole human organism is deranged, the mind perverted, the imagination corrupted. For want of moral force to overcome, the soul is debased.

To the heart that has become purified, all is changed. The Spirit of God produces a new life in the soul, bringing the thoughts and desires into obedience to the will of Christ; and the inward man is renewed in the image of God. Weak and erring men and women show to the world that the redeeming power of grace can cause the faulty character to develop into symmetry and fruitfulness.

The heart that receives the word of God is not like a broken cistern that loses it treasure; it is like the mountain stream, fed by unfailing springs, whose sparkling waters refresh the weary, the thirsty, the heavy-laden. It is like a river constantly flowing and, as it advances, becoming deeper and wider, until its life-giving waters are spread over all the earth. The stream leaves behind its gift of fruitfulness. When the earth lies bare and brown under summer's scorching heat, a line of verdure marks the river's course.

So with the true child of God. When the heart is opened to the heavenly influence of truth and love, these principles will flow forth like streams in the desert, causing fruitfulness to appear where now are barrenness and dearth.

Those who have been cleansed through a knowledge of Bible truth will daily drink of the inexhaustible fountain of grace and knowledge. They will find that their own hearts are filled to overflowing with the Spirit of their Master; and through their unselfish ministry many are benefited physically, mentally, and spiritually. The weary are refreshed, the sick restored to health, and the sin-burdened relieved.

"Give, and it shall be given unto you"; for the word of God is "a fountain of gardens, a well of living waters, and streams from Lebanon." Luke 6:38; Song of Solomon 4:15.

19 / Elisha, Gentle Prophet of Peace

To Elijah had been committed messages of condemnation and judgment. His was the voice of fearless reproof. Elisha's was a more peaceful mission—to strengthen the work Elijah had begun, to teach people the way of the Lord. Inspiration pictures him as coming into personal touch with the people, bringing healing and rejoicing.

Elisha was of mild and kindly spirit, but that he could also be stern is shown when, on the way to Bethel, he was mocked by ungodly youth. These youth had heard of Elijah's ascension and made this solemn event the subject of jeers, saying to Elisha, "Go up, thou bald head; go up, thou bald head." 2 Kings 2:23. Under the inspiration of the Almighty the prophet pronounced a curse on them. The awful judgment that followed was of God. "There came forth two she-bears out of the wood, and tare forty and two" of them. Verse 24.

Had Elisha allowed the mockery to pass unnoticed, he would have continued to be ridiculed by the rabble, and his mission in a time of national peril might have been defeated. This one instance of terrible severity was sufficient to command respect throughout his life. For fifty years he went from city to city, passing through crowds of rude, dissolute youth, but none mocked him as the prophet of the Most High.

Even kindness should have its limits. The so-called

This chapter is based on 2 Kings 4.

tenderness, the coaxing and indulgence toward youth by parents and guardians is one of the worst evils which can come on them. In every family, firmness and positive requirements are essential.

Every child should be taught to show true reverence for God. Never should His name be spoken lightly or thoughtlessly. Reverence should be shown for God's representatives—ministers, teachers, and parents, who are called to act in His stead. In the respect shown them, God is honored.

A Family's Hospitality Is Rewarded

The kindly spirit that enabled Elisha to exert a powerful influence over many in Israel is revealed in the story of his friendly relations with a family at Shunem. In his journeyings to and fro, "one day Elisha went on to Shunem, where a wealthy woman lived, who urged him to eat some food. So whenever he passed that way, he would turn in there to eat food." 2 Kings 4: 8, RSV. The mistress of the house perceived that Elisha was a "holy man of God," and she said to her husband, "Let us make a little chamber . . . on the wall; and let us set for him there a bed, and a table, a stool, and a candlestick: and it shall be, when he cometh to us, that he shall turn in thither." To this retreat Elisha often came. Nor was God unmindful of the woman's kindness. Her home had been childless, and now the Lord rewarded her hospitality by the gift of a son.

Years passed. The child was old enough to be out in the field with the reapers. One day he was stricken by the heat, "and he said unto his father, My head, my head." A lad carried the child to his mother, "and when he had . . . brought him to his mother, he sat on her knees till noon, and then died. And she went up, and laid him on the bed of the man of God, and shut the door upon him, and went out."

In her distress, the woman determined to go to Elisha for help. Accompanied by her servant, she set forth immediately. "When the man of God saw her afar off, . . . he said to Gehazi his servant, Behold, yonder is that Shunammite: run now . . . to meet her, and say unto her, Is it well with thee? is it well with thy husband? is it well with the child?" But not till she reached Elisha did the stricken mother reveal the cause of her sorrow. Upon hearing of her loss, Elisha told Gehazi: "Take my staff in thine hand, and go . . . and lay my staff upon the face of the child."

But the mother would not be satisfied till Elisha himself came with her. "I will not leave thee," she declared. So "he arose, and followed her. And Gehazi passed on before them, and laid the staff upon the face of the child; but there was neither voice, nor hearing. Wherefore he went again to meet him, and told him, saying, The child is not awaked."

When they reached the house, Elisha went into the room where the dead child lay, "and shut the door upon the two of them, and prayed to the Lord. Then he went up and lay upon the child, putting his mouth upon his mouth, his eyes upon his eyes, and his hands upon his hands; and as he stretched himself upon him, the flesh of the child became warm. Then he got up again, and walked once to and fro in the house, and went up, and stretched himself upon him; the child sneezed seven times, and the child opened his eyes." RSV. So was the faith of this woman rewarded. Christ, the great Life-giver, restored her son to her.

In like manner will His faithful ones be rewarded when, at His coming, the grave is robbed of the victory it has claimed. Then will He restore to His servants the children that have been taken from them by death.

Jesus comforts our sorrow for the dead with a message of infinite hope: "I am He that liveth, and was dead; and, behold, I am alive for evermore, . . . and have the keys of hell and of death." Revelation 1:18. "The Lord Himself shall descend from heaven with a shout, with the voice of the Archangel, and with the trump of God: and the dead in Christ shall rise first: then we which are alive and remain shall be caught up together with them in the clouds, to meet the Lord in the air: and so shall we ever be with the Lord." 1 Thessalonians 4:16, 17.

In his ministry Elisha combined the work of healing with teaching. Throughout his long and effective labors, Elisha fostered the educational work of the schools of the prophets. His instruction to the earnest groups of young men were confirmed by the deep movings of the Holy Spirit.

The Poisoned Pottage Made Edible

On one of his visits to the school at Gilgal he healed the poisoned pottage. "There was a dearth in the land; and the sons of the prophets were sitting before him: and he said unto his servant, Set on the great pot, and seethe pottage for the sons of the prophets. And one went out into the field to gather herbs, and found a wild vine, and gathered thereof wild gourds his lap full, and came and shred them into the pot of pottage: for they knew them not. So they poured out for the men to eat. And it came to pass, as they were eating of the pottage, that they cried out, and said, O thou man of God, there is death in the pot. And they could not eat thereof. But he said, Then bring meal. And he cast it into the pot; and he said, Pour out for the people, that they may eat. And there was no harm in the pot."

At Gilgal, also, while the famine was still in the land, Elisha fed one hundred men with the present brought to him by "a man from Baalshalisha"—"twenty loaves of barley, and full ears of corn in the husk." When the offering came, he said to his servant, "Give unto the people, that they may eat. And his servant said, What, should I set this before an hundred men? He said again, Give the people, that they may eat: for thus saith the Lord, They shall eat, and shall leave thereof. So he set it before them, and they did eat, and left thereof, according to the word of the Lord."

Again and again since that time, though not always in so marked and perceptible a manner, the Lord Jesus has worked to supply human need. If we had clearer spiritual discernment we would recognize more readily than we do God's compassionate dealing with the children of men.

In the days of Christ's earthly ministry, when He performed a similar miracle in feeding the multitudes, the same unbelief was manifested as was shown by those associated with the prophet: "What, should I set this before an hundred men?" And when Jesus told His disciples to give the multitude to eat, they answered, "We have no more than five loaves and two fish—unless we are to go and buy food for all these people." Luke 9:13, RSV. What is that among so many?

When the Lord gives a work to be done, let not men stop to inquire into the reasonableness of the command or the probable result of their efforts to obey. The supply in their hands may seem to fall short of the need to be filled, but in the hands of the Lord it will prove more than sufficient. The servant "set it before them, and they did eat, and left thereof, according to the word of the Lord."

Let none waste time deploring the scantiness of their visible resources. Energy and trust in God will develop resources. The gift brought to Him with thanksgiving and prayer for His blessing, He will multiply as He multiplied the food given to the sons of the prophets and to the weary multitude.

20 / Captain Naaman Healed of Leprosy

"Naaman, commander of the army of the king of Syria, was a great man with his master and in high favor because by him the Lord had given victory to Syria. He was a mighty man of valor, but he was a leper." RSV.

Ben-hadad, king of Syria, had defeated Israel in the battle which resulted in the death of Ahab. Since that time the Syrians had maintained against Israel a constant border warfare, and in one of their raids had carried away a little maid who, in the land of her captivity, "waited on Naaman's wife." A slave, far from her home; this little maid was one of God's witnesses, fulfilling the purpose for which God had chosen Israel as His people. In that heathen home, her sympathies were aroused in behalf of her master, and, remembering the wonderful miracles of healing wrought through Elisha, she said to her mistress, "Would God my lord were with the prophet that is in Samaria! for he would recover him of his leprosy." Verse 3. She believed that by the power of Heaven Naaman could be healed.

The conduct of the captive maid in that heathen home is a strong witness to the power of early home training. There is no higher trust than that committed to fathers and mothers in the care and training of their children.

Happy are the parents whose lives reflect the divine, so that the promises and commands of God awaken in

This chapter is based on 2 Kings 5.

the child gratitude and reverence, parents whose tenderness and justice and long-suffering interpret to the child the love and justice and long-suffering of God, and who teach the child to love and trust and obey his Father in heaven. They endow him with a treasure as enduring as eternity.

Our children may spend their lives in common vocations, but all are called to be ministers of mercy to the world. They are to stand by the side of Christ in unselfish service.

A Captive Girl Encourages Naaman to Seek Healing

Naaman heard of the words that the maid had spoken to her mistress, and, obtaining permission from the king, went forth to seek healing, taking "ten talents of silver, and six thousand pieces of gold, and ten changes of raiment." He also carried a letter from the king of Syria to the king of Israel: "I have . . . sent Naaman my servant to thee, that thou mayest recover him of his leprosy."

When the king of Israel read the letter, "he rent his clothes, and said, Am I God, to kill and to make alive, that this man doth send unto me to recover a man of his leprosy? Wherefore consider, I pray you, and see how he seeketh a quarrel against me."

Tidings of the matter reached Elisha, and he sent word to the king: "Wherefore hast thou rent thy clothes? let him come now to me, and he shall know that there is a prophet in Israel."

"So Naaman came with his horses and with his chariot, and stood at the door of the house of Elisha." Through a messenger the prophet told him, "Go and wash in Jordan seven times, and thy flesh shall come again to thee, and thou shalt be clean."

Naaman had expected to see some wonderful manifestation of power from heaven. "I thought," he said, "He will surely come out to me, and stand, and call on the name of the Lord his God, and strike his hand over the place, and recover the leper." When told to wash in the Jordan, his pride was touched: "Are not Abana and Pharpar, rivers of Damascus, better than all the waters of Israel? may I not wash in them, and be clean? So he turned and went away in a rage."

The rivers mentioned by Naaman were beautified by surrounding groves, and many flocked to the banks of these pleasant streams to worship their idol gods. It would have cost Naaman no humiliation of soul to descend into one of those streams. But only through following the specific directions of the prophet could he find healing.

Naaman's servants urged him to carry out Elisha's directions: "If the prophet had bid thee do some great thing, wouldest thou not have done it? how much rather then, when he saith to thee, Wash, and be clean?" The haughty Syrian yielded his pride and seven times dipped himself in Jordan, "according to the saying of the man of God." And his faith was honored: "His flesh came again like unto the flesh of a little child, and he was clean."

Gratefully "he returned to the man of God, he and all his company," with the acknowledgment, "Now I know that there is no God in all the earth, but in Israel."

In accordance with custom, Naaman asked Elisha to accept a costly present. But the prophet refused. It was not for him to take payment for a blessing that God had bestowed. "So he departed from him."

Elisha's Servant Has the Spirit of Judas

Gehazi, Elisha's servant, had had opportunity to develop the spirit of self-denial characterizing his master's lifework. The best gifts of Heaven had long been within his reach; yet, turning from these, he had coveted instead worldly wealth. And now the hidden longings of his avaricious spirit led him to yield to an overmastering temptation. "My master hath spared Naaman this Syrian, in not receiving at his hands that which he brought: . . . I will run after him, and take somewhat of him." In secrecy "Gehazi followed after Naaman."

"When Naaman saw him running after him, he lighted down from the chariot to meet him, and said, Is all well? And he said, All is well." Then Gehazi uttered a deliberate lie. "My master," he said, "hath sent me, saying, Behold, even now there be come to me from Mount Ephraim two young men of the sons of the prophets: give them, I pray thee, a talent of silver, and two changes of garments." To the request Naaman gladly acceded, pressing upon Gehazi two talents of silver instead of one, "with two changes of garments," and commissioning servants to bear the treasure back.

As Gehazi neared Elisha's home, he dismissed the servants and placed the silver and the garments in hiding. This accomplished, "he went in, and stood before his master." In response to the inquiry, "Where have you been, Gehazi?" he answered, "Your servant went nowhere." RSV.

Elisha knew all. "Did I not go with you in spirit," he asked, "when the man turned from his chariot to meet you? Was it a time to accept money and garments, olive orchards and vineyards, sheep and oxen, menservants and maidservants? Therefore the leprosy of Naaman shall cleave to you, and to your descendants forever." Swift was the retribution that overtook the guilty man. He went out from Elisha's presence, "a leper, as white as snow." RSV.

Solemn are the lessons taught by this experience. Gehazi placed a stumbling block in the pathway of Naaman, upon whose mind had broken a wonderful light and who was favorably disposed toward the service of the living God. For the deception practiced, there could be no excuse. To the day of his death Gehazi remained a leper.

"A false witness shall not be unpunished, and he that speaketh lies shall not escape." Proverbs 19:5. "All things are naked and opened unto the eyes of Him with whom we have to do." Hebrews 4:13. God re-

vealed to His prophet every detail of the scene between Gehazi and Naaman.

Truth is of God; deception in all its forms is of Satan,
and whoever in any way departs from the straight line
of truth is betraying himself into the power of the
wicked one. Those who have learned of Christ will be
straightforward and true, for they are preparing for the
fellowship of those holy ones in whose mouth is found
no guile. See Revelation 14:5.

Naaman's wonderful faith was commended by the
Saviour as an object lesson. "There were many lepers
in Israel in the time of the prophet Elisha," the Saviour
declared; "and none of them was cleansed, but only
Naaman the Syrian." Luke 4:27, RSV. God passed
over many lepers in Israel because their unbelief
closed the door to them. A heathen nobleman who had
been true to his convictions of right was in the sight of
God more worthy of His blessing than the afflicted in
Israel who had despised their God-given privileges.
God works for those who appreciate His favors and respond to the light given them from heaven.

If those who are honest in heart follow what they understand to be duty, they will be given increased light,
until, like Naaman, they will acknowledge that "there
is no God in all the earth," save the living God, the
Creator.

21 / Elisha's Closing Ministry

Elisha lived to see many changes in the kingdom of Israel. Hazael the Syrian had scourged the apostate nation. Jehu had slain all the house of Ahab. Jehoahaz, Jehu's successor, had lost some of the cities east of the Jordan. For a time it had seemed as if the Syrians might gain control of the entire kingdom. But the reformation carried forward by Elisha led many to inquire after God. The altars of Baal were being forsaken, and slowly yet surely God's purpose was being fulfilled in those who chose to serve Him with all the heart.

It was because of His love for erring Israel that God permitted the Syrians to scourge them. Because of His compassion for those whose moral power was weak He raised up Jehu to slay Jezebel and the house of Ahab. Once more, through a merciful providence, the priests of Baal and of Ashtoreth were set aside, and their heathen altars thrown down. God foresaw that if temptation were removed, some would forsake heathenism, and this is why He permitted calamity after calamity to befall them. And when His purpose was accomplished, He turned the tide in favor of those who had learned to inquire after Him.

While Satan was doing all in his power to complete the ruin he had wrought during the reign of Ahab and Jezebel, Elisha continued to bear his testimony. He met with opposition, yet none could gainsay his words. Many came to him for counsel. Joram, king of Israel, sought his advice; and once, when in Damascus, he was visited by messengers from Benhadad, king of

Syria. To all, the prophet bore faithful witness in a time when the great majority of the people were in open rebellion against Heaven.

And God never forsook His chosen messenger. On one occasion, the king of Syria sought to destroy Elisha because of his apprising the king of Israel of the plans of the enemy. The Syrian king had taken counsel with his servants, saying, "In such and such a place shall be my camp." This plan was revealed by the Lord to Elisha, who "sent unto the king of Israel, saying, Beware that thou pass not such a place; for thither the Syrians are come down. And the king of Israel sent to the place which the man of God told him and warned him of, and saved himself there, not once nor twice.

"Therefore the heart of the king of Syria was sore troubled for this thing; and he called his servants, and said unto them, Will ye not show me which of us is for the king of Israel? And one of his servants said, None, my lord, O king: but Elisha, the prophet that is in Israel, telleth the king of Israel the words that thou speakest in thy bedchamber." 2 Kings 6:8-12.

Determined to make away with the prophet, the Syrian king commanded, "Go and spy where he is, that I may send and fetch him." The prophet was in Dothan, and, learning this, the king sent "horses, and chariots, and a great host: and they came by night, and compassed the city about. And when the servant of the man of God was risen early, and gone forth, behold, an host compassed the city both with horses and chariots." Verses 13-15.

In terror Elisha's servant sought him. "Alas, my master!" he said. "How shall we do?"

"Fear not," was the answer of the prophet, "for they who be with us are more than they that be with them." Then, that the servant might know this for himself, Elisha prayed, "Lord, . . . open his eyes, that he may see." So "the Lord opened the eyes of the young man; and he saw: and, behold, the mountain was full of horses and chariots of fire round about Elisha." An encircling band of heavenly angels had come in mighty power to minister to the Lord's helpless ones. Verses 15-17.

As the Syrian soldiers boldly advanced, ignorant of the unseen hosts of heaven, "Elisha prayed unto the Lord, and said, Smite this people, I pray Thee, with blindness. And He smote them with blindness according to the word of Elisha. And Elisha said unto them, This is not the way, neither is this the city: follow me, and I will bring you to the man whom ye seek. But he led them to Samaria.

"And it came to pass, when they were come into Samaria, that Elisha said, Lord, open the eyes of these men, that they may see. And the Lord opened their eyes, and they saw; and, behold, they were in the midst of Samaria. And the king of Israel said unto Elisha, . . .shall I smite them? And he answered, Thou shalt not smite them: wouldest thou smite those whom thou hast taken captive with thy sword and with thy bow? set bread and water before them, that they may eat and drink, and go to their master." Verses 18-22.

God Honors Elisha's Prophecy

For a time after this, Israel was free from the attacks of the Syrians. But later, under king Hazael, the Syrian hosts surrounded Samaria and besieged it. Never had Israel been brought into so great a strait as during this siege. The horrors of prolonged famine were driving the king of Israel to desperate measures when Elisha predicted deliverance the following day.

The next morning the Lord "made the host of the Syrians to hear a noise of chariots, and a noise of horses, even the noise of a great host." Seized with fear, "they fled for their life," leaving "the camp as it was," with rich stores of food. 2 Kings 7:6, 7.

During the night, four leprous men at the gate of the city, made desperate by hunger, had proposed to visit the Syrian camp and throw themselves on the mercy of the besiegers, hoping to obtain food. What was their astonishment when, entering the camp, they found "no man there." Verse 10. With none to forbid, "they went into one tent, and did eat and drink, and carried thence silver, and gold, and raiment, and went and hid it; and came again, and entered into another tent, and carried thence also, and went and hid it. Then they said one to another, We do not well: this day is a day of good tidings, and we hold our peace." Verses 8, 9. Quickly they returned to the city with the glad news.

So abundant were the supplies that on that day "a measure of fine flour was sold for a shekel" (verse 16), as foretold by Elisha the day before.

Elijah's Message Reached the Honest in Heart

Thus the man of God labored from year to year, drawing close to the people, and in times of crisis standing by the side of kings as a wise counselor. The dark shadow of apostasy was still everywhere apparent, yet here and there were those who had steadfastly refused to bow to Baal. As Elisha continued his work, many learned to rejoice in the service of the true God. The prophet was cheered by these miracles of divine grace, and he was inspired with a great longing to reach all who were honest in heart.

From a human point of view the outlook for the spiritual regeneration of the nation was as hopeless as is the outlook today. But the church of Christ is empowered by Him to do a special work, and if she is loyal to God, obedient to His commandments, no power can stand against her. There is before her the dawn of a bright, glorious day, if she will put on the robe of Christ's righteousness, withdrawing from all allegiance to the world.

Talk Courage and Hope

God calls on His faithful ones, who believe in Him, to talk courage to those who are unbelieving and hopeless. Show humble faith in God's power and willingness to save. When in faith we take hold of His strength, He will change, wonderfully change, the most hopeless, discouraging outlook. He will do this for the glory of His name.

Elisha continued to take an active interest in the schools of the prophets. God was with him. On one occasion "the sons of the prophets said unto Elisha, Behold now, the place where we dwell with thee is too strait for us. Let us go, we pray thee, unto Jordan, and take thence every man a beam, and let us make us a place there, where we may dwell." 2 Kings 6:1, 2. Elisha went with them, encouraging them, giving instruction, and even performing a miracle to aid them.

"As one was felling a beam, the axhead fell into the water: and he cried, and said, Alas, master! for it was borrowed. And the man of God said, Where fell it? And he showed him the place. And he cut down a stick, and cast it in thither; and the iron did swim. Therefore said he, Take it up to thee. And he put out his hand, and took it." Verses 5-7.

Elisha's Last Days

So effectual had been his ministry that as Elisha lay on his deathbed, even the youthful King Joash, an idolater with little respect for God, recognized in the prophet a father in Israel and acknowledged that his presence among them was of more value in time of trouble than an army of horses and chariots. See 2 Kings 13:14.

To many a troubled soul the prophet had acted the part of a wise father. And in this instance he turned not from the godless youth before him, so unworthy of the position of trust he was occupying, and yet so greatly in need of counsel. God was bringing the king an opportunity to redeem the past and place his kingdom on vantage ground. The Syrian foe was to be repulsed. Once more the power of God was to be manifested in behalf of erring Israel.

The dying prophet told the king, "Take bow and arrows." Joash obeyed. Then the prophet said, "Put thine hand upon the bow." Joash "put his hand upon it: and Elisha put his hands upon the king's hands. And he said, Open the window eastward"—toward the cities beyond Jordan in possession of the Syrians. 2 Kings 13:15-17. The king having opened the window, Elisha told him to shoot. As the arrow sped on its way, the prophet was inspired to say, "The arrow of the Lord's . . . deliverance from Syria: for thou shalt smite the Syrians in Aphek, till thou have consumed them." 2 Kings 13:17.

And now the prophet tested the faith of the king. Bidding Joash take up the arrows, he said, "Smite upon the ground." Three times the king smote the ground. "Thou shouldest have smitten five or six times," Elisha cried in dismay, "then hadst thou smitten Syria till thou hadst consumed it: whereas now thou shalt smite Syria but thrice." Verses 18, 19.

The lesson is for all in positions of trust. When God gives assurance of success, the chosen instrument must do all in his power to bring about the promised result. In proportion to the enthusiasm and perseverance with which the work is carried forward will be the success given. God can work miracles for His people only as they act their part with untiring energy. Men of devotion, of moral courage, with a zeal that never flags will labor on undaunted until apparent defeat is turned to victory. Not even prison walls will cause them to swerve from their purpose of upbuilding God's kingdom.

Elisha Faithful to the End

With the counsel and encouragement given Joash, the work of Elisha closed. He had proved faithful to the end. Never had he lost his trust in the power of Omnipotence. Always he had advanced by faith, and God had honored his confidence.

It was not given Elisha to follow his master in a fiery chariot. Upon him the Lord permitted to come a lingering illness. As on the heights of Dothan he had seen the encircling hosts of heaven, so now he was conscious of the presence of sympathizing angels, and he was sustained. As he had advanced in a knowledge of God's merciful kindness, faith had ripened into an abiding trust in God, and when death called him he was ready.

"The righteous hath hope in his death." Proverbs 14:32. Elisha could say in all confidence, "As for me, I will behold Thy face in righteousness: I shall be satisfied, when I awake, with Thy likeness." Psalm 17: 15.

22 / Jonah, the Prophet Who Ran Away

One of the greatest cities of the ancient world was Nineveh, the capital of Assyria. Founded on the fertile bank of the Tigris, it had become "an exceeding great city of three days' journey."

Nineveh was a center of crime and wickedness—"the bloody city, . . . full of lies." The prophet Nahum compared the Ninevites to a cruel lion. "Upon whom," he inquired, "has not come your unceasing evil?" Nahum 3:1, 19, RSV.

Yet Nineveh was not wholly given over to evil. In that city many were reaching out after something better, and, if granted opportunity to learn of the living God, they would put away their evil deeds. And so God revealed Himself to them in an unmistakable manner to lead them to repentance.

To the prophet Jonah came the word of the Lord, "Arise, go to Nineveh, that great city, and cry against it; for their wickedness is come up before Me." The prophet was tempted to question the wisdom of the call. It seemed as if nothing could be gained by proclaiming such a message in that proud city. He forgot that God whom he served was all-wise and all-powerful. While he hesitated, Satan overwhelmed him with discouragement, and he "rose up to flee unto Tarshish." Finding a ship ready to sail, "he paid the fare thereof and went down into it, to go with them."

Jonah had been entrusted with a heavy responsibil-

This chapter is based on Jonah 1 to 4.

ity. Had the prophet obeyed unquestioningly, he would have been blessed abundantly. Yet in Jonah's despair the Lord did not desert him. Through trials and strange providences, the prophet's confidence in God was to be revived.

Not for long was he permitted to go undisturbed in his mad flight. "The Lord sent out a great wind into the sea, . . . so that the ship was like to be broken. Then the mariners were afraid, and cried every man unto his god, and cast forth the wares that were in the ship into the sea, to lighten it of them. But Jonah was gone down into the sides of the ship; and he lay, and was fast asleep."

The master of the ship, distressed beyond measure, sought out Jonah and said, "What meanest thou, O sleeper? arise, call upon thy God, if so be that God will think upon us, that we perish not."

Jonah Cast Overboard

But the prayers of the man who had turned aside from duty brought no help. The mariners proposed as a last resort the casting of lots, "that we may know," they said, "for whose cause this evil is upon us. So they cast lots, and the lot fell upon Jonah. Then said they unto him, Tell us, we pray thee, for whose cause this evil is upon us; what is thine occupation? and whence comest thou? what is thy country? and of what people art thou?

"And he said unto them, I am an Hebrew; and I fear the Lord, the God of heaven, which hath made the sea and the dry land.

"Then . . . the men knew that he fled from the presence of the Lord, because he had told them.

"Then they said to him, 'What shall we do to you, that the sea may be calm for us?'—for the sea was growing more tempestuous. And he said to them, 'Pick me up and throw me into the sea; then the sea will become calm for you. For I know that this great tempest is because of me.' " Jonah 1:11, 12, NKJV.

"So they took up Jonah, and cast him forth into the sea: and the sea ceased from her raging. . . .

"The Lord had prepared a great fish to swallow up Jonah. And Jonah was in the belly of the fish three days and three nights."

"Then Jonah prayed to the Lord his God from the belly of the fish, saying:

> I called to the Lord, out of my distress,
>   And He answered me. . .
>
> For Thou didst cast me into the deep,
>   Into the heart of the seas,
> And the flood was round about me;
>   All Thy waves and Thy billows passed over me.
>
> Then I said, "I am cast out from Thy presence;
>   How shall I again look upon Thy holy
>   temple?" . . .
>
> When my soul fainted within me,
>   I remembered the Lord;
> And my prayer came to Thee,
>   Into Thy holy temple. . . .
>
> What I have vowed I will pay.
>   Deliverance belongs to the Lord!
>   RSV

At last Jonah had learned that "salvation belongeth unto the Lord." Psalm 3:8. With penitence and a recognition of the saving grace of God, came deliverance. Jonah was released from the perils of the mighty deep and was cast upon the dry land.

Once more the servant of God was commissioned to warn Nineveh: "Arise, go to Nineveh, that great city, and proclaim to it the message that I tell you." This time he did not question or doubt, but "arose and went to Nineveh, according to the word of the Lord." RSV.

As Jonah entered the city, he began at once to "cry against" it the message: "Yet forty days, and Nineveh shall be overthrown!" From street to street he went, sounding the warning. The cry rang through the streets of the godless city until all the inhabitants heard the startling announcement. The Spirit of God pressed the message home to every heart, and multitudes repented in deep humiliation.

"Then tidings reached the king of Nineveh, and he arose from his throne, removed his robe, and covered himself with sackcloth, and sat in ashes. And he made proclamation and published through Nineveh, 'By the decree of the king and his nobles: Let . . . every one turn from his evil way and from the violence which is in his hands. Who knows, God may yet repent and turn from His fierce anger, so that we perish not?' " RSV.

As king and nobles, the high and the low, "repented at the preaching of Jonas" (Matthew 12:41), mercy was granted them. "God repented of the evil which He had said He would do to them; and He did not do it." RSV. Their doom was averted, the God of Israel was honored throughout the heathen world, and His law was revered. Not until many years later was Nineveh to fall a prey to the surrounding nations through forget-fulness of God and through boastful pride.

When Jonah learned of God's purpose to spare the city, he should have been the first to rejoice. But he allowed his mind to dwell on the possibility of his being regarded as a false prophet. The compassion shown by God toward the repentant Ninevites "displeased Jonah exceedingly, and he was angry." "Is not this what I said," he inquired of the Lord, "when I was yet in my country? That is why I made haste to flee to Tarshish; for I knew that Thou art a gracious God and merciful, slow to anger, and abounding in steadfast love, and repentest of evil." RSV.

Once more he was overwhelmed with discourage-ment. Losing sight of the interests of others, in dissat-isfaction he exclaimed, "Therefore now, O Lord, take my life from me, I beseech Thee, for it is better for me to die than to live." RSV.

"And the Lord said, 'Do you well to be angry?' Then Jonah went out of the city . . . and made a booth for himself there. He sat under it in the shade, till he should see what would become of the city. And the Lord God appointed a plant, and made it come up over Jonah, that it might be a shade over his head, to save him from his discomfort. So Jonah was exceedingly glad because of the plant." RSV.

Then the Lord gave Jonah an object lesson. He "appointed a worm which attacked the plant, so that it withered. When the sun rose, God appointed a sultry east wind; and the sun beat upon the head of Jonah so that he was faint; and he asked that he might die, and said, 'It is better for me to die than to live.' " RSV.

Again God spoke to His prophet: " 'Do you do well to be angry for the plant?' And he said, 'I do well to be angry, angry enough to die.'

"And the Lord said, 'You pity the plant, . . . and should not I pity Nineveh, that great city, in which there are more than a hundred and twenty thousand persons who do not know their right hand from their left?' " RSV.

Jonah had fulfilled the commission given him to warn that great city; and though the event predicted did not come to pass, yet the message of warning was nonetheless from God, and it accomplished the purpose God designed. His grace was revealed among the heathen. The Lord "delivered them from their distress; He brought them out of darkness and gloom." "He sent forth His word, and healed them, and delivered them from destruction." Psalm 107:13, 14, 20, RSV.

Christ referred to the preaching of Jonah and compared the inhabitants of Nineveh with the professed people of God in His day: "The men of Nineveh shall rise in judgment with this generation, and shall condemn it: because they repented at the preaching of Jonas; and, behold, a greater than Jonas is here.'' Matthew 12:41. Into the busy world where men were trying to get all they could for self, Christ had come; and above the confusion His voice was heard: "What shall a man give in exchange for his soul?" Mark 8:37.

Jonah's Day, and Ours

Today the cities are in need of knowledge of the true God as were the Ninevites. Christ's ambassadors are to point men to the nobler world. According to the Scriptures, the only city that will endure is the city whose builder and maker is God. Through His servants the Lord is calling on men to secure the immortal inheritance.

There is coming rapidly an almost universal guilt on the cities, because of the steady increase of determined wickedness. Every day brings fresh revelations of strife, bribery, fraud, violence, lawlessness, indifference to human suffering, and brutal destruction of human life. Every day testifies to the increase of insanity, murder, and suicide. Men boast of the progress and enlightenment of the age in which we now live; but God sees the earth filled with iniquity and violence. Men declare that the law of God has been abrogated, and as a result, a tide of evil is sweeping over the world. Nobility of soul, gentleness, piety, are bartered away to gratify the lust for forbidden things.

With long-sufferance and tender compassion God deals with the transgressors of His law. And yet, the end of God's forbearance with those who persist in disobedience is approaching rapidly.

Ought men to be surprised over a sudden change in the dealings of the Supreme Ruler with the inhabitants of a fallen world? Ought they be surprised that God should bring destruction on those whose ill-gotten gains have been obtained through fraud? Many have chosen to remain under the banner of the originator of rebellion against the government of heaven.

The forbearance of God has been so great that we

marvel. The Omnipotent One has been exerting a restraining power over His own attributes. God allows men a period of probation, but there is a point beyond which divine patience is exhausted. The Lord bears long with men, giving warnings to save them, but a time will come when the rebellious element will be blotted out, in mercy to themselves and to those who would be influenced by their example.

The Spirit of God is being withdrawn. Disasters follow one another in quick succession—earthquakes, tornadoes, fire, and flood. Apparently these calamities are capricious outbreaks of disorganized unregulated forces of nature, beyond the control of man; but they are among the agencies by which God seeks to arouse men and women to a sense of their danger.

God's messengers in the great cities are not to become discouraged over the wickedness and depravity they face while proclaiming the glad tidings of salvation. The Lord gave Paul in wicked Corinth a message: "Do not be afraid, . . . for I am with you. . . ; I have many people in this city." Acts 18:9, 10, RSV. In every city there are many who with proper teaching may learn to become followers of Jesus.

God's message for the inhabitants of earth today is, "Be ye also ready: for in such an hour as ye think not the Son of man cometh." Matthew 24:44. The conditions in the great cities proclaim in thunder tones that the hour of God's judgment is come and that the end of all things earthly is at hand. In quick succession the judgments of God will follow one another—fire, and flood, and earthquake, with war and bloodshed. The angel of mercy cannot much longer shelter the impenitent. The storm is gathering; and those only will stand who respond to the invitations of mercy, as did the inhabitants of Nineveh under the preaching of Jonah, and become sanctified through obedience to the laws of the divine Ruler.

23 / The Decline and Fall of Israel

The closing years of the kingdom of Israel were marked with violence and bloodshed not witnessed even in the worst periods under the house of Ahab. For two centuries the ten tribes had been sowing the wind; now they were reaping the whirlwind. King after king was assassinated. "They made kings, but not through Me," the Lord declared of the godless usurpers. "They set up princes, but without My knowledge." Hosea 8:4, RSV. Those who should have stood before the nations of earth as the depositaries of divine grace "dealt treacherously against the Lord" and with one another. Hosea 5:7.

Through Hosea and Amos God sent message after message, urging repentance and threatening disaster. "Ye have plowed wickedness," declared Hosea, "ye have reaped iniquity; ye have eaten the fruit of lies: because thou didst trust in thy way, in the multitude of thy mighty men." "In a morning shall the king of Israel utterly be cut off." Hosea 10:13, 15. Unable to discern the disastrous outcome of their evil course, the ten tribes were soon to be "wanderers among the nations." Hosea 9:17.

Some leaders felt keenly their loss of prestige and wished that this might be regained. But they continued in iniquity, flattering themselves that they would attain the political power they desired by allying themselves with the heathen—making "a covenant with the Assyrians." Hosea 12:1.

The Lord had repeatedly set before the ten tribes the

evils of disobedience. But notwithstanding reproof and entreaty, Israel had sunk still lower in apostasy. The Lord declared, "My people are bent on turning away from Me." Hosea 11:7, RSV.

The iniquity in Israel during the last half century before the Assyrian captivity was like that of the days of Noah. In their worship of Baal and Ashtoreth the people severed their connection with all that is uplifting and ennobling and fell an easy prey to temptation. The misguided worshipers had no barrier against sin and yielded themselves to the evil passions of the human heart.

The prophets lifted their voices against the marked oppression, flagrant injustice, luxury and extravagance, the shameless feasting and drunkenness, and the gross licentiousness. But in vain were their protests. "Him that rebuketh in the gate," declared Amos, "they hate . . . and they abhor him that speaketh uprightly." Amos 5:10. Finally nearly all the inhabitants of the land had given themselves over to the alluring practices of nature worship. Forgetting their Maker, Israel "deeply corrupted themselves." Hosea 9:9.

Hosea's Gracious Appeals

The transgressors were given many opportunities to repent. In their hour of deepest apostasy God's message was one of forgiveness and hope. "O Israel," He declared, "thou hast destroyed thyself; but in Me is thine help. I will be thy King: where is any other that may save thee?" Hosea 13:9, 10. "Come, and let us return unto the Lord," the prophet entreated, "for He hath torn, and He will heal us. . . . Then shall we know, if we follow on to know the Lord: His going forth is prepared as the morning; and He shall come unto us as the rain, as the latter and former rain unto the earth." Hosea 6:1-3.

"I will heal their backsliding, I will love them freely," the Lord declared. "I will be as the dew unto

Israel: he shall grow as the lily. . . . They that dwell under His shadow shall return. . . . For the ways of the Lord are right, and the just shall walk in them: but the transgressors shall fall therein.'' Hosea 14:4-9.

"Seek ye Me," the Lord invited, "and ye shall live." "And so the Lord, the God of hosts, shall be with you, as ye have spoken. Hate the evil, and love the good, and establish judgment in the gate: it may be that the Lord God of hosts will be gracious unto the remnant of Joseph." Amos 5:4, 14, 15.

So contrary to the evil desires of the impenitent were the words of God's messengers, that the idolatrous priest at Bethel sent to the ruler in Israel, saying, "Amos hath conspired against thee in the midst of the house of Israel: the land is not able to bear all his words." Amos 7:10.

The evils that overspread the land had become incurable, and on Israel was pronounced the dread sentence: "Ephraim is joined to idols: let him alone." "The days of visitation are come, the days of recompense are come; Israel shall know it." Hosea 4:17; 9:7. The ten tribes of Israel were now to reap the fruitage of the apostasy that had taken form with the setting up of the strange altars at Bethel and at Dan. God's message was: "All the sinners of My people shall die by the sword, which say, The evil shall not overtake nor prevent us." Amos 9:10.

"The houses of ivory shall perish, and the great houses shall have an end." "Israel shall surely go into captivity forth of his land." "Because I will do this unto thee, prepare to meet thy God, O Israel." Amos 3:15; 7:17; 4:12.

Judgments Stayed for a Season

For a season these predicted judgments were stayed, and during the long reign of Jeroboam II the armies of Israel gained signal victories. But this time of apparent prosperity wrought no change in the hearts of the impenitent, and it was finally decreed, "Jeroboam shall

die by the sword, and Israel shall surely be led away
captive out of their own land." Amos 7:11.

The boldness of this utterance was lost on king and
people. Amaziah, a leader among the idolatrous priests
at Bethel, stirred by the plain words spoken against the
nation and their king, said to Amos, "O thou seer, go,
flee thee away into the land of Judah, and there eat
bread, and prophesy there: but prophesy not again any
more at Bethel: for it is the king's chapel, and it is the
king's court." Verses 12, 13.

To this the prophet firmly responded: "Israel shall
surely go into captivity." Verse 17.

The words spoken against the apostate tribes were
literally fulfilled, yet the destruction of the kingdom
came gradually. In judgment the Lord remembered
mercy. When "the king of Assyria came against the
land" (2 Kings 15:19), Menahem, then king of Israel,
was permitted to remain on the throne as a vassal of
the Assyrian realm. The Assyrians, having humbled
the ten tribes, returned for a season to their own land.

Menahem, far from repenting of the evil that had
wrought ruin in his kingdom, continued in "the sins of
Jeroboam the son of Nebat, who made Israel to sin."
Verse 18. "In the days of Pekah" (verse 29), his successor, Tiglath-pileser, king of Assyria, invaded Israel
and carried away a multitude of captives living in Galilee and east of the Jordan. These were scattered among
the heathen in lands far removed from Palestine. From
this terrible blow the northern kingdom never recov-
ered. Only one more ruler, Hoshea, was to follow Pekah. Soon the kingdom was to be swept away forever.

In that time of sorrow and distress God still remembered mercy. In the third year of Hoshea's reign, good
King Hezekiah began to rule in Judah and instituted
important reforms in the temple service at Jerusalem.
A Passover celebration was arranged for, and to this
feast were invited not only Judah and Benjamin, but
the northern tribes as well.

"So couriers went throughout all Israel and Judah,"

with the pressing invitation, "O people of Israel, return to the Lord, the God of Abraham, Isaac, and Israel, that He may turn again to the remnant of you who have escaped from the hand of the kings of Assyria. . . . Do not now be stiffnecked as your fathers were, but yield yourselves to the Lord, and come to His sanctuary. . . . For if you return to the Lord, your brethren and your children will find compassion with their captors, and return to this land. For the Lord your God is gracious and merciful, and will not turn away His face from you, if you return to Him." 2 Chronicles 30:6-9, RSV.

From city to city the couriers sent by Hezekiah carried the message. But the remnant of the ten tribes still dwelling within the once-flourishing northern kingdom treated the royal messengers with indifference, even with contempt. "They laughed them to scorn, and mocked them." A few, however, "of Asher and Manasseh and of Zebulun humbled themselves, and came to Jerusalem . . . to keep the feast of unleavened bread." Verses 10, 11-13.

Swiftly the End Came

About two years later, Samaria was besieged by the hosts of Assyria, and multitudes perished miserably of hunger and disease, as well as by the sword. The city and nation fell, and the broken remnant of the ten tribes were scattered in the provinces of the Assyrian realm.

The destruction that befell the northern kingdom was a direct judgment from Heaven. Through Isaiah the Lord referred to the Assyrian hosts as "the rod of Mine anger." "The staff in their hand," He said, "is Mine indignation." Isaiah 10:5.

Because the children of Israel refused steadfastly to repent, the Lord "afflicted them, and delivered them into the hand of spoilers, until He had cast them out of His sight," in harmony with the plain warnings He had sent them "by all His servants the prophets."

"So was Israel carried away out of their own land to Assyria," "because they obeyed not the voice of the Lord their God, but transgressed His covenant." 2 Kings 17:20, 23; 18:12.

In the terrible judgments on the ten tribes the Lord had a wise and merciful purpose. That which He could no longer do through them in the land of their fathers He would seek to accomplish by scattering them among the heathen. Not all who were carried captive were impenitent. Some had remained true to God, and others had humbled themselves before Him. Through these, He would bring multitudes in Assyria to a knowledge of the attributes of His character and the beneficence of His law.

24 / A Nation "Destroyed for Lack of Knowledge"

God's favor toward Israel had always been conditional on their obedience. At Sinai they had entered into covenant with Him as His "own possession among all peoples." "All that the Lord has spoken we will do," they had promised. Exodus 19:5, 8, RSV. God had chosen Israel as His people, and they had chosen Him as their King.

Near the close of the wilderness wandering, on the very borders of the Promised Land, those who remained faithful renewed their vows of allegiance. Through Moses they were exhorted to remain separate from the surrounding nations and to worship God alone. See Deuteronomy 4.

The Israelites had been specially charged not to lose sight of the commandments of God. Plain and decided were the warnings given them against the idolatrous customs prevailing among the neighboring nations. "Take heed unto yourselves, lest ye forget the covenant of the Lord your God, which He made with you, and make you a graven image, or the likeness of anything, which the Lord thy God hath forbidden thee." Deuteronomy 4:23.

Calling heaven and earth to witness, Moses declared that if, after having dwelt long in the Land of Promise, the people should bow down to graven images and refuse to return to the worship of the true God, they would be carried away captive and scattered among the heathen. "Ye shall soon utterly perish from off the land whereunto ye go over Jordan to possess it," he warned them. "Ye shall not prolong your days upon it, but shall utterly be destroyed. And the Lord shall scatter you among the nations, and ye shall be left few in number among the heathen, whither the Lord shall lead you." Verses 26, 27.

This prophecy, fulfilled in part in the time of the judges, met a more complete and literal fulfillment in the captivity of Israel in Assyria and of Judah in Babylon. Satan had made repeated attempts to cause the chosen nation to forget "the commandments, the statutes, and the judgments" that they had promised to keep forever. Deuteronomy 6:1. He knew that if he could lead Israel to "walk after other gods, and serve them, and worship them," they would "surely perish." Deuteronomy 8:19.

The enemy of God's church on the earth had not, however, taken into account the compassionate nature of Him whose glory it is to be "merciful and gracious, long-suffering, and abundant in goodness and truth, keeping mercy for thousands, forgiving iniquity." Exodus 34:6, 7. Even in the darkest hours of their history, the Lord graciously spread before Israel the things that were for the welfare of the nation. "It was I who taught Ephraim to walk," He declared through Hosea. "I took them up in My arms; but they did not know that I healed them." Hosea 11:3, RSV.

Tenderly had the Lord dealt with them, instructing them by His prophets. If Israel had heeded the messages of the prophets, they would have been spared humiliation. But because they persisted in turning aside from His law, God was compelled to let them go into captivity. "My people are destroyed for lack of knowledge," was His message. "Because thou hast rejected knowledge, I will also reject thee . . . : seeing thou hast forgotten the law of thy God." Hosea 4:6.

In every age, transgression of God's law has been followed by the same result. In the days of Noah, when iniquity became so deep and widespread that God could no longer bear with it, the decree went forth, "I will destroy man whom I have created from the face of the earth." Genesis 6:7. In Abraham's day the people of Sodom openly defied God and His law; they passed the limits of divine forbearance, and there was kindled against them the fire of God's vengeance.

The time preceding the captivity of the ten tribes of Israel was one of similar wickedness. Hosea declared: "The Lord has a controversy with the inhabitants of the land. There . . . is swearing, lying, killing, stealing, and committing adultery; they break all bounds and murder follows murder." Hosea 4:1, 2, RSV.

Israel, "Wanderers Among the Nations"

To the ten tribes, long impenitent, no promise of complete restoration to their former power in Palestine was given. Until the end of time, they were to be "wanderers among the nations." But through Hosea a prophecy set before them the privilege of having a part in the final restoration to be made to the people of God at the close of earth's history. "Many days," the prophet declared, the ten tribes were to abide "without a king, and without a prince, and without a sacrifice, and without an image, and without an ephod, and without teraphim. Afterward," the prophet continued, "shall the children of Israel return, and seek the Lord their God, and David their king; and shall fear the Lord and His goodness in the latter days." Hosea 3:4, 5.

In symbolic language Hosea set forth God's plan of restoring to every penitent soul the blessings granted Israel in the days of their loyalty to Him in the Promised Land. Referring to Israel the Lord declared, "I will give her her vineyards, and make the Valley of Achor a door of hope. And there she shall answer as in the days of her youth, as at the time when she came out of the land of Egypt. And in that day, says the Lord, you will call Me, 'My husband,' and no longer will you call Me, 'My Baal.' " Hosea 2:15, 16, RSV.

In the last days of earth's history, God's covenant with His commandment-keeping people is to be re-

newed, "And I will betroth thee unto Me forever;
. . . in righteousness, and in judgment, and in loving-
kindness, and in mercies. . . . And thou shalt know
the Lord." "And I will have mercy upon her that had
not obtained mercy; and I will say to them which were
not My people, Thou art My people; and they shall
say, Thou art my God." Verses 19, 20, 23.

From "every nation, and kindred, and tongue, and
people" some will gladly respond to the message,
"Fear God, and give glory to Him; for the hour of His
judgment is come." They will turn from every idol that
binds them to earth, and will "worship Him that made
heaven, and earth, and the sea, and the fountains of
waters." They will free themselves from every entan-
glement and will stand before the world as monuments
of God's mercy. Obedient to the divine requirements,
they will be recognized as those who have kept "the
commandments of God, and the faith of Jesus." Revelation 14:6, 7, 12.

"I will restore the fortunes of My people Israel. . . .
I will plant them upon their land, and they shall never
again be plucked up out of the land which I have given
them." Amos 9:14, 15, RSV.

25 / Prophet With a Message of Hope

For many years King Uzziah ruled with discretion in the land of Judah and Benjamin. Cities were rebuilt and fortified, and the riches of the nations flowed into Jerusalem. Uzziah's name "spread far abroad; for he was marvelously helped, till he was strong." 2 Chronicles 26:15.

Outward prosperity, however, was not accompanied by spiritual power. The temple services were continued, and multitudes assembled to worship the living God; but pride and formality took the place of humility and sincerity. Of Uzziah it is written: "When he was strong, his heart was lifted up to his destruction: for he transgressed against the Lord his God." Verse 16. In violation of a plain command of the Lord, the king entered the sanctuary "to burn incense upon the altar." Azariah the high priest and his associates remonstrated with him: "Thou hast trespassed," they urged; "neither shall it be for thine honor." Verses 16, 18.

Uzziah was filled with wrath that he should be rebuked. But he was not permitted to profane the sanctuary against the united protest of those in authority. While standing there in wrathful rebellion, he was smitten with leprosy. To the day of his death, he remained a leper, a living example of the folly of departing from a plain "Thus said the Lord." Neither his position nor his long service could be pleaded as an excuse for the presumptuous sin which brought upon him the judgment of Heaven. God is no respecter of persons. See Numbers 15:30.

161

Uzziah's son Jotham succeeded to the throne after his father's death. "He did that which was right in the sight of the Lord: he did according to all that his father Uzziah had done. Howbeit the high places were not removed." 2 Kings 15:34, 35.

The reign of Uzziah was drawing to a close when Isaiah, a young man of the royal line, was called to the prophetic mission. He was to witness the invasion of Judah by the armies of Israel and Syria; he was to behold the Assyrian hosts encamped before the chief cities of the kingdom. Samaria was to fall, and the ten tribes were to be scattered among the nations. Judah was to be invaded by Assyrian armies, and Jerusalem suffer a siege that would have resulted in her downfall had not God miraculously interposed. The divine protection was being removed, and Assyrian forces were about to overspread Judah.

Isaiah Sent When God's Purposes Seemed to Be Failing

But the dangers from without were not so serious as the dangers from within. By their apostasy and rebellion the people who should have been light bearers among the nations were inviting the judgments of God. Many of the evils of the northern kingdom, which had been denounced by Hosea and Amos, were fast corrupting Judah. In their desire for gain, men were adding house to house and field to field. See Isaiah 5:8. Justice was perverted, and no pity was shown the poor. God declared, "The spoil of the poor is in your houses." Isaiah 3:14. Even magistrates turned a deaf ear to the cries of the poor, the widows, and the fatherless. See Isaiah 10:1, 2.

With wealth came love of display, drunkenness, and revelry. See Isaiah 2:11, 12; 3:16, 18-23; 5:22, 11, 12. And idolatry itself no longer provoked surprise. See Isaiah 2:8, 9. The few who remained true to God were tempted to give way to despair. It seemed as if God's purpose for Israel was about to fail.

It is not surprising that when Isaiah was called to

bear God's messages of reproof, he shrank from the responsibility. He knew he would encounter resistance. As he thought of the stubbornness and unbelief of the people, his task seemed hopeless. Should he in despair leave Judah undisturbed to their idolatry? Were the gods of Nineveh to rule the earth in defiance of the God of heaven?

Such thoughts as these were crowding through Isaiah's mind as he stood under the portico of the temple. Suddenly there rose up before him a vision of the Lord sitting on a throne high and lifted up, while the train of His glory filled the temple. On each side of the throne the seraphim united in the solemn invocation, "Holy, holy, holy, is the Lord of hosts: the whole earth is full of His glory," until pillar and cedar gate seemed shaken with the sound, and the house was filled with praise. Isaiah 6:3.

Isaiah was overwhelmed with a sense of the purity and holiness of God. "Woe is me!" he cried; "for I am undone; because I am a man of unclean lips, and I dwell in the midst of a people of unclean lips: for mine eyes have seen the King, the Lord of hosts." Verse 5. He realized that if left to his own inefficiency, he would be utterly unable to accomplish the mission to which he had been called. But a living coal from the altar was laid upon his lips, with the words, "Lo, this hath touched thy lips; and thine iniquity is taken away, and thy sin purged." Then the voice of God was heard saying, "Whom shall I send, and who will go for Us?" and Isaiah responded, "Here am I; send me." Verses 7, 8.

Final Success Assured

The prophet's duty was plain—he was to lift his voice against the prevailing evils. But he dreaded to undertake the work without some assurance of hope. "Lord, how long?" he inquired. Verse 11. Are none of Thy chosen people ever to repent and be healed?

His mission was not to be wholly fruitless, yet the evils that had been multiplying for generations could not be removed in his day. He must be a patient, coura-geous teacher—a prophet of hope as well as of doom. A remnant should be saved. That this might be brought about, messages of entreaty were to be delivered to the rebellious nation.

The ten tribes of the northern kingdom were soon to be scattered among the nations; the destroying armies of hostile nations were to sweep over the land again and again; even Jerusalem was finally to fall and Judah to be carried away captive; yet the Promised Land was not to remain forsaken forever. The assurance of the heavenly visitant to Isaiah was:

> In it shall be a tenth,
> And it shall return, and shall be eaten:
> As a teil tree, and as an oak,
> Whose substance is in them, when they cast their
>   leaves:
> So the holy seed shall be the substance thereof.
>   Verse 13

This assurance brought courage to Isaiah. He had seen the King, the Lord of hosts; he had heard the song of the seraphim, ''The whole earth is full of His glory.'' Verse 3. He had the promise that the messages of Jeho-vah would be accompanied by the convicting power of the Holy Spirit, and the prophet was nerved for the work before him. Throughout his long, arduous mis-sion he carried the memory of this vision. For sixty years or more he stood as a prophet of hope, predicting the future triumph of the church.

26/ Isaiah's Message: "Behold Your God!"

Long had Satan sought to lead men to look on their Creator as the author of suffering and death. Those whom he had thus deceived regarded Him as watching to condemn, unwilling to receive the sinner so long as there was a legal excuse for not helping him. The law of love by which heaven is ruled had been misrepresented as a restriction on men's happiness, a yoke from which they should be glad to escape. The archdeceiver declared that its precepts could not be obeyed.

In losing sight of God's true character, the Israelites were without excuse. Often had God revealed Himself to them as "merciful and gracious, slow to anger and abounding in steadfast love and faithfulness." Psalm 86:15, RSV. Tenderly had the Lord dealt with Israel in their deliverance from Egyptian bondage and in their journey to the Promised Land. "In all their affliction He was afflicted, and the angel of His presence saved them: in His love and in His pity He redeemed them." Isaiah 63:9. Moses instructed them fully concerning the attributes of their invisible King. See Exodus 34:6, 7.

At the height of Israel's rebellion the Lord had proposed to make of the descendants of Moses "a greater nation and mightier than they." Numbers 14:12. But the prophet pleaded the promises of God in behalf of the chosen nation. And then, as the strongest of all pleas, he urged the love of God for fallen man. See verses 17-19.

Graciously the Lord responded, "I have pardoned

165

according to thy word." Then He imparted to Moses a knowledge of His purpose concerning the final triumph of Israel: "Truly as I live, all the earth shall be filled with the glory of the Lord." Verses 20, 21. God's glory, His character, His tender love, were to be revealed to all mankind. And this promise was confirmed by an oath. As surely as God lives and reigns, His glory should be declared "among the nations, His marvelous works among all the peoples!" Psalm 96:3, RSV.

The Gospel to All the World

Today this prophecy is meeting rapid fulfillment. Soon the gospel message will have been proclaimed to all nations. Men and women from every kindred, tongue, and people are being "accepted in the Beloved," "that in the ages to come He might show the exceeding riches of His grace in His kindness toward us through Christ Jesus." Ephesians 1:6; 2:7.

In the vision in the temple court, Isaiah was given a clear view of the character of God. "The high and lofty One that inhabiteth eternity, whose name is Holy," had appeared before him in great majesty; yet he was made to understand the compassionate nature of his Lord. He who dwells "in the high and holy place" dwells "with him also that is of a contrite and humble spirit, to revive the spirit of the humble, and to revive the heart of the contrite ones." Isaiah 57:15.

In beholding God the prophet had not only been given a view of his own unworthiness, there had come to his humbled heart the assurance of forgiveness, full and free; and he had arisen a changed man. He could testify of the transformation wrought through beholding Infinite Love. Henceforth he longed to see erring Israel set free from the burden and penalty of sin. "Why should ye be stricken any more?" "Come now, and let us reason together, saith the Lord: though your sins be as scarlet, they shall be as white as snow; though they be red like crimson, they shall be as wool." Isaiah 1:5, 18.

The God whose character they had misunderstood was set before them as the great Healer of spiritual disease. He who had been backsliding in the way of his heart might find healing by turning to the Lord. "I have seen his ways," the Lord declared, "and will heal him." Isaiah 57:18.

The prophet exalted God as Creator. His message to the cities of Judah was, "Behold your God!" Isaiah 40:9. "To whom then will ye liken Me, or shall I be equal? saith the Holy One. Lift up your eyes on high, and behold who hath created these things, that bringeth out their host by number: He calleth them all by names by the greatness of His might, for that He is strong in power; not one faileth." Isaiah 40:25, 26.

God Will Accept Unworthy Sinners

To those who feared they would not be received if they should turn to God, the prophet declared: "Hast thou not known? hast thou not heard, that the everlasting God, the Lord, the Creator of the ends of the earth, fainteth not, neither is weary? there is no searching of His understanding. He giveth power to the faint; and to them that have no might He increaseth strength. Even the youths shall faint and be weary, and young men shall utterly fall: but they that wait upon the Lord shall renew their strength; they shall mount up with wings as eagles; they shall run, and not be weary; they shall walk, and not faint." Verses 28-31.

The heart of Infinite Love yearns after those who feel powerless to free themselves from the snares of Satan. "Fear thou not," He bids them, "for I am with thee: be not dismayed; for I am thy God: I will strengthen thee; yea, I will help thee; yea, I will uphold thee with the right hand of My righteousness." "Fear not; I will help thee." Isaiah 41:10, 13.

Many who were wholly unacquainted with God's attributes were yet to behold the glory of the divine character. For the purpose of making plain His merciful designs He kept sending His prophets with the message, "Turn ye again now everyone from his evil way." Jeremiah 25:5. "For My name's sake," He declared through Isaiah, "will I defer Mine anger, and for My praise will I refrain for thee, that I cut thee not off." Isaiah 48:9.

The Lord Will Receive You

The call to repentance was clear, and all were invited to return. "Seek ye the Lord while He may be found," the prophet pleaded; "call ye upon Him while He is near: let the wicked forsake his way, and the unrighteous man his thoughts: and let him return unto the Lord, and He will have mercy upon him; and to our God, for He will abundantly pardon." Isaiah 55:6, 7.

Have you wandered far from God? Have you sought to feast on the fruits of transgression, only to find them turn to ashes upon your lips? And now, your plans thwarted and your hopes dead, do you sit alone and desolate? That voice comes to you distinct and clear, "Arise ye, and depart; for this is not your rest: because it is polluted, it shall destroy you." Micah 2:10. Your Father invites you saying, "Return unto Me; for I have redeemed thee." "Come unto Me: hear, and your soul shall live." Isaiah 44:22; 55:3.

Do not listen to the enemy's suggestion to stay away from Christ until you have made yourself better, until you are good enough to come. Repeat the promise of the Saviour, "Him that cometh to Me I will in no wise cast out." John 6:37. Tell the enemy that the blood of Jesus Christ cleanses from all sin. Make the prayer of David your own: "Wash me, and I shall be whiter than snow." Psalm 51:7.

The exhortations of the prophet to Judah were not in vain. Some turned from their idols. They learned to see in their Maker love, mercy, and tender compassion. And in the dark days that were to come, the prophet's words were to continue bearing fruit in decided reformation. Many were to behold the One altogether lovely. Their sins were to be forgiven, and they were to make their boast in God alone. They would exclaim, "The Lord is our judge, the Lord is our lawgiver, the Lord is our king; He will save us." Isaiah 33:22.

The messages borne by Isaiah to those who chose to turn from their evil ways were full of comfort and encouragement:

> O Israel, thou shalt not be forgotten of Me.
> I have blotted out, as a thick cloud, thy transgressions,
> And, as a cloud, thy sins:
> Return unto Me; for I have redeemed thee.
> Isaiah 44:21, 22

> You will say in that day:
> "I will give thanks to Thee, O Lord,
> For though Thou wast angry with me,
> Thy anger turned away, and Thou didst comfort me. . . .
> Shout, and sing for joy, O inhabitant of Zion,
> For great in your midst is the Holy One of Israel."
> Isaiah 12:1-6, RSV

27 / Ahaz Almost Ruins the Kingdom

The accession of Ahaz to the throne brought Isaiah face to face with conditions more appalling than any that had hitherto existed in Judah. Many were now being persuaded to worship heathen deities. Princes were untrue to their trust; false prophets were leading astray; some priests were teaching for hire. Yet the leaders in apostasy still kept up the forms of divine worship and claimed to be the people of God.

The prophet Micah declared that sinners in Zion, while blasphemously boasting, "Is not the Lord in the midst of us? No evil shall come upon us," continued to "build Zion with blood and Jerusalem with wrong." Micah 3:11, 10, RSV. Isaiah lifted his voice in stern rebuke: "What to Me is the multitude of your sacrifices? . . . When you come to appear before Me, who requires of you this trampling of My courts?" Isaiah 1:11, 12, RSV.

Inspiration declares, "The sacrifice of the wicked is abomination: how much more, when he bringeth it with a wicked mind?" Proverbs 21:27. It is not because God is unwilling to forgive that He turns from the transgressor; because the sinner refuses the abundant provisions of grace, God is unable to deliver from sin. "Your iniquities have separated between you and your God, and your sins have hid His face from you, that He will not hear." Isaiah 59:2.

Isaiah called the attention of the people to the weakness of their position among the nations and showed that this was the result of wickedness in high places:

"The Lord, the Lord of hosts, is taking away from Jerusalem and Judah stay and staff, the whole stay of bread, and the whole stay of water; the mighty man and the soldier, the judge and the prophet, the diviner and the elder, the captain of fifty and the man of rank, the counselor and the skilful magician and the expert in charms. And I will make boys their princes, and babes shall rule over them." "For Jerusalem has stumbled, and Judah has fallen; because their speech and their deeds are against the Lord." Isaiah 3:1-4, 8, RSV.

"They which lead thee," the prophet continued, "cause thee to err." Verse 12. Of Ahaz it is written: "He walked in the way of the kings of Israel. He even burned his son as an offering, according to the abominable practices of the nations whom the Lord drove out before the people of Israel." 2 Kings 16:3, RSV.

Great Peril for the Chosen Nation

In the kingdom of Judah the outlook was dark. The forces for evil were multiplying. The prophet Micah was constrained to exclaim: "The good man is perished out of the earth: and there is none upright among men." "The best of them is as a brier: the most upright is sharper than a thorn hedge." Micah 7:2, 4.

In every age, because of His infinite love, God has borne long with the rebellious and urged them to return to Him. Thus it was during the reign of Ahaz. Invitation upon invitation was sent to erring Israel. And as the prophets stood before the people, earnestly exhorting to repentance and reformation, their words bore fruit.

Through Micah came the wonderful appeal, "O My people, what have I done unto thee? and wherein have I wearied thee? testify against Me. For I brought thee up out of the land of Egypt, and redeemed thee out of the house of servants." Micah 6:3, 4.

Throughout probationary time God's Spirit is entreating men to accept the gift of life. "Turn ye, turn ye from your evil ways; for why will ye die?" Ezekiel

33:11. Satan leads man into sin and then leaves him there, helpless and hopeless, fearing to seek pardon. But God invites, "Let him take hold of My strength, that he may make peace with Me." Isaiah 27:5. In Christ every provision has been made, every encouragement offered.

In Judah and Israel many were inquiring: "Shall I come before the Lord . . . with burnt offerings? . . . Will the Lord be pleased with thousands of rams, or with ten thousands of rivers of oil?" The answer is plain: "He hath showed thee, O man, what is good; and what doth the Lord require of thee, but to do justly, and to love mercy, and to walk humbly with thy God?" Micah 6:6-8.

From age to age these counsels were repeated to those who were falling into habits of formalism and of forgetting to show mercy. When Christ Himself was approached by a lawyer with the question, "Which is the great commandment in the law?" He said, "Thou shalt love the Lord thy God with all thy heart, and with all thy soul, and with all thy mind. This is the first and great commandment. And the second is like unto it, Thou shalt love thy neighbor as thyself." Matthew 22:36-39.

These plain utterances should be received by us as the voice of God. We should lose no opportunity of performing deeds of mercy, of tender forethought and Christian courtesy for the burdened and oppressed. If we can do no more, we may speak words of courage and hope to those who are unacquainted with God. Rich are the promises to those who bring joy and blessing into the lives of others: "If you pour yourself out for the hungry and satisfy the desire of the afflicted, then shall your light rise in the darkness and your gloom be as the noonday. And the Lord will guide you continually, and satisfy your desire with good things, and make your bones strong; and you will be like a watered garden, like a spring of water, whose waters fail not." Isaiah 58:10, 11, RSV.

The idolatrous course of Ahaz in the face of the earnest appeals of the prophets could have but one result: "The wrath of the Lord was upon Judah and Jerusalem, and He . . . delivered them to trouble, to astonishment, and to hissing." 2 Chronicles 29:8. The kingdom suffered a rapid decline, and its very existence was soon imperiled by invading armies. "Rezin king of Syria and Pekah son of Remaliah king of Israel came up to Jerusalem to war." 2 Kings 16:5.

Had Ahaz and the men of his realm been true servants of the Most High, they would have had no fear of so unnatural an alliance as had been formed against them. But stricken with a nameless dread of the judgments of an offended God, the heart of the king "and the heart of his people shook as the trees of the forest shake before the wind." Isaiah 7:2, RSV. In this crisis the word of the Lord came to Isaiah to meet the trembling king and say: "Fear not, neither be fainthearted. . . . Because Syria, Ephraim, and the son of Remaliah, have taken evil counsel against thee. . . . Thus saith the Lord God, It shall not stand, neither shall it come to pass." Verses 4-7.

Well would it have been for Judah had Ahaz received this message as from heaven. But choosing to lean on the arm of flesh, he sought help from the heathen. In desperation he sent word to Tiglath-pileser, king of Assyria: "I am thy servant and thy son: come up, and save me out of the hand of the king of Syria, and out of the hand of the king of Israel, which rise up against me." 2 Kings 16:7. The request was accompanied by a rich present from the king's treasure and the temple storehouse.

The help was sent and King Ahaz was given temporary relief, but at what a cost to Judah! Assyria soon threatened to overflow and spoil Judah. Ahaz and his unhappy subjects were now harassed by the fear of falling completely into the hands of the cruel Assyrians. "The Lord brought Judah low" (2 Chronicles 28:19) because of continued transgression.

In this time of chastisement, instead of repenting, Ahaz trespassed "yet more against the Lord: . . . for he sacrificed unto the gods of Damascus." "Because the gods of the kings of Syria help them," he said, "therefore will I sacrifice to them, that they may help me." 2 Chronicles 28:22, 23.

As the apostate king neared the end of his reign, he caused the doors of the temple to be closed. No longer were offerings made for the sins of the people. Deserting the house of God and locking its doors, the inhabitants of the godless city boldly worshiped heathen deities on the street corners throughout Jerusalem. Heathenism had seemingly triumphed.

But in Judah there dwelt some who maintained their allegiance to Jehovah. To these Isaiah and Micah looked in hope as they surveyed the ruin wrought during the last years of Ahaz. Their sanctuary was closed, but the faithful ones were assured: "God is with us." "Sanctify the Lord of hosts Himself; and let Him be your fear. . . . And He shall be for a sanctuary." Isaiah 8:10, 13, 14.

28 / King Hezekiah Repairs the Damage

Hezekiah came to the throne determined to save Judah from the fate that was overtaking the northern kingdom. The prophets offered no halfway measures. Only by decided reformation could the threatened judgments be averted.

No sooner had he ascended the throne than he began to plan and execute. He first turned to the restoration of the temple services and solicited the cooperation of priests and Levites who had remained true. "Our fathers have trespassed," he confessed, "and done that which was evil in the eyes of the Lord our God, and have forsaken Him." "Now it is in mine heart to make a covenant with the Lord God of Israel, that His fierce wrath may turn away from us." 2 Chronicles 29:6, 10.

The king reviewed the situation—the closed temple and the cessation of services; idolatry practiced in the streets of the city and throughout the kingdom; the apostasy of multitudes who might have remained true had the leaders set a right example; and the decline of the kingdom and loss of prestige in the estimation of surrounding nations. Soon the northern kingdom would fall completely into the hands of the Assyrians and be ruined; and this fate would befall Judah as well, unless God should work mightily through chosen representatives.

Hezekiah appealed to the priests to unite with him in bringing about reform. "Be not now negligent," he exhorted them, "for the Lord hath chosen you to stand before Him, to serve Him." "Sanctify now yourselves, and sanctify the house of the Lord God of your fathers." Verses 11, 5.

The priests began at once. Enlisting the cooperation of others, they engaged heartily in cleansing and sanctifying the temple. Within a remarkably short time they were able to report their task completed. The temple doors had been repaired and thrown open; the sacred vessels had been assembled and put in place; and all was in readiness for the reestablishment of the sanctuary services.

In the first service held, the rulers of the city united with King Hezekiah and the priests in seeking forgiveness for the sins of the nation. Upon the altar were placed sin offerings "to make an atonement for all Israel." Once more the temple courts resounded with praise. The songs of David and Asaph were sung with joy, as the worshipers realized that they were being delivered from the bondage of sin and apostasy. "Hezekiah and all the people rejoiced because of what God had done for the people; for the thing came about suddenly." Verses 24, 36, RSV.

God had prepared the hearts of the chief men of Judah to lead out in a decided reformatory movement, that the apostasy might be stayed. His messages had been rejected by the kingdom of Israel, but in Judah there remained a good remnant, and to these the prophets continued to appeal. Hear Isaiah urging, "Turn ye unto Him from whom the children of Israel have deeply revolted." Isaiah 31:6. Hear Micah declaring with confidence: "I will bear the indignation of the Lord, because I have sinned against Him, until He plead my cause, and execute judgment for me: He will bring me forth to the light, I shall behold His righteousness." Micah 7:9.

These and like messages had brought hope to many in the dark years when the temple doors remained closed; and now, as the leaders began a reform, a multitude of the people, weary of the thralldom of sin, were ready to respond.

Those who sought forgiveness had wonderful encouragement offered in Scripture. "You will return to the Lord," Moses had said, "and obey His voice, for the Lord your God is a merciful God; He will not fail you or destroy you or forget the covenant with your fathers which He swore to them." Deuteronomy 4:30, 31, RSV.

And at the dedication of the temple Solomon had prayed, "When Thy people Israel be smitten down before the enemy, because they have sinned against Thee, and shall turn again to Thee, and confess Thy name, and pray, and make supplication unto Thee in this house: then hear Thou in heaven, and forgive the sin of Thy people Israel." 1 Kings 8:33, 34. By night the Lord had appeared to Solomon to tell him that mercy would be shown those who should worship there: "If My people, which are called by My name, shall humble themselves, and pray, and seek My face, and turn from their wicked ways; then will I hear from heaven, and will forgive their sin, and will heal their land." 2 Chronicles 7:14. These promises met abundant fulfillment during the reformation under Hezekiah.

Celebrating the Passover

In his zeal to make the temple services a real blessing, Hezekiah determined to gather the Israelites together for the Passover feast. For many years the Passover had not been observed as a national festival. The division of the kingdom after Solomon's reign had made this seem impracticable. But the stirring messages of the prophets were having their effect. By royal couriers the invitation to the Passover at Jerusalem was heralded "from city to city through the country of Ephraim and Manasseh even unto Zebulun." The bearers of the invitation were usually repulsed; nevertheless some "humbled themselves, and came to Jerusalem." 2 Chronicles 30:10, 11.

In Judah the response was very general, for God

gave "them one heart to do the commandment of the king and of the princes"—a command in accord with the will of God as revealed through His prophets. Verse 12.

The desecrated streets of the city were cleared of the idolatrous shrines placed there during the reign of Ahaz. The Passover was observed, and the week was spent by the people in offering peace offerings and in learning what God would have them do. Those who had prepared their hearts to seek God found pardon. A great gladness possessed the multitude. "The Levites and the priests praised the Lord day by day, singing with loud instruments." All were united in their desire to praise Him. Verse 21.

The seven days allotted to the feast passed all too quickly, and the worshipers determined to spend another seven days in learning more fully the way of the Lord. The teaching priests continued their instruction from the book of the law; daily the people assembled to offer praise and thanksgiving; and as the great meeting drew to a close, it was evident that God had wrought marvelously in the conversion of backsliding Judah. "There was great joy in Jerusalem: for since the time of Solomon the son of David king of Israel there was not the like in Jerusalem." Verse 26.

The Reformation Spreads

The time had come for the worshipers to return to their homes. God had accepted those who with broken hearts had confessed their sins and with resolute purpose had turned to Him for forgiveness and help.

There now remained an important work in which those who were returning to their homes must take part, and the accomplishment of this work bore evidence to the genuineness of the reformation: "Now when all this was finished, all Israel who were present went out to the cities of Judah and broke in pieces the pillars and hewed down the Asherim and broke down the high places and the altars throughout all Judah and

Benjamin, and in Ephraim and Manasseh, until they had destroyed them all. Then all the people of Israel returned to their cities, every man to his possession." 2 Chronicles 31:1, RSV.

"Throughout all Judah" the king "wrought that which was good and right and truth before the Lord his God. And in every work that he began. . . , he did it with all his heart, and prospered." Verses 20, 21.

The success of the Assyrians in scattering the remnant of the ten tribes among the nations was leading many to question the power of the God of the Hebrews. Emboldened by their successes, the Ninevites had long since set aside the message of Jonah and had become defiant in their opposition to Heaven. A few years after the fall of Samaria the victorious armies reappeared in Palestine, directing their forces against the fenced cities of Judah; but they withdrew for a season because of difficulties in other portions of their realm. Not until near the close of Hezekiah's reign was it to be demonstrated before the world whether the gods of the heathen were finally to prevail.

29/ Visitors From Babylon See the Wrong Things

In the midst of his prosperous reign King Hezekiah was suddenly stricken with a malady beyond the power of man to help. His last hope seemed removed when Isaiah appeared with the message, "Thus saith the Lord, Set thine house in order: for thou shalt die, and not live." Isaiah 38:1.

The outlook seemed dark, yet the king could still pray. So Hezekiah "turned his face to the wall, and prayed unto the Lord, saying, I beseech Thee, O Lord, remember now how I have walked before Thee in truth and with a perfect heart, and have done that which is good in Thy sight. And Hezekiah wept sore." 2 Kings 20:2, 3.

The dying ruler had served God faithfully and strengthened the confidence of the people in their Supreme Ruler. Like David, he could now plead:

Let my prayer come before Thee:
Incline Thine ear unto my cry;
For my soul is full of troubles.
            Psalm 88:2, 3

Forsake me not when my strength faileth.

O God, forsake me not;
Until I have showed Thy strength unto this
    generation,
And Thy power to everyone that is to come.
            Psalm 71:9, 18

"Afore Isaiah was gone out into the middle court, . . . the word of the Lord came to him, saying, Turn again, and tell Hezekiah the captain of My people, Thus saith the Lord, the God of David thy father, I have heard thy prayer, I have seen thy tears: behold, I will heal thee: on the third day thou shalt go up unto the house of the Lord. And I will add unto thy days fifteen years; and I will deliver thee and this city out of the hand of the king of Assyria; and I will defend this city for Mine own sake, and for My servant David's sake." 2 Kings 20:4-6. Directing that a lump of figs be laid on the diseased part, Isaiah delivered the message of mercy.

Hezekiah pleaded for some sign that the message was from heaven. "What shall be the sign that the Lord will heal me, and that I shall go up into the house of the Lord the third day?" "This sign shalt thou have from the Lord," the prophet answered, "that the Lord will do the thing that He hath spoken: shall the shadow go forward ten degrees, or go back ten degrees?" "It is a light thing," Hezekiah replied, "for the shadow to go down ten degrees: nay, but let the shadow return backward ten degrees."

Only by the interposition of God could the shadow on the sundial be made to turn *back* ten degrees. Accordingly, "the prophet cried unto the Lord: and He brought the shadow ten degrees backward, by which it had gone down in the dial of Ahaz." Verses 8-11.

Restored to strength, Hezekiah vowed to spend his remaining days in willing service to the King of kings:

I said, in the noontide of my days I must depart.

But Thou hast held back my life from the pit of destruction,
For Thou has cast all my sins behind Thy back.

We will sing to stringed instruments
All the days of our life, at the house of the Lord.
Isaiah 38:10, 17, 20, RSV

In the fertile valleys of the Tigris and the Euphrates dwelt an ancient race which was destined to rule the world. Among its people were wise men who gave attention to astronomy. They noticed the shadow on the sundial turn back ten degrees. When King Merodach-baladan learned that this miracle was a sign to the king of Judah that the God of heaven had granted him a new lease of life, he sent ambassadors to Hezekiah to congratulate him and to learn, if possible, more of the God who was able to perform so great a wonder.

The visit of these messengers gave Hezekiah an opportunity to extol the living God, the upholder of all created things, through whose favor his own life had been spared when all other hope had fled. What momentous transformations might have taken place had these seekers after truth been led to the living God!

Hezekiah's Tragic Pride

But pride and vanity took possession of Hezekiah's heart. In self-exaltation the king "showed them his treasure house, the silver, the gold, the spices, the precious oil, his whole armory, all that was found in his storehouses. There was nothing in his house or in all his realm that Hezekiah did not show them." Isaiah 39:2, RSV. He did not stop to consider that these men of a powerful nation had not the love of God in their hearts and that it was imprudent to show them the temporal riches of the nation.

The visit of the ambassadors was a test of Hezekiah's gratitude and devotion. "And so in the matter of the envoys of the princes of Babylon, who had been sent to him to inquire about the sign that had been done in the land, God left him to himself, in order to try him and to know all that was in his heart." 2 Chronicles 32:31, RSV. Had Hezekiah borne witness to the goodness, the compassion of God, the report of the ambassadors would have been as light piercing darkness. But he magnified himself above the Lord of hosts, "for his heart was lifted up." Verse 25.

How disastrous the results! To Isaiah it was revealed that the king of Babylon and his counselors would plan to enrich their own country with the treasures of Jerusalem. Hezekiah had grievously sinned. "Therefore there was wrath upon him, and upon Judah and Jerusalem." Verse 25.

"Then came Isaiah the prophet unto King Hezekiah, and said unto him, ... What have they seen in thine house? And Hezekiah answered, All that is in mine house have they seen: there is nothing among my treasures that I have not showed them." Then Isaiah said, "Behold, the days come, that all that is in thine house, and that which thy fathers have laid up in store until this day, shall be carried to Babylon: nothing shall be left, saith the Lord. And of thy sons . . . shall they take away; and they shall be eunuchs in the palace of the king of Babylon." Isaiah 39:3-7.

Filled with remorse, "Hezekiah humbled himself for the pride of his heart, both he and the inhabitants of Jerusalem, so that the wrath of the Lord came not upon them in the days of Hezekiah." 2 Chronicles 32:26. But the evil seed sown was to yield a harvest of woe. His faith was to be severely tried, and he was to learn that only by putting his trust fully in Jehovah could he triumph over the powers plotting his ruin and the destruction of his people.

Our Words Can Help Others

Far more than we do, we need to speak of the mercy and loving-kindness of God, of the matchless depths of the Saviour's love. When mind and heart are filled with the love of God, it will not be difficult. Noble aspirations, clear perceptions of truth, yearnings for holiness, will find expression in words that reveal the character of the heart treasure.

Those with whom we associate day by day need our help, our guidance. Tomorrow some may be where we can never reach them again. Every day our words and acts are making impressions on those with whom we associate. One reckless movement, one imprudent step, and the surging waves of strong temptation may sweep a soul into the downward path. If the thoughts we have planted in human minds have been evil, we may have set in motion a tide of evil we are powerless to stay.

On the other hand, if by our example we aid others in the development of good principles, we give them power to do good. In their turn they exert the same beneficial influence over others. Thus hundreds and thousands are helped by our unconscious influence. Before an unbelieving, sin-loving world, true followers of Christ reveal the power of God's grace and the perfection of His character.

30 / An Angel Slays the Assyrian Army

When the hosts of Assyria were invading Judah and it seemed as if nothing could save Jerusalem, Hezekiah rallied the forces of his realm to resist their oppressors and to trust in the power of Jehovah to deliver: "Be strong and courageous, be not afraid nor dismayed for the king of Assyria, nor for all the multitude that is with him: with him is an arm of flesh; but with us is the Lord our God to help us, and to fight our battles." 2 Chronicles 32:7, 8.

The boastful Assyrian, while used by God for a season for the punishment of the nations, was not always to prevail. See Isaiah 10:5, 24-27. In a prophetic message given "in the year that King Ahaz died," Isaiah had declared: "The Lord of hosts hath sworn, . . . I will break the Assyrian in My land, and upon My mountains tread him underfoot. . . . For the Lord of hosts hath purposed, and who shall disannul it?" Isaiah 14:28, 24-27.

Hezekiah, in the earlier years of his reign, had continued to pay tribute to Assyria, in harmony with the agreement entered into by Ahaz. Meanwhile the king had done everything possible for the defense of his kingdom. He had made sure of a bountiful supply of water within Jerusalem. "He also made weapons and shields in abundance. And he set combat commanders over the people." 2 Chronicles 32:5, 6, RSV. Nothing had been left undone in preparation for a siege.

At the time of Hezekiah's accession to the throne of Judah, the Assyrians had already carried captive a large number from the northern kingdom; and while he was strengthening the defenses of Jerusralem, the Assyrians captured Samaria and scattered the ten tribes among the Assyrian provinces. Jerusalem was less than fifty miles away; and the rich spoils in the temple would tempt the enemy to return.

The king of Judah had determined to resist, and having accomplished all that human ingenuity and energy could do, he had exhorted his forces to be of good courage. The king with unwavering faith declared, "With us is the Lord our God to help us, and to fight our battles." 2 Chronicles 32:8.

Faith Inspires Faith

Nothing more quickly inspires faith than the exercise of faith. Confident that the prophecy against the Assyrians would be fulfilled, the king stayed his soul upon God. "And the people took confidence from the words of Hezekiah king of Judah." 2 Chronicles 32:8, RSV. What though the armies of Assyria, fresh from the conquest of the greatest nations, and triumphant over Samaria, should now turn against Judah? What though they should boast, "Shall I not do to Jerusalem and her idols as I have done to Samaria and her images?" Isaiah 10:11, RSV. Judah had nothing to fear, for their trust was in Jehovah.

The long-expected crisis finally came. The forces of Assyria appeared in Judea. Confident of victory, the leaders divided their forces. One army was to meet the Egyptian army to the south, while the other was to besiege Jerusalem.

Judah's only hope now was in God. All possible help from Egypt had been cut off, and no other nations were near to lend a friendly hand.

The Assyrian officers insolently demanded the surrender of the city. This demand was accompanied by blasphemous revilings against the God of the Hebrews. Because of the weakness and apostasy of Israel and Judah, the name of God was no longer feared among the nations, but had become a subject for continual reproach. See Isaiah 52:5.

"Speak ye now to Hezekiah," said Rabshakeh, one of Sennacherib's chief officers, "Thus saith the great king, the king of Assyria, What confidence is this wherein thou trustest? Thou sayest, (but they are but vain words,) I have counsel and strength for the war. Now on whom dost thou trust, that thou rebellest against me?" 2 Kings 18:19, 20.

The officers were outside the city, but within the hearing of the sentries on the wall. As the representatives of the Assyrian king loudly urged their proposals upon the chief men of Judah, the latter requested them to speak in the Syrian rather than the Jewish language, in order that those on the wall might not have knowledge of the proceedings of the conference. Rabshakeh, scorning this suggestion, lifted his voice still higher in the Jewish language:

"Hear ye the words of the great king, the king of Assyria. Thus saith the king, Let not Hezekiah deceive you: for he shall not be able to deliver you. Neither let Hezekiah make you trust in the Lord, saying, The Lord will surely deliver us: this city shall not be delivered into the hand of the king of Assyria. . . . Beware lest Hezekiah persuade you, saying, The Lord will deliver us. Hath any of the gods of the nations delivered his land out of the hand of the king of Assyria? . . . Have they delivered Samaria out of my hand? Who are they among all the gods of these lands, that have delivered their land out of my hand, that the Lord should deliver Jerusalem out of my hand?" Isaiah 36:13-20.

Judah's Leaders Pray With Contrition

The Jewish representatives returned to Hezekiah "with their clothes rent, and told him the words of Rabshakeh." Verse 22. The king "rent his clothes, and covered himself with sackcloth, and went into the house of the Lord." 2 Kings 19:1.

A messenger was dispatched to Isaiah: "This day is

a day of trouble, and of rebuke, and blasphemy. . . . It may be the Lord thy God will hear all the words of Rabshakeh, whom the king of Assyria his master has sent to reproach the living God; and will reprove the words which the Lord thy God hath heard: wherefore lift up thy prayer for the remnant that are left." Verses 3, 4.

"For this cause Hezekiah the king, and the prophet Isaiah the son of Amoz, prayed and cried to heaven." 2 Chronicles 32:20.

God answered His servants. To Isaiah was given the message for Hezekiah: "Thus saith the Lord, Be not afraid of the words which thou hast heard, with which the servants of the king of Assyria have blasphemed Me. Behold, I will send a blast upon him, and he shall hear a rumor, and shall return to his own land; and I will cause him to fall by the sword in his own land." 2 Kings 19:6, 7.

The Taunts of the Enemy

The Assyrian representatives communicated direct with their king who was with his army guarding the approach from Egypt. Sennacherib wrote "letters to rail on the Lord God of Israel, and to speak against Him, saying, As the gods of the nations of other lands have not delivered their people out of mine hand, so shall not the God of Hezekiah deliver His people out of mine hand." 2 Chronicles 32:17.

The boastful threat was accompanied by the message: "Let not thy God in whom thou trustest deceive thee, saying, Jerusalem shall not be delivered into the hand of the king of Assyria." 2 Kings 19:10.

When the king of Judah received the taunting letter, he took it into the temple and "spread it before the Lord" and prayed with strong faith for help from heaven, that the nations of earth might know that the God of the Hebrews still lived and reigned. Verse 14. The honor of Jehovah was at stake; He alone could bring deliverance.

"O Lord God of Israel," Hezekiah pleaded, "hear the words of Sennacherib, which hath sent [Rabshakeh] to reproach the living God. Of a truth, Lord, the kings of Assyria have destroyed the nations and their lands, and have cast their gods into the fire: for they were no gods. . . . Now therefore, O Lord our God, I beseech Thee, save Thou us out of his hand, that all the kingdoms of the earth may know that Thou art the Lord God, even Thou only." Verses 15-19.

> Give ear, O Shepherd of Israel, . . .
> And come and save us.
> Turn us again, O God,
> And cause Thy face to shine; and we shall be
>   saved.
>   Psalm 80:1-3

The Lord Responds to Judah's Pleadings

Hezekiah's pleadings in behalf of Judah and of the honor of their Supreme Ruler were in harmony with the mind of God. Solomon had prayed the Lord to maintain "the cause of His people Israel, . . . that all the people of the earth may know that the Lord is God, and that there is none else." 1 Kings 8:59, 60. Especially was the Lord to show favor when, in times of war or oppression by an army, the chief men of Israel should enter the house of prayer and plead for deliverance. See verses 33, 34.

Isaiah sent to Hezekiah saying, "Thus saith the Lord God of Israel, That which thou hast prayed to Me against Sennacherib king of Assyria I have heard. This is the word that the Lord hath spoken concerning him:

Isaiah's Message Concerning Sennacherib

"Whom hast thou reproached and blasphemed? and against whom hast thou exalted thy voice, and lifted up thine eyes on high? even against the Holy One of Israel. By thy messengers thou hast reproached the Lord." "I know thy abode, and thy going out, and thy coming in, and thy rage against Me. Because thy rage against Me and thy tumult is come up into Mine ears, therefore I will put My hook in thy nose, and My bridle in thy lips, and I will turn thee back by the way by which thou camest." 2 Kings 19:20-23, 27, 28.

Judah had been laid waste by the army of occupation, but God had promised to provide miraculously for the people. To Hezekiah came the message: "The king of Assyria . . . shall not come into this city, nor shoot an arrow there, nor come before it with a shield, nor cast a bank against it. By the way that he came, by the same shall he return, and shall not come into this city, saith the Lord. For I will defend this city, to save it, for Mine own sake, and for My servant David's sake." Verses 32-34.

Deliverance Comes

That very night deliverance came. "The angel of the Lord went out, and smote in the camp of the Assyrians an hundred fourscore and five thousand." Verse 35. "All the mighty men of valor, and the leaders and captains in the camp of the king of Assyria" were slain. 2 Chronicles 32:21.

Tidings of this terrible judgment upon the army that had been sent to take Jerusalem soon reached Sennacherib, who was still guarding the approach to Judea from Egypt. Stricken with fear, the Assyrian king hasted to depart and "returned with shame of face to his own land." Verse 21. But he had not long to reign. In harmony with the prophecy concerning his sudden end, he was assasinated by those of his own home, "and Esarhaddon his son reigned in his stead." Isaiah 37:38.

The God of the Hebrews had prevailed. His honor was vindicated in the eyes of the surrounding nations. In Jerusalem the people were filled with holy joy. Their entreaties for deliverance had been mingled with confession of sin and with many tears. They had trusted wholly in the power of God to save, and He had not failed them. The temple courts resounded with songs of solemn praise.

> The stouthearted were stripped of their spoil;
> They sank into sleep;
> All the men of war
> Were unable to use their hands.
> At Thy rebuke, O God of Jacob,
> Both rider and horse lay stunned.

> But Thou, terrible art Thou!
> Who can stand before Thee
> When once Thy anger is roused?. . .

> Make your vows to the Lord your God, and perform them;
> Let all around Him bring gifts
> To Him who is to be feared,
> Who cuts off the spirit of princes,
> Who is terrible to the kings of the earth.
> Psalm 76:5-12, RSV

Lessons From the Proud Assyrian Empire

Inspiration has likened Assyria at the height of her prosperity to a noble tree in the garden of God, towering above the surrounding trees: "Under his shadow dwelt all great nations." "All the trees of Eden . . . envied him." Ezekiel 31:6, 9.

But the rulers of Assyria, instead of using their blessings for the benefit of mankind, became the scourge of many lands. Merciless, with no thought of God or their fellowmen, they pursued the fixed policy of causing all nations to acknowledge the supremacy of gods of Nineveh, whom they exalted above the Most High. God had sent Jonah to them with a message of warning, and for a season they humbled themselves before the Lord of hosts and sought forgiveness. But soon they turned again to idol worship and to the conquest of the world.

The prophet Nahum, in his arraignment of the evildoers in Nineveh, exclaimed:

> Woe to the bloody city,
> All full of lies and booty—
> No end to the plunder!
>
> Horsemen charging,
> Flashing sword and glittering spear,
> Hosts of slain, heaps of corpses,
> Dead bodies without end—
> They stumble over the bodies!
>
> Behold, I am against you, says the Lord of hosts.
> Nahum 3:1, 3, 5, RSV

With unerring accuracy the Infinite One still keeps account with the nations. While His mercy is tendered, with calls to repentance, this account remains open; but when the figures reach a certain amount which God has fixed, the ministry of His wrath begins. The account is closed.

"The Lord is slow to anger, and great in power, and will not at all aquit the wicked." "Who can stand before His indignation? and who can abide in the fierceness of His anger?" Nahum 1:3, 6.

It was thus that Nineveh became a desolation, "where the lion brought his prey, where his cubs were, with none to disturb." Nahum 2:11, RSV.

Zephaniah prophesied of Nineveh: "Herds shall lie down in the midst of her, all the beasts of the field; the vulture and the hedgehog shall lodge in her capitals; the owl shall hoot in the window, the raven croak on the threshold; for her cedar work will be laid bare." Zephaniah 2:14, RSV.

The pride of Assyria and its fall are to serve as an object lesson to the end of time. "The Lord is good, a stronghold in the day of trouble; and He knoweth them that trust in Him. But with an overrunning flood He will make an utter end" of all who endeavor to exalt themselves above the Most High. Nahum 1:7, 8.

This is true not only of the nations that arrayed themselves against God in ancient times, but also of nations today who fail of fulfilling the divine purpose. In the day of final awards, when the righteous Judge of all the earth shall "sift the nations" (Isaiah 30:28), heaven's arches will ring with the triumphant songs of the redeemed. "Ye shall have a song," the prophet declares, "as in the night when a holy solemnity is kept; and gladness of heart, as when one goeth with a pipe to come into the mountain of the Lord, to the Mighty One of Israel. . . . Through the voice of the Lord shall the Assyrian be beaten down, which smote with a rod." Verses 29-31.

31 / Isaiah's "Good News" for All the Nations

To Isaiah it was given to make very plain to Judah that many who were not descendants of Abraham after the flesh were to be numbered among the Israel of God. This teaching was not in harmony with the theology of his age, yet he fearlessly proclaimed the message and brought hope to many a heart reaching out after the spiritual blessings promised to the seed of Abraham.

Isaiah "is very bold," Paul declares, "and saith, I was found of them that sought Me not; I was made manifest unto them that asked not after Me." Romans 10:20. Often the Israelites seemed unable or unwilling to understand God's purpose for the heathen. Yet it was this very purpose that had established them as an independent nation. Abraham, their father, had been called to go forth to the regions beyond, that he might be a light bearer to the heathen. The promise to him included a posterity as numerous as the sand by the sea, yet it was for no selfish purpose that he was to become the founder of a great nation in Canaan. God's covenant with him embraced all the nations of earth: "I will make of you a great nation, and I will bless you, and make your name great, so that you will be a blessing." Genesis 12:2, RSV.

Shortly before the birth of Isaac, the child of promise, God's purpose for mankind was again made plain: "All the nations of the earth shall be blessed in him." Genesis 18:18. The all-embracing terms of this covenant were familiar to Abraham's children and grandchildren. That the Israelites might be a blessing to the nations and God's name might be made known "throughout all the earth" (Exodus 9:16), they were delivered from Egyptian bondage. If obedient, they were to be far in advance of other peoples in wisdom. But this supremacy was to be maintained only in order that through them the purpose of God for "all nations of earth" might be fulfilled.

The marvelous providences connected with Israel's deliverance from Egyptian bondage and with their occupancy of the Promised Land led many of the heathen to recognize the God of Israel as the Supreme Ruler. Even proud Pharaoh was constrained to acknowledge His power: "Go, serve the Lord," he urged Moses, "and bless me also!" Exodus 12:31, 32.

The advancing hosts of Israel found that the mighty workings of God had gone before them. In wicked Jericho a heathen woman said, "The Lord your God, He is God in heaven above, and in earth beneath." Joshua 2:11. By faith "Rahab perished not with them that believed not." Hebrews 11:31. And her conversion was not an isolated case. The Gibeonites renounced heathenism and united with Israel, sharing the blessings of the covenant.

No distinction of nationality, race, or caste is recognized by God. All men are one by creation; all are one through redemption. Christ came to demolish every wall of partition, to throw open every compartment of the temple courts, that every soul may have free access to God. His love is so broad, so deep, so full, that it penetrates everywhere. It lifts out of Satan's influence those who have been deluded by his deceptions and places them within reach of the throne of God. "All the ends of the world," the psalmist was inspired to sing, "shall remember and turn unto the Lord: and all the kindreds of the nations shall worship before Thee." "Ethiopia shall soon stretch out her hands unto God." "The heathen shall fear the name of the Lord, and all the kings of the earth Thy glory." "From heaven did the Lord behold the earth; to hear the groaning of the prisoner; to loose those that are appointed to death; to declare the name of the Lord in Zion, and His praise in Jerusalem; when the people are gathered together, and the kingdoms, to serve the Lord.'' Psalm 22:27; 68:31; 102:15, 19-22.

Had Israel been true to her trust, all the nations of earth would have shared in her blessings. But as God's purpose was lost sight of, the heathen came to be looked on as beyond the pale of His mercy. The nations were overspread with a veil of ignorance; the love of God was little known; error and superstition flourished.

Such was the prospect that greeted Isaiah. Yet he was not discouraged, for ringing in his ears was the chorus of the angels, ''The whole earth is full of His glory.'' Isaiah 6:3. And his faith was strengthened by visions of glorious conquests by the church of God when ''the earth shall be full of the knowledge of the Lord, as the waters cover the sea.'' Isaiah 11:9.

The Captivity Brought "Good News" to Many

To the prophet was given a revelation of the beneficent design of God in scattering impenitent Judah among the nations of earth. ''My people shall know My name,'' the Lord declared. Isaiah 52:6. In their exile they were to impart to others a knowledge of the living God. Many among the strangers were to learn to love Him as their Creator and Redeemer; they were to begin the observance of His holy Sabbath as a memorial of His creative power. ''All the ends of the earth shall see the salvation of our God.'' Verse 10. Many of these converts from heathenism would unite with the Israelites and accompany them on the return journey to Judea. They should thenceforth be numbered among spiritual Israel—His church on earth.

''The sons of the stranger, that join themselves to the Lord, to serve Him, and to love the name of the Lord, to be His servants, everyone that keepeth the

Sabbath from polluting it, and taketh hold of My covenant; even them will I bring to My holy mountain, and make them joyful in My house of prayer: . . . for Mine house shall be called an house of prayer for all people." Isaiah 56:6, 7.

The prophet was permitted to look down the centuries to the advent of the promised Messiah. Many were being led astray by false teachers; others were not bringing true holiness into the life practice. The outlook seemed hopeless; but soon before the eyes of the prophet was spread a wondrous vision. He saw the Sun of Righteousness, and, lost in admiration, he exclaimed: "The people that walked in darkness have seen a great light: they that dwell in the land of the shadow of death, upon them hath the light shined." Isaiah 9:2.

This glorious Light of the world was to bring salvation to every nation and people. The prophet heard the eternal Father declare: "It is too light a thing that You should be My servant to raise up the tribes of Jacob and to restore the preserved of Israel; I will give You as a light to the nations, that My salvation may reach to the end of the earth." Isaiah 49:6, RSV; see also verses 8, 9, 12.

Looking on still farther through the ages, the prophet saw the bearers of the glad tidings of salvation going to the ends of the earth. He heard the commission, "Enlarge the place of your tent, and let the curtains of your habitations be stretched out; hold not back, lengthen your cords and strengthen your stakes. For . . . your descendants will possess the nations." Isaiah 54:2, 3, RSV.

> How beautiful upon the mountains
> Are the feet of him who bringeth good tidings, . . .
> That publisheth salvation;
> That saith unto Zion, thy God reigneth!
> Isaiah 52:7

The prophet [Isaiah] heard the voice of God calling, that the way might be prepared for the ushering in of His everlasting kingdom. The message was plain.

> Arise, shine; for thy light is come,
> And the glory of the Lord is risen upon thee.
>
> For, behold, the darkness shall cover the earth,
> And gross darkness the people:
> But the Lord shall arise upon thee,
> And His glory shall be seen upon thee.
> And the Gentiles shall come to thy light,
> And kings to the brightness of thy rising.
>
> Look unto Me, and be ye saved, all the ends of the
>   earth:
> For I am God, and there is none else.
>   Isaiah 60:1-3; 45:22

The Church Takes the "Good News" to the World

These prophecies are today meeting fulfillment in the benighted regions of earth. Missionaries have been likened by the prophet to ensigns set up for the guidance of those looking for the light of truth: "In that day the Lord will extend His hand yet a second time to recover the remnant which is left of His people. . . . He will raise an ensign for the nations, and will assemble the outcasts of Israel, and gather the dispersed of Judah from the four corners of the earth." Isaiah 11:11, 12, RSV.

Among all nations the Lord sees men and women praying for light. They grope as blind men. But they are honest in heart. With no knowledge of the written law of God nor of His Son Jesus, they have revealed the working of a divine power on mind and character. At times those who have no knowledge of God aside from that which they have received under the operations of divine grace have protected His servants at the risk of their own lives. The Holy Spirit is implanting the grace of Christ in the heart of many a noble seeker after truth, quickening his sympathies contrary to his former education. The "Light, which lighteth every man" (John 1:9) is shining in his soul, and, if heeded, will guide his feet to the kingdom of God.

God will not permit any soul to be disappointed in his longing for something higher and nobler than anything the world can offer. Constantly He is sending His angels to those who, surrounded by discouraging circumstances, pray in faith for some power higher than themselves to bring deliverance and peace. In various ways God will place them in touch with providences that will establish their confidence in the One who has given Himself a ransom for all.

Unto all "the upright" in heathen lands "there ariseth light in the darkness." Psalm 112:4. God hath spoken: "I will bring the blind by a way that they knew not; I will lead them in paths that they have not known: I will make darkness light before them, and crooked things straight." Isaiah 42:16.

32 / Manasseh and Josiah: The Worst and the Best

The kingdom of Judah was once more brought low during Manasseh's wicked reign. Paganism was revived, and many were led into idolatry. "Manasseh made Judah and the inhabitants of Jerusalem to err, and to do worse than the heathen." 2 Chronicles 33:9. Gross evils sprang up and flourished—tyranny, oppression, hatred of all that is good. Justice was perverted; violence prevailed.

Yet the trying experiences through which Judah had safely passed during Hezekiah's reign had developed a sturdiness of character in many that now served as a bulwark against iniquity. Their testimony in behalf of truth aroused the anger of Manasseh, who endeavored to silence every voice of disapproval. "Manasseh shed innocent blood . . . till he had filled Jerusalem from one end to another." 2 Kings 21:16.

One of the first to fall was Isaiah, who for more than half a century had stood as the appointed messenger of Jehovah. "Others suffered mocking and scourging, and even chains and imprisonment. They were stoned, they were sawn in two, they were killed with the sword." Hebrews 11:36, 37, RSV.

Some who suffered persecution during Manasseh's reign were commissioned to bear special messages of reproof. The king of Judah, the prophets declared, "hath done wickedly above all . . . which were before him." 2 Kings 21:11. Because of this, the inhabitants of the land were to be carried captive to Babylon, there to become "a prey and a spoil to all their enemies."

Verse 14. But those who in a strange land should put their trust wholly in the Lord would find a sure refuge.

Faithfully the prophets spoke to Manasseh and his people, but backsliding Judah would not heed. As an earnest of what would befall the people should they continue impenitent, the Lord permitted their king to be captured by Assyrian soldiers who "bound him with fetters, and carried him to Babylon." 2 Chronicles 33:11. This affliction brought the king to his senses. He "humbled himself greatly before the God of his fathers, and . . . He was entreated of him, and heard his supplication, and brought him again to Jerusalem into his kingdom. Then Manasseh knew that the Lord He was God." Verses 12, 13. But this repentance came too late to save the kingdom from the influence of years of idolatrous practices.

Among those whose life had been shaped beyond recall was Manasseh's own son, who came to the throne at the age of twenty-two. King Amon "walked in all the way that his father walked in." "He forsook the Lord, the God of his fathers." 2 Kings 21:21. The wicked king was not permitted to reign long. Only two years from the time he ascended the throne, he was slain in the palace by his own servants, and "the people of the land made Josiah his son king in his stead." 2 Chronicles 33:25.

Josiah Resolves to Be True to His Trust

With the accession of Josiah to the throne, where he was to rule for thirty-one years, those who had maintained their faith began to hope that the downward course of the kingdom was checked; for the new king, though only eight years old, "did that which was right in the sight of the Lord, and walked in all the way of David his father, and turned not aside to the right hand or to the left." 2 Kings 22:2. Warned by the errors of past generations, Josiah chose to do right. His obedience made it possible for God to use him as a vessel unto honor.

At the time Josiah began to rule, and for many years before, the truehearted were questioning whether God's promises to Israel could ever be fulfilled. The apostasy of former centuries had gathered strength; ten tribes had been scattered among the heathen; only Judah and Benjamin remained, and these now seemed on the verge of moral and national ruin. The prophets had begun to foretell the destruction of their fair city, where stood the temple built by Solomon. Was God about to turn aside from His purpose of bringing deliverance to those who should put their trust in Him? Could those who had remained true to God hope for better days?

These anxious questions were voiced by Habakkuk: "O Lord, how long shall I cry, and Thou wilt not hear! even cry out unto Thee of violence, and Thou wilt not save! . . . Spoiling and violence are before me: and there are that raise up strife and contention. Therefore the law is slacked, and judgment doth never go forth: for the wicked doth compass about the righteous; therefore wrong judgment proceedeth." Habakkuk 1:2-4.

God answered His loyal children. Through His mouthpiece He revealed His determination to bring chastisement upon the nation that had turned to serve the gods of the heathen. Within the lifetime of some who were even then making inquiry regarding the future, He would bring the Chaldeans upon the land of Judah as a divinely appointed scourge. The princes and fairest of the people were to be carried captive to Babylon; the Judean cities, villages, and cultivated fields were to be laid waste.

Habakkuk Bows in Submission to the Lord

"Art Thou not from everlasting, O Lord my God, mine Holy One?" Habakkuk exclaimed. And then, his faith laying hold on the precious promises that reveal God's love for His children, the prophet added, "We shall not die." Verse 12. With this declaration of faith he rested the case of every believing Israelite in the hands of a compassionate God.

This was not Habakkuk's only experience in the exercise of strong faith. On one occasion he said, "I will stand upon my watch, and set me upon the tower, and will watch to see what He will say unto me." Graciously the Lord answered: "Write the vision, and make it plain upon tables, that he may run that readeth it. For the vision is yet for an appointed time, but at the end it shall speak, and not lie: though it tarry, wait for it; because it will surely come, it will not tarry. Behold, his soul which is lifted up is not upright in him: but the just shall live by his faith." Habakkuk 2:1-4.

Faith Will Sustain God's People Today

The faith that strengthened Habakkuk in those days of trial was the same faith that sustains God's people today. Under circumstances the most forbidding, the believer may keep his soul stayed on the Source of all light and power. Through faith in God, his courage may be renewed. "The just shall live by his faith." The Lord will more than fulfill the highest expectations of those who put their trust in Him. He will give the wisdom their necessities demand.

We must cultivate the faith that lays hold on the promises of God and waits for deliverance in His appointed time and way. The sure word of prophecy will meet its final fulfillment in the glorious advent of our Saviour as King of kings and Lord of lords. The time of waiting may seem long, many in whom confidence has been placed may fall by the way; but with the prophet who endeavored to encourage Judah in a time of apostasy, let us declare, "The Lord is in His holy temple: let all the earth keep silence before Him." Verse 20.

> O Lord, revive Thy work in the midst of the years,
> In the midst of the years make it known;
> In wrath remember mercy.
> Habakkuk 3:2

Though the fig tree do not blossom,
Nor fruit be on the vines,
The produce of the olive fail
And the fields yield no food,
The flock be cut off from the fold
And there be no herd in the stalls,
Yet I will rejoice in the Lord,
I will joy in the God of my salvation.
God, the Lord, is my strength.
                    Habakkuk 3:17-19, RSV

Habakkuk was not the only one through whom was given a message of hope and of future triumph as well as of present judgment. During the reign of Josiah the word of the Lord came to Zephaniah, specifying the results of continued apostasy and calling attention to the glorious prospect beyond. His prophecies of judgment on Judah apply with equal force to the judgments to fall on an impenitent world at the second advent of Christ:

The great day of the Lord is near,
    It is near, and hasteth greatly,
Even the voice of the day of the Lord:
    The mighty man shall cry there bitterly.

That day is a day of wrath,
    A day of trouble and distress,
A day of wasteness and desolation,
    A day of darkness and gloominess.

A day of clouds and thick darkness,
    A day of the trumpet and alarm
Against the fenced cities,
    And against the high towers.
                    Zephaniah 1:14-16

"Neither their silver nor their gold shall be able to

deliver them in the day of the Lord's wrath. In the fire of His jealous wrath, all the earth shall be consumed; for a full, yea, sudden end He will make of all the inhabitants of the earth.'' Verse 18, RSV.

> Seek ye the Lord, all ye meek of the earth,
> Which have wrought His judgment;
> Seek righteousness,
> Seek meekness:
> It may be ye shall be hid
> In the day of the Lord's anger.
> Zephaniah 2:3

> In that day it shall be said to Jerusalem,
> Fear thou not:
> And to Zion, Let not thine hands be slack.
> The Lord thy God in the midst of thee
> Is mighty; He will save,
> He will rejoice over thee with joy;
> He will rest in His love,
> He will joy over thee with singing.
> Zephaniah 3:16, 17

33 / The Long-lost Law Book Discovered

The messages of the prophets regarding the Babylonian captivity did much to prepare the way for a reformation in the eighteenth year of Josiah's reign. This reform movement was brought about in a wholly unexpected manner through the discovery of a portion of Holy Scripture that for many years had been misplaced and lost.

Nearly a century before, during the first Passover celebrated by Hezekiah, provision had been made for the public reading of the book of the law. Observance of the statutes recorded in the book of the covenant (a part of Deuteronomy), had made the reign of Hezekiah prosperous. But during Manasseh's reign the temple copy of the book had become lost.

The long-lost manuscript was found in the temple by Hilkiah, the high priest, while the building was undergoing repairs. He handed the precious volume to Shaphan, a learned scribe, who took it to the king with the story of its discovery.

Josiah was deeply stirred as he heard for the first time the warnings recorded in this ancient manuscript. Never before had he realized how repeatedly Israel had been urged to choose the way of life, that they might become a blessing to all nations. See Deuteronomy 31:6. The book abounded in assurances of God's willingness to save those who should place their trust fully in Him. As He had wrought in their deliverance from Egyptian bondage, so would He work mightily in placing them at the head of the nations of earth.

As the king heard the inspired words, he recognized, in the picture set before him, conditions similar to those existing in his kingdom. In prophetic portrayals of departure from God, he was startled to find plain statements that the day of calamity would follow and that there would be no remedy. There could be no mistaking the meaning of the words. And at the close of the volume, in a rehearsal of the events of the future, Moses had declared:

> [Israel] forsook God who made him,
>   And scoffed at the Rock of his salvation. . . .
> They sacrificed to demons which were no gods. . . .
> You were umindful of the Rock that begot you,
>   And you forgot the God who gave you birth.
> The Lord saw it, and spurned them,
>   Because of the provocation of His sons and His
>   daughters.
> And He said, ''I will hide My face from them,
>   I will see what their end will be,
> For they are a perverse generation,
>   Children in whom is no faithfulness.''
>
> How should one chase a thousand,
>   And two put ten thousand to flight,
> Unless their Rock had sold them,
>   And the Lord had given them up?
>
> Vengeance is Mine, and recompense,
>   For the time when their foot shall slip;
> For the day of their calamity is at hand,
>   And their doom comes swiftly.
>
>   Deuteronomy 32:15-20, 30, 35, RSV

Young Josiah Does All He Can Do

As King Josiah read the prophecies of swift judgment, he trembled for the future. The perversity of Judah had been great; what was to be the outcome of their continued apostasy?

"In the eighth year of his reign, while he was yet young," he had consecrated himself fully to the service of God. At the age of twenty he had removed "the high places, and the groves, and the carved images, and the molten images." "They brake down the altars of Baalim in his presence; and the images . . . and the groves . . . he brake in pieces, and made dust of them, and strowed it upon the graves of them that had sacrificed unto them. And he burnt the bones of the priests upon the altars, and cleansed Judah and Jerusalem." 2 Chronicles 34:3-5.

The youthful ruler extended his efforts to the portions of Palestine formerly occupied by the ten tribes of Israel, only a feeble remnant of which now remained. "So did he," the record reads, "in the cities of Manasseh, and Ephraim, and Simeon, even unto Naphtali." Verse 6. Not until he had traversed the length and breadth of this region of ruined homes, and "had broken down the altars and the groves, and had beaten the graven images into powder, and cut down all the idols throughout all the land of Israel," did he return to Jerusalem. Verse 7.

Thus Josiah had endeavored as king to exalt God's holy law. And now, while Shaphan the scribe was reading to him out of the book of the law, the king discerned in this volume a powerful ally in the work of reform he so much desired to see. He resolved to do all in his power to acquaint his people with its teachings and to lead them, if possible, to reverence and love the law of heaven.

The King Consults the Lord's Prophetess

But was it possible to bring about the needed reform? Israel had almost reached the limit of divine forbearance. Overwhelmed with sorrow and dismay, Josiah bowed before God in agony of spirit, seeking pardon for the sins of an impenitent nation.

At that time the prophetess Huldah was living in Jerusalem near the temple. The king determined to inquire of the Lord through this chosen messenger whether by any means within his power he might save erring Judah, now on the verge of ruin.

The respect in which he held the prophetess led him to choose as his messengers to her the first men of the kingdom: "Go ye, inquire of the Lord for me, and for the people, and for all Judah, concerning the words of this book that is found." 2 Kings 22:13.

Through Huldah the Lord sent Josiah word that Jerusalem's ruin could not be averted. The people could not escape their punishment. So long had their senses been deadened by wrongdoing that, if judgment should not come, they would soon return to the same sinful course. "Tell the man that sent you to me," the prophetess declared, "Thus saith the Lord, Behold, I will bring evil upon this place, and upon the inhabitants thereof, even all the words of the book which the king of Judah hath read: . . . My wrath shall be kindled against this place, and shall not be quenched." Verses 15-17.

But because the king had humbled his heart before God, to him was sent the message: "Because thine heart was tender, and thou hast humbled thyself before the Lord, when thou heardest what I spake against this place, and against the inhabitants thereof, that they should become a desolation and a curse, and hast rent thy clothes and wept before Me; I also have heard thee, saith the Lord. Behold therefore, I will gather thee unto thy fathers, and thou shalt be gathered into thy grave in peace; and thine eyes shall not see all the evil which I will bring upon this place." Verses 19, 20.

The king must leave with God the events of the future. But the Lord had not withdrawn opportunity for repentance and reformation, and Josiah determined to do all in his power to bring about decided reforms. He arranged at once for a great convocation, to which were invited the elders, magistrates, and the common people.

To this vast assembly the king himself read "all the

words of the book of the covenant which was found in the house of the Lord." 2 Kings 23:2. The royal reader was deeply affected, and he delivered his message with the pathos of a broken heart. His hearers were profoundly moved. The intensity of feeling revealed in the countenance of the king, the solemnity of the message itself, the warning of judgments impending—all these had their effect. Many determined to join the king in seeking forgiveness.

Josiah now proposed that those highest in authority unite with the people in solemnly covenanting before God to institute decided changes. The response was more hearty than the king had dared hope for: "All the people joined in the covenant." Verse 3, RSV.

So long had they followed the customs of the surrounding nations in bowing down to images that it seemed almost beyond the power of man to remove every trace of these evils. But Josiah persevered in his effort to cleanse the land. See verses 20, 24.

Three-Hundred-Year-Old Prophecy Fulfilled

Centuries before, Jeroboam in bold defiance of God had set up an unconsecrated altar at Bethel. During the dedication of this altar, there had suddenly appeared a man of God from Judea who "cried against the altar," declaring: "O altar, altar, thus saith the Lord; Behold, a child shall be born unto the house of David, Josiah by name; and upon thee shall he offer the priests of the high places that burn incense upon thee, and men's bones shall be burnt upon thee." 1 Kings 13:2.

Three centuries had passed. Josiah the king found himself in Bethel, where stood this ancient altar. The prophecy uttered so many years before was now to be literally fulfilled.

"The altar at Bethel, the high place erected by Jeroboam the son of Nebat, who made Israel to sin, that altar with the high place he pulled down and he broke in pieces its stones, crushing them to dust. . . . And as Josiah turned, he saw the tombs there on the mount;

and he sent and took the bones out of the tombs, and burned them upon the altar, and defiled it, according to the word of the Lord which the man of God proclaimed, who had predicted these things.'' 2 Kings 23:15, 16, RSV.

On the southern slopes of Olivet, opposite the beautiful temple of Jehovah on Mount Moriah, were shrines and images placed there by Solomon to please his idolatrous wives. See 1 Kings 11:6-8. For upwards of three centuries the great, misshapen images had stood, mute witness to the apostasy of Israel's wisest king. These, too, were destroyed by Josiah.

The king sought further to establish the faith of Judah by holding a great Passover in harmony with the provisions made in the book of the law. ''For no such passover had been kept since the days of the judges who judged Israel, or during all the kings of Israel or the kings of Judah.'' 2 Kings 23:22, RSV. But the zeal of Josiah could not atone for the sins of past generations, nor could the piety displayed by the king's followers effect a change of heart in many who stubbornly refused to turn from idolatry to worship the true God.

For more than a decade following the Passover, Josiah continued to reign. At thirty-nine he met death in battle with the forces of Egypt. ''All Judah and Jerusalem mourned for Josiah. And Jeremiah lamented'' for him. 2 Chronicles 35:24, 25.

The time was rapidly approaching when Jerusalem was to be utterly destroyed and the inhabitants of the land carried captive to Babylon, there to learn lessons they ad refused to learn under circumstances more favorable.

34 / Jeremiah, the Man Who Felt God's Anguish

Jeremiah had hoped for a permanent reformation under Josiah. Called of God to the prophetic office while still a youth, a member of the priesthood, Jeremiah had been trained from childhood for holy service. In those happy years he little realized that he had been ordained from birth to be "a prophet unto the nations." When the divine call came, he was overwhelmed. "Ah, Lord God!" he exclaimed, "I do not know how to speak, for I am only a youth." Jeremiah 1:5, 6, RSV.

In the youthful Jeremiah, God saw one who would be true to his trust and stand for the right against great opposition. In childhood he had proved faithful, and now he was to endure hardness as a soldier of the cross. "Do not say, 'I am only a youth.' . . . Be not afraid of them, for I am with you to deliver you." "Say to them everything that I command you. Do not be dismayed by them, lest I dismay you before them. And I, behold, I make you this day a fortified city, an iron pillar, and bronze walls, against the whole land. . . . They will fight against you; but they shall not prevail against you, for I am with you, says the Lord, to deliver you." Verses 7, 8, 17-19, RSV.

For forty years Jeremiah was to stand as a witness for truth and righteousness. In a time of unparalleled apostasy he was to exemplify in life and character the worship of the true God. He was to be the mouthpiece of Jehovah. He was to predict the downfall of the house of David and the destruction of the beautiful temple built by Solomon. Imprisoned, despised, hated, rejected of men, he was finally to share in the sorrow and woe that should follow the destruction of the fated city.

Yet Jeremiah was often permitted to look beyond the distressing scenes of the present to the glorious future, when God's people should be planted again in Zion. "Their soul shall be as a watered garden; and they shall not sorrow any more at all." Jeremiah 31:12. Jeremiah wrote: "The Lord said unto me, Behold, I have put My words in thy mouth. See, I have this day set thee over the nations and over the kingdoms, to root out, and to pull down, and to destroy, and to throw down, to build, and to plant." Jeremiah 1:9, 10.

A True Prophet Always "Builds"

Thank God for the words, "to build, and to plant." The Lord's purpose was to restore and to heal. Prophecies of swift-coming judgments were to be fearlessly delivered, yet the prophet was to accompany these messages with assurances of forgiveness to all who should turn from their evil-doing.

Jeremiah sought to encourage the men of Judah to lay spiritual foundations broad and deep, by thorough repentance. Long had they been building with material likened by Jeremiah to dross: "Refuse silver they are called, for the Lord has rejected them." Jeremiah 6:30, RSV. Now they were urged to build for eternity, casting aside the rubbish of apostasy and using as material pure gold, refined silver, precious stones—faith, obedience, and good works—which alone are acceptable to God.

The word of the Lord was, "Return, thou backsliding Israel, . . . and I will not cause Mine anger to fall upon you: for I am merciful, saith the Lord, . . . for I am married unto you." Jeremiah 3:12-14.

And in addition the Lord gave His erring people the very words with which they might turn to Him: "We come unto Thee; for Thou art the Lord our God." "We lie down in our shame, and our confusion covereth us:

for we have sinned against the Lord our God, we and our fathers, from our youth even unto this day, and have not obeyed the voice of the Lord our God." Verses 22, 25.

The reformation under Josiah had cleansed the land of idolatrous shrines, but the hearts of the multitude had not been transformed. The seeds of truth that had sprung up and given promise of an abundant harvest had been choked by thorns. Another such backsliding would be fatal.

Jeremiah called attention repeatedly to the counsels given in Deuteronomy. He showed how these might bring the highest spiritual blessing to the nation. "Ask for the old paths, where is the good way, and walk therein, and ye shall find rest for your souls." Jeremiah 6:16.

On one occasion, at one of the principal entrances to the city the prophet urged the importance of keeping holy the Sabbath day: "If ye diligently hearken unto Me, saith the Lord, to bring in no burden through the gates of this city on the Sabbath day, but hallow the Sabbath day, to do no work therein; then shall there enter into the gates of this city kings and princes sitting upon the throne of David, . . . and this city shall remain for ever." Jeremiah 17:24, 25. If the admonitions to obey the God of their fathers to hallow His Sabbath were not heeded, the city and its palaces would be utterly destroyed by fire. Only by the most decided measures could a change for the better be brought about; therefore the prophet labored most earnestly for the impenitent. "O Jerusalem, wash thine heart from wickedness, that thou mayest be saved." Jeremiah 4:14.

But by the great mass of the people the call to repentance was unheeded. Those who ruled the nation had been untrue to their trust and had been leading many astray. From the beginning of Jehoiakim's reign, Jeremiah had little hope of saving his beloved land from destruction and captivity. Yet he was not to remain silent while utter ruin threatened the kingdom. Those loyal to God must be encouraged to persevere in rightdoing, and sinners must be induced, if possible, to turn from iniquity.

Jeremiah was commanded by the Lord to stand in the court of the temple and speak to all who might pass in and out. He must diminish not a word!

The prophet obeyed; he lifted his voice in warning and entreaty. "Hear the word of the Lord, all ye of Judah, that enter in at these gates. . . . Amend your ways and your doings, and I will cause you to dwell in this place. Trust ye not in lying words, saying, The temple of the Lord, The temple of the Lord, The temple of the Lord." Jeremiah 7:2-4.

God's Marvelous Loving-Kindness

The unwillingness of the Lord to chastise is here vividly shown. He yearns over His erring children; in every way possible He seeks to teach them the way of life. See Jeremiah 9:24. Though the Israelites had wandered long in idolatry and slighted His warnings, yet He now declares His willingness to defer chastisement and grant yet another opportunity for repentance. He makes plain that only by thorough heart reformation could the impending doom be averted. In vain would be their trust in the temple and its services. Ceremonies could not atone for sin. Reformation of heart and of the life practice alone could save them from the result of transgression.

Thus "in the cities of Judah, and in the streets of Jerusalem" the message of Jeremiah was, "Hear ye the words of this covenant"—the precepts of God as recorded in the Scriptures—"and do them." Jeremiah 11:6. "Why," the Lord inquired, "is this people of Jerusalem slidden back by a perpetual backsliding?" Jeremiah 8:5. It was because they had refused to be corrected. See Jeremiah 5:3. "The stork in the heavens knows her appointed times; and the turtledove, the swift, and the swallow observe the time of their coming. But My people know not the judgment of the Lord." "Shall I not avenge Myself on such a nation as this?" Jeremiah 8:7; 9:9, NKJV.

While Josiah had been their ruler, the people had some ground for hope. But he had fallen in battle. The time for intercession had all but passed. "Though Moses and Samuel stood before Me," the Lord declared, "yet My mind could not be toward this people: cast them out of My sight." Jeremiah 15:1.

A refusal to heed the invitation that God was now offering would bring the judgments that had befallen the northern kingdom more than a century before. The message now was: "If ye will not hearken to . . . the words of My servants the prophets, whom I sent unto you, . . . then will I make this house like Shiloh, and will make this city a curse to all the nations of the earth." Jeremiah 26:4-6.

Those who stood in the temple court listening to Jeremiah understood clearly this reference to Shiloh, when in the days of Eli the Philistines had carried away the ark of the testament. The sin of Eli consisted in passing lightly over the evils prevailing in the land. His neglect to correct these evils had brought on Israel a fearful calamity. Eli lost his life, the ark had been taken from Israel, thirty thousand people had been slain—all because sin had flourished unrebuked and unchecked. Israel had vainly thought that, notwithstanding their sinful practices, the ark would ensure victory over the Philistines. In like manner, during the days of Jeremiah, the people of Judah were prone to believe that observance of the appointed temple services would preserve them from punishment for their wicked course.

What a lesson is this to men holding positions of responsibility in the church! What a warning to deal faithfully with wrongs that bring dishonor to the cause of truth! Let none charge the servants of God with being too zealous in endeavoring to cleanse the camp from evil-doing. The desolation of Jerusalem in the days of Jeremiah is a solemn warning that the admonitions given through chosen instrumentalities cannot be disregarded with impunity.

Jeremiah's message aroused the antagonism of many. They cried out, "Why hast thou prophesied in the name of the Lord, saying, This house shall be like Shiloh, and this city shall be desolate without an inhabitant? And all the people were gathered against Jeremiah in the house of the Lord." Verse 9. Priests, false prophets, and people turned on him who would not speak smooth things or prophesy deceit. God's servant was threatened with death.

Jeremiah's Courage Saves His Life

Tidings of the words of Jeremiah were carried to the princes, and they hastened from the palace to learn for themselves the truth of the matter. "Then spake the priests and the prophets unto the princes and to all the people, saying, This man is worthy to die; for he hath prophesied against this city, as ye have heard with your ears." Verse 11. But Jeremiah boldly declared: "The Lord sent me to prophesy against this house and against this city all the words that ye have heard. Therefore now . . . obey the voice of the Lord your God; and the Lord will repent Him of the evil that He hath pronounced against you. As for me, behold, I am in your hand: do with me as seemeth good and meet unto you. But know ye for certain, that if ye put me to death, ye shall surely bring innocent blood upon yourselves, and upon this city, and upon the inhabitants thereof: for of a truth the Lord hath sent me unto you." Verses 12-15.

Had the prophet been intimidated by those high in authority, he would have lost his life. But the courage with which he delivered the solemn warning commanded the respect of the people and turned the princes in his favor. They reasoned with the priests and false prophets. Thus God raised up defenders for His servant.

The elders also united in protesting against the decision of the priests regarding Jeremiah. Through the pleading of these men of influence the prophet's life was spared, although many priests and false prophets would gladly have seen him put to death on the plea of sedition.

To the close of his ministry, Jeremiah stood as "a tower and a fortress" (Jeremiah 6:27) against which the wrath of man could not prevail. "They shall fight against thee," the Lord had forewarned His servant, "but they shall not prevail against thee." Jeremiah 15:20.

Jeremiah's Peaceful, Shrinking Disposition

Naturally timid, Jeremiah longed for the quiet of retirement, where he need not witness the continued impenitence of his beloved nation. His heart was wrung with anguish over the ruin wrought by sin. "O that my head were waters, and mine eyes a fountain of tears," he mourned, "that I might weep day and night for the slain of the daughter of my people! O that I had in the wilderness a lodging place of wayfaring men; that I might leave my people, and go from them." Jeremiah 9:1, 2.

His sensitive soul was pierced by the arrows of derision hurled at him. "I have become a laughingstock all the day; every one mocks me." "Say all my familiar friends, watching for my fall . . . 'Perhaps he will be deceived, then we can overcome him.' " Jeremiah 20:7, 10, RSV.

But the faithful prophet was daily strengthened. "The Lord is with me as a dread warrior," he declared in faith. "Therefore my persecutors will stumble, they will not overcome me. They will be greatly shamed." Jeremiah 20:11, RSV. He learned to pray, "Correct me, O Lord, but in just measure; not in Thy anger, lest Thou bring me to nothing." Jeremiah 10:24, RSV.

When tempted in his misery to say, "My strength and my hope is perished from the Lord" (Lamentations 3:18), Jeremiah recalled the providences of God in his behalf and exclaimed: "The steadfast love of the Lord never ceases, His mercies never come to an end; they are new every morning; great is Thy faithfulness. 'The Lord is my portion,' says my soul, 'therefore I will hope in Him.' The Lord is good to those who wait for Him, to the soul that seeks Him. It is good that one should wait quietly for the salvation of the Lord." Lamentations 3:22-26, RSV.

35 / Judah's Amazing Stubbornness

The first years of Jehoiakim's reign were filled with warnings of approaching doom. All unexpectedly a new world power, the Babylonian empire, was rising to the eastward and swiftly overshadowing Assyria, Egypt, and all other nations.

The king of Babylon was to be the instrument of God's wrath on impenitent Judah. Again and again Jerusalem was to be entered by the armies of Nebuchadnezzar. Tens of thousands were to be taken captive in enforced exile. Jehoiakim, Jehoiachin, and Zedekiah were in turn to become vassals of the Babylonian ruler, and all in turn were to rebel. Severe chastisements were to be inflicted on the rebellious nation, until at last Jerusalem would be burned, the temple Solomon built destroyed, and Judah fall, never again to occupy its former position among the nations.

Those times of change were marked with many messages from Heaven through Jeremiah. The Lord gave the children of Judah ample opportunity of freeing themselves from alliances with Egypt and of avoiding controversy with Babylon. Jeremiah taught the people by acted parables, hoping to arouse them to a sense of obligation to God and to encourage them to maintain friendly relations with the Babylonian government.

To illustrate the importance of obedience to God, Jeremiah gathered some Rechabites into the temple and set wine before them. As expected, he met with absolute refusal: "We will drink no wine: for Jonadab the son of Rechab our father commanded us, saying,

Ye shall drink no wine, neither ye, nor your sons forever." "Then came the word of the Lord unto Jeremiah, saying, Thus saith the Lord of hosts, . . . The words of Jonadab the son of Rechab, that he commanded his sons not to drink wine, are performed; for unto this day they drink none, but obey their father's commandment." Jeremiah 35:6, 12-14. But the men of Judah had hearkened not to the words of the Lord and were about to suffer severe judgments.

The Lord declared, "I have sent to you all My servants the prophets, sending them persistently, saying, 'Turn now every one of you from his evil way, and amend your doings, and do not go after other gods to serve them, and then you shall dwell in the land which I gave to you and your fathers.' But you did not incline your ear or listen to Me." "Therefore, . . . I am bringing on Judah and all the inhabitants of Jerusalem all the evil that I have pronounced against them." Verses 15, 17, RSV.

When men turn from admonition until their hearts become hardened, the Lord permits them to be led by other influences. Refusing the truth, they accept falsehood to their own destruction. The Chaldeans were to be the instrument by which God would chastise His disobedient people. Their sufferings were to be in proportion to the light they had despised and rejected. God now would visit His displeasure on them as a last effort to check their evil course.

Upon the Rechabites was pronounced a continued blessing: "Because ye have obeyed the commandment of Jonadab your father, . . . Jonadab the son of Rechab shall not want a man to stand before Me forever." Verses 18, 19. The lesson is for us. If the requirements of a wise father, who took the most effectual means to secure his posterity against the evils of intemperance, were worthy of strict obedience, surely God's authority should be held in much greater reverence! By His servants He predicts the dangers of disobedience; He sounds the warning and reproves sin.

His people are kept in prosperity only by His mercy, through the vigilant watchcare of chosen instrumentalities. He cannot uphold a people who reject His counsel.

The Faithful Youth Were Encouraged

Never did Jeremiah lose sight of the importance of heart holiness in the service of God. He foresaw the scattering of Judah among the nations, but with faith he looked beyond to restoration. "The days come, saith the Lord, that I will raise unto David a righteous Branch, and a King shall reign and prosper, and shall execute judgment and justice in the earth. In His days Judah shall be saved, and Israel shall dwell safely: and this is His name whereby He shall be called, THE LORD OUR RIGHTEOUSNESS." Jeremiah 23:5, 6.

Those who should choose to live holy lives amid apostasy would be enabled to witness for Him. The days were coming, the Lord declared, when people would no longer say, "The Lord liveth, which brought up the children of Israel out of the land of Egypt; but, The Lord liveth, which brought up and which led the seed of the house of Israel out . . . from all countries whither I had driven them; and they shall dwell in their own land." Verses 7, 8. Such were the prophecies uttered by Jeremiah when the Babylonians were bringing their besieging armies against the walls of Zion.

Like sweetest music these promises fell on the ears of those who were steadfast in their worship of God. In homes where the counsels of a covenant-keeping God were still held in reverence, even the children were mightily stirred, and on their receptive minds lasting impressions were made. Their observance of Holy Scripture brought to Daniel and his fellows opportunities to exalt the true God before the nations of earth. The instruction these Hebrew children received in the homes of their parents made them strong in faith. When Nebuchadnezzar for the first time besieged Jerusalem and carried away Daniel and his companions, the faith of the Hebrew captives was tried to the utmost. But those who had learned to place their trust in the promises of God found these all-sufficient, a guide and a stay.

As an interpreter of the judgments beginning to fall on Judah, Jeremiah stood nobly in defense of the justice of God. He extended his influence beyond Jerusalem by frequent visits to various parts of the kingdom. In his testimonies he constantly emphasized the importance of maintaining a covenant relationship with the compassionate Being who on Sinai had spoken the Decalogue. His words reached every part of the kingdom.

The Perversity of King Jehoiakim

At the very time messages of impending doom were urged upon princes and people, Jehoiakim, who should have been foremost in reformation, was spending his time in selfish pleasure: "I will build me a wide house and large chambers," he proposed; and this house, "cieled with cedar, and painted with vermilion" (Jeremiah 22:14), was built with money and labor secured through fraud and oppression.

The prophet was inspired to pronounce judgment on the faithless ruler: "Woe unto him that buildeth his house by unrighteousness, and his chambers by wrong; that useth his neighbor's service without wages, and giveth him not for his work." "Therefore thus saith the Lord concerning Jehoiakim the son of Josiah king of Judah; They shall not lament for him. . . . He shall be buried with the burial of an ass, drawn and cast forth beyond the gates of Jerusalem." Verses 13, 18, 19.

Within a few years this terrible judgment was to be visited on Jehoiakim; but first the Lord in mercy informed the impenitent nation of His purpose: "Jeremiah the prophet spake unto all the people of Judah," pointing out that for more than twenty years he had borne witness of God's desire to save, but that his messages had been despised. See Jeremiah 25:1-3. And now, "thus saith the Lord of hosts; Because ye have not heard My words, behold, I will send and take all the families of the north, . . . and Nebuchadnezzar the king of Babylon, My servant, and will bring them against this land. . . . This whole land shall become a desolation, and an astonishment; and these nations shall serve the king of Babylon seventy years." Verses 8-11.

The Lord likened the fate of the nation to the draining of a cup filled with the wine of divine wrath. Among the first to drink of this cup was to be "Jerusalem, and the cities of Judah, and the kings thereof." Verse 18. Others were to partake of the same cup—Egypt and many other nations. See Jeremiah 25.

To illustrate further the coming judgments the prophet was bidden to "take some of the elders of the people and some of the senior priests, and go out to the valley of the son of Hinnom" (Jeremiah 19:1, 2, RSV) and there dash to pieces a "potter's earthen bottle" (verse 1) and declare in behalf of the Lord, "Even so will I break this people and this city, as one breaketh a potter's vessel, that cannot be made whole again." Verse 11. Returning to the city, he stood in the court of the temple and declared, "Thus saith the Lord of hosts, the God of Israel; Behold, I will bring upon this city and upon all her towns all the evil that I have pronounced against it, because they have hardened their necks, that they might not hear My words." Verse 15.

The prophet's words aroused the anger of those high in authority, and Jeremiah was imprisoned, and placed in the stocks. Nevertheless, his voice could not be silenced. The word of truth, he declared, "was in mine heart as a burning fire shut up in my bones, and I was weary with forbearing, and I could not stay." Jeremiah 20:9.

About this time the Lord commanded Jeremiah to write the messages. "Take a scroll and write on it all the words that I have spoken to you against Israel and

Judah and all the nations, from the day I spoke to you, from the days of Josiah until today. It may be that the house of Judah will hear all the evil which I intend to do to them, so that every one may turn from his evil way, and that I may forgive their iniquity and their sin." Jeremiah 36:2, 3, RSV.

In obedience to this command, Jeremiah called his faithful friend, Baruch the scribe, and dictated "all the words of the Lord, which He had spoken unto him." Verse 4. These were written on a roll of parchment and constituted a warning of the sure result of continual apostasy and an earnest appeal for the renunciation of all evil.

Jeremiah, still a prisoner, sent Baruch to read the roll to the multitudes at the temple on a national fast day. "It may be," the prophet said, "their supplication will come before the Lord, and that every one will turn from his evil way, for great is the anger and wrath that the Lord has pronounced against this people." Verse 7, RSV.

The roll was read before all the people. Afterward the scribe was summoned before the princes to read the words to them. They listened with great interest and promised to inform the king, but counseled the scribe to hide himself, for they feared the king would seek to slay those who had prepared and delivered the message.

Jehoiakim immediately ordered the roll read in his hearing. One of the royal attendants, Jehudi, began reading the words of reproof and warning. It was winter, and the king and princes were gathered about an open fire. The king, far from trembling at the danger hanging over himself and his people, seized the roll and in a frenzy of rage "cut it with the penknife, and cast it into the fire . . . until all the roll was consumed." Verse 23.

Neither the king nor his princes "was afraid, nor rent their garments." Certain of the princes, however, "had made intercession to the king that he would not burn the roll: but he would not hear them." The wicked king sent for Jeremiah and Baruch to be taken, "but the Lord hid them." Verses 24-26.

God was graciously seeking to warn the men of Judah for their good. He pities men struggling in the blindness of perversity. He seeks to enlighten the darkened understanding. He endeavors to help the self-complacent to become dissatisfied and seek for a close connection with heaven.

How God Tries to Save Us

God's plan is not to send messengers who will please and flatter sinners. Instead, He lays heavy burdens on the conscience of the wrongdoer to prompt the agonizing cry, "What must I do to be saved?" Acts 16:30. But the Hand that humbles to the dust is the Hand that lifts up the penitent one. He who permits the chastisement to fall inquires, "What wilt thou that I shall do unto thee?" Mark 10:51.

But King Jehoiakim and his lords, in their arrogance and pride, would not heed the warning and repent. The gracious opportunity offered them at the time of the burning of the sacred roll was their last. God declared He would visit with special wrath the man who had proudly lifted himself up against the Almighty. "Thus saith the Lord of Jehoiakim king of Judah; He shall have none to sit upon the throne of David: and his dead body shall be cast out in the day to the heat, and in the night to the frost." Jeremiah 36:30.

Jeremiah's Second Book

The burning of the roll was not the end of the matter. The written words were more easily disposed of than the swift-coming punishment God had pronounced against rebellious Israel. But even the written roll was reproduced. "Take thee again another roll," the Lord commanded His servant, "and write in it all the former words that were in the first roll, which Jehoiakim the king of Judah hath burned." Verse 28. The words were still living in the heart of Jeremiah, "as a burning fire," and the prophet reproduced that which the wrath of man had destroyed.

Taking another roll, Baruch wrote therein "all the words of the book which Jehoiakim king of Judah had burned in the fire." Verse 32. The means by which Jehoiakim had endeavored to limit the influence of the prophet gave further opportunity for making plain the divine requirements.

The spirit that led to the persecution of Jeremiah exists today. Many refuse to heed warnings, preferring to listen to false teachers who flatter their vanity and overlook their evil-doing. In the day of trouble such will have no sure refuge. God's chosen servants should meet with courage the sufferings that befall them through reproach, neglect, and misrepresentation. They should discharge faithfully the work God has given them, ever remembering that the prophets, the Saviour, and His apostles also endured persecution for the Word's sake.

It was God's purpose that Jehoiakim should heed the counsels of Jeremiah and thus win favor in the eyes of Nebuchadnezzar and save himself much sorrow. The youthful king had sworn allegiance to the Babylonian ruler, and had he remained true to his promise he would have commanded the respect of the heathen. But Judah's king willfully violated his word of honor, and rebelled. This brought against him bands of marauders. Within a few years he closed his disastrous reign in ignominy, rejected of Heaven, unloved by his people, and despised by the rulers of Babylon, whose confidence he had betrayed.

Jehoiachin [also known as Jeconiah, and Coniah], the son of Jehoiakim, occupied the throne only three months and ten days when he surrendered to the Chaldean armies which were once more besieging the fated city. Nebuchadnezzar "carried away Jehoiachin to Babylon, and the king's mother, and the king's wives, and his officers, and the mighty of the land," several thousand in number, together with "craftsmen and smiths a thousand," and "all the treasures of the house of the Lord, and the treasures of the king's house." 2 Kings 24:15, 16, 13.

The kingdom of Judah, broken in power and robbed of its strength, was nevertheless still permitted to exist as a separate government. At its head Nebuchadnezzar placed Mattaniah, a younger son of Josiah, changing his name to Zedekiah.

36 / Zedekiah, Judah's Last King

At the beginning of his reign Zedekiah was trusted fully by the king of Babylon and had as a counselor the prophet Jeremiah. He could have kept the respect of many in high authority and communicated to them a knowledge of the true God. Thus the captive exiles already in Babylon would have been granted many liberties; God's name would have been honored; and those that remained in Judah would have been spared the terrible calamities that finally came.

Through Jeremiah, Zedekiah and all Judah were counseled to submit quietly to the temporary rule of their conquerors. Those in captivity should seek the peace of the land into which they had been carried. However, Satan, taking advantage of the circumstances, caused false prophets to arise in Jerusalem and in Babylon who declared that the yoke of bondage would soon be broken and the former prestige of the nation restored.

Heeding such flattering prophecies would have led to fatal moves on the part of king and exiles. Lest insurrection be incited, the Lord commanded Jeremiah to meet the crisis without delay by warning the king of Judah of the sure consequence of rebellion. The captives also were admonished not to be deluded into believing their deliverance near. "Let not your prophets and your diviners, that be in the midst of you, deceive you," he urged. Jeremiah 29:8. Mention was made of the Lord's purpose to restore Israel at the close of seventy years of captivity.

God knew that should His captive people be persuaded by false prophets to look for a speedy deliverance, their position in Babylon would be made very difficult. Any insurrection on their part would lead to further restriction of their liberties. Suffering and disaster would result.

Why Submission Was So Important

God desired them to submit and make their servitude as pleasant as possible. His counsel was: "Build ye houses, and dwell in them; and plant gardens. . . . Seek the peace of the city whither I have caused you to be carried away captives, and pray unto the Lord for it: for in the peace thereof shall ye have peace." Verses 5-7.

Among the false teachers in Babylon were two men whose lives were corrupt. Jeremiah had warned them of their danger. Angered by reproof, they sought to stir up the people to act contrary to the counsel of God in the matter of submitting to the king of Babylon. The Lord testified through Jeremiah that these false prophets should be delivered to Nebuchadnezzar and slain. Not long afterward, this prediction was fulfilled.

To the end of time, people will arise to create confusion and rebellion among those who claim to be representatives of God. Those who prophesy lies will encourage men to look on sin as a light thing. They will seek to make the one who has warned them responsible for their difficulties, even as the Jews charged Jeremiah with their evil fortunes. But, as anciently, the certainty of God's messages will be established today.

Jeremiah had followed a consistent course in counseling submission to the Babylonians. Ambassadors from Edom, Moab, Tyre, and other nations visited Zedekiah to learn whether he would join them in a united revolt against Babylon. While these ambassadors were awaiting a response, the word of the Lord came to Jeremiah: "Make yourself thongs and yoke-bars, and put them on your neck. Send word to the [neighboring kings] . . . by the hand of the envoys who have come to Jerusalem." Jeremiah 27:2, 3, RSV. God had given them all into the hand of Nebuchadnezzar, and they were to "serve him, and his son, and his son's son, until the very time of his land come." Verse 7.

The ambassadors were further instructed that if they refused to serve the Babylonian king, they should be punished "with the sword, with famine, and with pestilence." "Do not listen to your prophets," the Lord declared, "your diviners, your dreamers. . . . For it is a lie which they are prophesying to you, with the result that you will be removed far from your land. . . . But any nation which will bring its neck under the yoke of the king of Babylon and serve him, I will leave on its own land, to till it and dwell there, says the Lord." Verses 8-11, RSV. The lightest punishment a merciful God could inflict on so rebellious a people was submission to the rule of Babylon, but if they warred against this they were to feel the full rigor of His chastisement. The amazement of the assembled council of nations knew no bounds when Jeremiah made known the will of God.

Jeremiah Opposed by Arrogant False Prophets

Jeremiah stood firmly for the policy of submission. Prominent among those who opposed the counsel of the Lord was Hananiah, one of the false prophets. Thinking to gain the favor of the royal court, he declared that God had given him words of encouragement for the Jews: "Thus speaketh the Lord of hosts, the God of Israel, . . . Within two full years will I bring again unto this place all the vessels of the Lord's house, that Nebuchadnezzar king of Babylon took away from this place, and carried them to Babylon: and I will bring again to this place Jeconiah the son of Jehoiakim king of Judah, with all the captives of Judah, . . . for I will break the yoke of the king of Babylon." Jeremiah 28:2-4.

Jeremiah cited the prophecies of Hosea, Habakkuk,

and Zephaniah, whose messages had been similar to his own. He referred to events which had taken place in exact fulfillment of God's purpose as revealed through His messengers. "The prophet which prophesieth of peace," Jeremiah proposed in conclusion, "when the word of the prophet shall come to pass, then shall the prophet be known, that the Lord hath truly sent him." Verse 9.

The words of Jeremiah aroused Hananiah to a daring challenge. Taking the symbolic yoke from Jeremiah's neck, Hananiah broke it, saying, "Thus saith the Lord; Even so will I break the yoke of Nebuchadnezzar king of Babylon from the neck of all the nations within the space of two full years." Verse 11.

Apparently Jeremiah could do nothing more than to retire from the scene of conflict. But he was given another message: "Go, tell Hananiah, 'Thus says the Lord: You have broken wooden bars, but I will make in their place bars of iron. . . . I have put upon the neck of all these nations an iron yoke of servitude to Nebuchadnezzar king of Babylon, and they shall serve him. . . .'

"And Jeremiah the prophet said to the prophet Hananiah, 'Listen, Hananiah, the Lord has not sent you, and you have made this people trust in a lie. Therefore thus says the Lord: . . . "This very year you shall die, because you have uttered rebellion against the Lord." ' In that same year, in the seventh month, the prophet Hananiah died." Verses 13-17, RSV. The false prophet had wickedly declared himself the Lord's messenger, and suffered death in consequence.

The unrest caused by the false prophets brought Zedekiah under suspicion of treason, and only by quick action on his part was he permitted to continue reigning as a vassal. The king accompanied a prince on a mission to Babylon. Jeremiah 51:59. During this visit to the Chaldean court, Zedekiah renewed his oath of allegiance to Nebuchadnezzar.

Through Daniel and other Hebrew captives, the Babylonian monarch had been made acquainted with the power and supreme authority of the true God; and when Zedekiah once more solemnly promised to remain loyal, Nebuchadnezzar required him to swear to this in the name of the Lord God of Israel. Had Zedekiah respected this renewal of his covenant oath, his loyalty would have had a profound influence on many who were watching those who claimed to honor the God of the Hebrews. But of Zedekiah it is recorded: "He also rebelled against King Nebuchadnezzar, who had made him swear by God; he stiffened his neck and hardened his heart against turning to the Lord, the God of Israel." 2 Chronicles 36:13, RSV.

Ezekiel Shown Abominations in the Temple

While Jeremiah continued to bear testimony in the land of Judah, the prophet Ezekiel was raised up among the captives in Babylon to warn and to comfort the exiles. Ezekiel made plain the folly of trusting the predictions of an early return to Jerusalem. He also was instructed to foretell by a variety of symbols the siege and destruction of Jerusalem.

In the sixth year of the reign of Zedekiah, the Lord revealed to Ezekiel some of the abominations being practiced in Jerusalem, even within the inner court of the Lord's house. See Ezekiel 8:10. Those who should have been spiritual leaders—"elders of the house of Israel" (verse 11, RSV)—were seen offering incense before the idolatrous representations introduced into hidden chambers within the temple court. "The Lord seeth us not," they blasphemously declared. Verse 12.

The prophet was shown "women weeping for Tammuz," and "about five and twenty men, with their backs toward the temple of the Lord, and their faces toward the east; and they worshiped the sun toward the east." Verses 14, 16. Now the glorious Being who accompanied Ezekiel throughout this astonishing vision inquired of the prophet: "Is it a light thing to the house of Judah that they commit the abominations which they commit here? . . . Mine eye shall not spare, neither will I have pity: and though they cry in Mine ears with a loud voice, yet will I not hear them." Verses 17, 18.

Through Jeremiah the Lord had declared: "Both prophet and priest are profane; yea, in My house have I found their wickedness." Jeremiah 23:11. In the closing narrative of Zedekiah's reign, this charge of violating the temple was repeated: "All the chief of the priests, and the people, transgressed very much after all the abominations of the heathen; and polluted the house of the Lord which He had hallowed in Jerusalem." 2 Chronicles 36:14.

The day of doom for the kingdom of Judah was fast approaching. Again "the word of the Lord came to" Ezekiel: " 'Son of man, what is this proverb that you have about the land of Israel, saying, . . . "Every vision comes to nought"? ' " "Therefore say to them, . . . The word which I speak will be performed, says the Lord God." Ezekiel 12:21, 22, 28, RSV.

Foremost among those rapidly leading the nation to ruin was Zedekiah their king. Forsaking the counsels of the Lord, forgetting the debt of gratitude he owed Nebuchadnezzar, violating his solemn oath of allegiance taken in the name of the God of Israel, Judah's king rebelled against the prophets, against his benefactor, and against his God. In his own wisdom he turned to the ancient enemy of Israel, "sending his ambassadors into Egypt, that they might give him horses and much people." Ezekiel 17:15.

"Will he succeed?" the Lord inquired. "Can a man escape who does such things? Can he break the covenant and yet escape? . . . Pharaoh with his mighty army and great company will not help him in war. . . . Because he despised the oath and broke the covenant, because he gave his hand and yet did all these things, he shall not escape." Verses 15-18, RSV. "Remove the diadem," the Lord decreed, "and take off the crown." Not until Christ Himself should set up His kingdom was Judah again to have a king. "I will overturn, overturn, overturn, it," was the divine edict concerning the throne, "and it shall be no more, until He come whose right it is; and I will give it Him." Ezekiel 21:26, 27.

37/ Zedekiah Fails His Last Chance

In the ninth year of Zedekiah's reign "Nebuchadnezzar king of Babylon came, he, and all his host, against Jerusalem." 2 Kings 25:1. The outlook for Judah was hopeless. "Behold, I am against thee," the Lord Himself declared through Ezekiel. "I will pour out Mine indignation upon thee, I will blow against thee in the fire of My wrath, and deliver thee into the hand of brutish men, and skillful to destroy." Ezekiel 21:3, 31.

The Egyptians endeavored to come to the rescue, and the Chaldeans, in order to keep them back, abandoned for a time their siege. Hope sprang up in the heart of Zedekiah, and he sent a messenger to Jeremiah, asking him to pray to God in behalf of the Hebrew nation.

The prophet's fearful answer was: "Do not deceive yourselves. . . . For even if you should defeat the whole army of Chaldeans who are fighting against you, and there remained of them only wounded men, every man in his tent, they would rise up and burn this city with fire." Jeremiah 37:9, 10, RSV. The remnant of Judah were to go into captivity and learn through adversity the lessons they had refused to learn under more favorable circumstances.

Among the righteous still in Jerusalem were some who determined to place beyond the reach of ruthless hands the sacred ark containing the tables of stone on which had been traced the Decalogue. With mourning they secreted the ark in a cave. It was hidden from Israel because of their sins and was to be no more restored to them. That sacred ark is yet hidden.

Now, as the fated city was about to pass into the hands of the heathen, Jeremiah considered his work done and attempted to leave, but was prevented by one who reported that he was about to join the Babylonians. The prophet denied the lying charge, but "the princes were wroth with Jeremiah, and smote him, and put him in prison." Verse 15.

The hopes that had sprung up when the armies of Nebuchadnezzar turned to meet the Egyptians were soon dashed to the ground. The might of Egypt was but a broken reed. Inspiration had declared, "I will strengthen the arms of the king of Babylon, but the arms of Pharaoh shall fall down; and they shall know that I am the Lord, when I shall put my sword into the hand of the king of Babylon, and he shall stretch it out upon the land of Egypt." Ezekiel 30:25.

A Vascillating King's Secret Rendezvous

While the princes were still vainly looking toward Egypt for help, King Zedekiah was thinking of the prophet of God that had been thrust into prison. After many days the king sent for him and asked him secretly, "Is there any word from the Lord?" Jeremiah answered, "There is: for, said He, thou shalt be delivered into the hand of the king of Babylon.

"Moreover Jeremiah said unto King Zedekiah, . . . Where are now your prophets which prophesied unto you, saying, The king of Babylon shall not come against you, nor against this land? Therefore hear now, I pray thee, O my lord the king: . . . that thou cause me not to return to the house of Jonathan the scribe, lest I die there." Jeremiah 37:17-20.

At this Zedekiah commanded that they commit "Jeremiah into the court of the prison, and that they should give him daily a piece of bread out of the bakers' street, until all the bread in the city were spent." Verse 21.

The king dared not openly manifest any faith in Jeremiah. Though fear drove him to seek information privately, he was too weak to brave the disapprobation of his princes and people by submitting to the will of God as declared by the prophet.

Jeremiah continued to advise submission to the Babylonian rule: "He that remaineth in this city shall die by the sword, by the famine, and by the pestilence: but he that goeth forth to the Chaldeans shall live." Jeremiah 38:2.

At last the princes, enraged over the counsels that were contrary to their policy of resistance, made a vigorous protest before the king. The prophet was an enemy to the nation. He should be put to death!

An Ethiopian Saves Jeremiah's Life

The cowardly king knew that the charges were false, but to propitiate those high and influential in the nation, he gave Jeremiah into their hands to do as they pleased. The prophet was cast "into the dungeon of Malchiah . . . : and they let down Jeremiah with cords. And in the dungeon there was no water, but mire: and Jeremiah sunk in the mire." But God raised up friends for him, who besought the king and had him again removed to the court of the prison. Verse 6.

Once more the king sent privately for Jeremiah and bade him relate the purpose of God toward Jerusalem. Jeremiah inquired, "If I declare it unto thee, wilt thou not surely put me to death? and if I give thee counsel, wilt thou not hearken unto me?" The king entered into a secret compact with the prophet. "As the Lord liveth, . . . I will not put thee to death, neither will I give thee into the hand of these men that seek thy life." Verses 15, 16.

There was still opportunity for the king to heed the warnings, and thus to temper with mercy the judgments falling on city and nation. "If you will surrender to the princes of the king of Babylon," was the message given the king, "then your life shall be spared, and this city shall not be burned with fire, and you and your house shall live. But if you do not surrender . . . , then this city shall be given into the hand of the Chaldeans, and they shall burn it with fire, and you shall not escape from their hand." Verses 17, 18, RSV.

"I am afraid of the Jews who have deserted to the Chaldeans," the king replied, "lest I be handed over to them and they abuse me." But the prophet promised, "You shall not be given to them." And he added the earnest entreaty, "Obey now the voice of the Lord in what I say to you, and it shall be well with you, and your life shall be spared." Verses 19, 20, RSV.

Had the king chosen to obey, lives might have been spared and the city saved from conflagration; but he thought he had gone too far to retrace his steps. He was afraid of ridicule, afraid for his life. After years of rebellion against God, Zedekiah thought it too humiliating to say to his people, I accept the word of the Lord, as spoken through the prophet Jeremiah; I dare not venture to war against the enemy.

Zedekiah Has No Moral Stamina

With tears Jeremiah entreated Zedekiah to save himself and his people. He assured him that unless he should heed the counsel of God, he could not escape with his life, and all his possessions would fall to the Babylonians. But the king would not retrace his steps. He decided to follow the counsel of the false prophets. He became a cringing slave to public opinion. With no fixed purpose to do evil, he was also without resolution to stand boldly for the right.

The king was even too weak to be willing that his people know that he had held a conference with Jeremiah. If Zedekiah had bravely declared that he believed the words of the prophet, already half fulfilled, what desolation might have been averted! He should have said, I will obey the Lord and save the city from utter ruin. I love truth, I hate sin, and I will follow the counsel of the Mighty One of Israel.

The people would have respected Zedekiah's courageous spirit, and those who were wavering between faith and unbelief would have taken a firm stand for the right. The fearlessness and justice of this course would have inspired admiration and loyalty. Judah would have been spared the untold woe of carnage, famine, and fire.

The weakness of Zedekiah was a sin for which he paid a fearful penalty. The enemy swept down like a resistless avalanche and devastated the city. The Hebrew armies were beaten back in confusion. Zedekiah was taken prisoner, his sons slain before his eyes. The king was led from Jerusalem a captive, his eyes were put out, and after arriving in Babylon he perished miserably. The beautiful temple that for centuries had crowned Mount Zion was not spared. "They burnt the house of God, and brake down the wall of Jerusalem, and burnt all the palaces thereof with fire, and destroyed all the goodly vessels thereof." 2 Chronicles 36:19. The chief of the priests, officers, and princes were taken to Babylon and executed as traitors. Others were carried captive to live in servitude to Nebuchadnezzar and his sons.

The Babylonians Respect Jeremiah

Of Jeremiah it is recorded: "Nebuchadnezzar king of Babylon gave charge concerning Jeremiah to Nebuzar-adan the captain of the guard, saying, Take him . . . and do him no harm; but do unto him even as he shall say unto thee." Jeremiah 39:11, 12.

Released from prison by the Babylonian officers, the prophet chose to cast his lot with the feeble remnant left by the Chaldeans to be "vinedressers and husbandmen." Jeremiah 52:16. Over these the Babylonians set Gedaliah as governor. Only a few months passed before the governor was treacherously slain. The people, after passing through many trials, were persuaded to take refuge in Egypt. Against this move, Jeremiah lifted his voice in protest: "Go not into

Egypt,'' he pleaded. But the inspired counsel was not heeded, and "all the remnant of Judah" took flight into Egypt. "They obeyed not the voice of the Lord." Jeremiah 43:2, 5, 7.

The sorrow of the prophet over the utter perversity of those who should have been the light of the world and over the fate of Zion and the people carried captive to Babylon is revealed in the lamentations he has left on record as a memorial of the folly of turning from the counsels of Jehovah to human wisdom. Amid the ruin, Jeremiah could still declare, "It is of the Lord's mercies that we are not consumed." His constant prayer was, "Let us search and try our ways, and turn again to the Lord!" Lamentations 3:22, 40.

But now Zion was utterly destroyed; the people of God were in captivity. Overwhelmed with grief, the prophet exclaimed:

> How lonely sits the city
>   that was full of people!
> How like a widow has she become,
>   she that was great among the nations!
> She that was a princess among the cities
>   has become a vassal.
>
> She weeps bitterly in the night,
>   tears on her cheeks;
> among all her lovers
>   she has none to comfort her;
> all her friends have dealt treacherously with her,
>   they have become her enemies.
>
> Judah . . . finds no resting place; . . .
> All her gates are desolate,
>   her priests groan;
> her maidens have been dragged away,
>   and she herself suffers bitterly.
> Her foes have become the head,
>   her enemies prosper.

How the Lord in His anger has set the daughter
    of Zion under a cloud!
He has cast down from heaven to earth
    the splendor of Israel;
He has not remembered His footstool
    in the day of His anger.

He has bent His bow like an enemy,
    with His right hand set like a foe;
and He has slain all the pride of our eyes
    in the tent of the daughter of Zion;
He has poured out His fury like fire.

Remember, O Lord, what has befallen us; . . .
Our fathers sinned, and are no more;
    and we bear their iniquities.
Slaves rule over us;
    there is none to deliver us from their hand.

Restore us to Thyself, O Lord, that we may be
    restored!
    Renew our days as of old!
            Lamentations 1:1-5; 2:1, 4;
            5:1-8, 21, RSV

38 / Not All Was Lost!

Through Jeremiah in Jerusalem, Daniel in Babylon, and Ezekiel on the banks of the Chebar, the Lord in mercy made clear His eternal purpose. That which He had said He would do for those who proved true to Him, He would surely bring to pass.

In the wilderness wandering the Lord had made abundant provision for His children to keep in remembrance His law. After settlement in Canaan the divine precepts were to be repeated daily in every home. They were to be set to music. Priests were to teach them, and the rulers were to make them their daily study. The Lord commanded Joshua concerning the book of the law: "Do according to all that is written therein: for then thou shalt make thy way prosperous, and then thou shalt have good success." Joshua 1:8.

Had this counsel been heeded through the centuries that followed, how different would have been Israel's history! It was regard for the law that gave Israel strength during the reign of David and the earlier years of Solomon's rule. Through faith in the living word, reformation was wrought in the days of Elijah and Josiah. And to these same Scriptures, Israel's richest heritage, Jeremiah appealed in his efforts toward reform. He met the people with the plea, "Hear ye the words of this covenant." Jeremiah 11:2.

As the armies of the Chaldeans came for the last time to besiege Jerusalem, hope fled from every heart. But God left not to hopeless despair the faithful remnant in the city. Even while Jeremiah was under close surveillance in prison, there came to him fresh revelations concerning Heaven's willingness to forgive and to save.

Jeremiah, by an acted parable, illustrated before the inhabitants of the fated city his faith in the ultimate fulfillment of God's purpose for His people. In the presence of witnesses, he purchased an ancestral field in the neighboring village of Anathoth. From every human point of view this purchase of land already under the control of the Babylonians appeared to be folly. The prophet himself had been foretelling the destruction of Jerusalem and a long period of captivity in Babylon. Already advanced in years, he could never hope to receive benefit from the purchase he had made.

However, he had a firm conviction that the Lord purposed to restore to the children of the captivity the Land of Promise. With the eye of faith Jeremiah saw the exiles returning and reoccupying the land of their fathers. Through the purchase of the Anathoth estate he would inspire others with the hope that brought comfort to his own heart.

Having signed the deeds of transfer and secured the countersignatures of witnesses, Jeremiah charged Baruch his secretary: "Take these deeds, . . . and put them in an earthenware vessel, that they may last for a long time. For thus says the Lord of hosts . . . : Houses and fields and vineyards shall again be bought in this land." Jeremiah 32:14, 15, RSV.

Jeremiah Overwhelmed With Temptation to Doubt

After arranging for the preservation of the written records, the faith of Jeremiah was now sorely tried. Had he acted presumptuously? Had he given ground for false hope? Could the promises to the chosen nation ever meet with complete fulfillment?

Perplexed in spirit, the prophet appealed to God for further enlightenment concerning the divine purpose. Nebuchadnezzar's armies were about to take the walls of Zion by storm. Thousands were perishing in a last desperate defense of the city. More thousands were dying of hunger and disease. The besieging towers of the enemy's forces were already overlooking the walls. "Behold, the siege mounds," the prophet prayed to God, "have come up to the city to take it, and because of sword and famine and pestilence the city is given into the hands of the Chaldeans who are fighting against it. What Thou didst speak has come to pass, and behold, Thou seest it. Yet Thou, O Lord God, hast said to me, 'Buy the field for money and get witnesses'—though the city is given into the hands of the Chaldeans." Verses 24, 25, RSV.

The prayer was graciously answered. "The word of the Lord unto Jeremiah" in that hour of distress was: "Behold, I am the Lord, the God of all flesh: is there anything too hard for Me?" Verses 26, 27. Soon the city's gates and palaces were to be burned; destruction was imminent and the inhabitants were to be carried away captive; nevertheless the eternal purpose of the Lord was yet to be fulfilled. The Lord declared concerning those on whom His chastisements were falling:

"I will bring them again unto this place, and I will cause them to dwell safely: and they shall be My people, and I will be their God: I will give them one heart, and one way, that they may fear Me forever, for the good of them, and of their children after them."

"Like as I have brought all this great evil upon this people, so will I bring upon them all the good that I have promised them. And fields shall be bought in this land, whereof ye say, It is desolate without man or beast; it is given into the hand of the Chaldeans. Men shall buy fields for money, and subscribe evidences, and seal them." Verses 37-39, 42-44.

Encouragement When All Seemed Lost

"Concerning the houses of this city, and concerning the houses of the kings of Judah, which are thrown down by the mounts, and by the sword. . . . Behold, I will bring it health and cure, and I will cure them, and will reveal unto them the abundance of peace and truth. And I will cause the captivity of Judah and the captivity of Israel to return, and will build them, as at the first. And I will cleanse them from all their iniquity, whereby they have sinned against Me; and I will pardon all their iniquities. . . .

"Again there shall be heard in this place, which ye say shall be desolate without man and without beast, even in the cities of Judah, and in the streets of Jerusalem, . . . the voice of joy, and the voice of gladness, the voice of the bridegroom, and the voice of the bride, the voice of them that shall say, Praise the Lord of hosts: for the Lord is good; for His mercy endureth forever. . . . For I will cause to return the captivity of the land, as at the first, saith the Lord." Jeremiah 33:4, 6-8, 10, 11.

The Church of God Comforted

Thus was the church of God comforted in one of the darkest hours of her long conflict with the forces of evil. Satan had seemingly triumphed, but the Lord was overruling events. His message to the church was: "I am with thee, . . . to save thee." "I will restore health unto thee, and I will heal thee of thy wounds." Jeremiah 30: 11, 17.

In the glad day of restoration, the tribes of divided Israel were to be reunited as one people. The Lord declared: "I will bring them from the north country, and gather them from the coasts of the earth, and with them the blind and the lame. . . . They shall come with weeping, and with supplications will I lead them: . . . for I am a Father to Israel." Jeremiah 31:8, 9.

The New Covenant Will Solve the Problem of Apostasy

Humbled in the sight of the nations, those who once had been favored of Heaven above all other peoples of the earth were to learn in exile the lesson of obedience. "I will correct thee in measure, and will not leave thee altogether unpunished," He declared. Jeremiah 30:11.

Yet before all the nations of earth He would demonstrate His plan to bring victory out of apparent defeat, to save rather than to destroy. To the prophet was given the message:

> He who scattered Israel will gather him,
>   and will keep him as a shepherd keeps his
>   flock. . . .
> They shall come and sing aloud on the height of
>   Zion, . . .
> Their life shall be like a watered garden,
>   and they shall languish no more. . . .
> I will turn their mourning into joy,
>   I will comfort them, and give them gladness for
>   sorrow.
>   Jeremiah 31:10-13, RSV

"Behold, the days come . . . that I will make a new covenant with the house of Israel, and with the house of Judah: not according to the covenant that I made with their fathers in the day that I took them by the hand to bring them out of the land of Egypt; which My covenant they brake, although I was an husband unto them, saith the Lord: but this shall be the covenant that I will make with the house of Israel; After those days, saith the Lord, I will put My law in their inward parts, and write it in their hearts; and will be their God, and they shall be My people. And they shall teach no more every man his neighbor, and every man his brother, saying, Know the Lord: for they shall all know Me, from the least of them unto the greatest of them, saith the Lord: for I will forgive their iniquity, and I will remember their sin no more." Verses 31-34.

39 / Daniel a Captive in Babylon

Among the children of Israel carried captive to Babylon were men as true as steel to principle, men who would honor God at the loss of all things. In the land of their captivity these were to carry out God's purposes as His representatives. Their faith and their name as worshipers of the living God they were to bear as a high honor.

The fact that they were captives and that the vessels of God's house had been placed in the temple of the Babylonish gods was cited by the victors as evidence that their religion was superior to that of the Hebrews. Yet God gave Babylon evidence of His supremacy, of the holiness of His requirements, and of the sure results of obedience.

Daniel and his three companions were illustrious examples of what men may become who unite with God. From the simplicity of their home, these youth of royal line were taken to the most magnificent of cities and into the court of the world's greatest monarch. They were "children in whom was no blemish, but well favored, and skillful in all wisdom, and cunning in knowledge, and understanding science."

Seeing in these youth remarkable ability, Nebuchadnezzar determined that they should be trained to fill important positions. He arranged for them to learn the language of the Chaldeans and for three years to be granted the unusual educational advantages afforded princes of the realm.

This chapter is based on Daniel 1.

The king did not compel the Hebrew youth to renounce their faith in favor of idolatry, but he hoped to bring this about gradually.

By giving them names significant of idolatry, by bringing them daily into close association with idolatrous customs, and under the influence of the seductive rites of heathen worship, he hoped to induce them to renounce their religion and to unite with the worship of the Babylonians.

Idolatry and Seductive Temptation

At the very outset there came a decisive test of character. It was provided that they should eat the food and drink the wine that came from the king's table. In this the king thought to express his solicitude for their welfare. But the food from the king's table was consecrated to idolatry, and partaking of it would be regarded as offering homage to the gods of Babylon. In such homage, Daniel and his companions would deny their faith and dishonor the principles of the law of God. Nor dared they risk the enervating effect of luxury and dissipation on physical, mental, and spiritual development. They were acquainted with the intemperance of Nadab and Abihu and its results and knew that their own physical and mental powers would be injuriously affected by wine.

Daniel and his associates had been taught that God would hold them accountable for their capabilities and that they must never dwarf or enfeeble their powers. Strong were the temptations in that corrupt and luxurious court, but they remained uncontaminated. No influence could sway them from the principles they had learned in early life by a study of the Word and works of God.

Daniel might have found a plausible excuse for departing from strictly temperate habits. He might have argued that should he adhere to the divine teaching, he would offend the king and probably lose his position and his life. If he should disregard the commandment of the Lord he would secure intellectual advantages and flattering worldly prospects.

But Daniel did not hesitate. He determined to stand firm. He "purposed in his heart that he would not defile himself with the portion of the king's meat, nor with the wine which he drank." In this he was supported by his three companions.

In reaching this decision the Hebrew youth did not act presumptuously. They did not choose to be singular, but they would be so rather than dishonor God. The first wrong step would lead to others, until, their connection with Heaven severed, they would be swept away by temptation.

"God had brought Daniel into favor and tender love with the prince of the eunuchs," and the request was received with respect. Yet the prince hesitated. "I fear my lord the king," he explained to Daniel, "for why should he see your faces worse liking than the children which are of your sort? then shall ye make me endanger my head to the king."

Daniel Appeals to Another Authority

Daniel then appealed to Melzar, the officer in special charge of the Hebrew youth. He asked that the matter be tested by a ten days' trial, the Hebrew youth being supplied with simple food, while their companions ate the king's dainties.

Melzar, though fearful, consented. At the end of ten days, the result was the opposite of the prince's fears. "Their countenances appeared fairer and fatter in flesh than all the children which did eat the portion of the king's meat." As a result, Daniel and his associates were permitted their simple diet during their entire course of training.

For three years the Hebrew youth studied, depending constantly on God's power. It was not pride or ambition that had brought them to the king's court; they were captives in a strange land. Separated from home, they sought to acquit themselves creditably, for the honor of their downtrodden people and for the glory of Him whose servants they were.

The Lord regarded with approval their purity of motive, and He "gave them knowledge and skill in all learning and wisdom: and Daniel had understanding in all visions and dreams." The promise was fulfilled, "Them that honor Me I will honor." 1 Samuel 2:30. While receiving instruction from man in the duties of court life, Daniel was being taught by God to read the mysteries of the future and to record for coming generations, through figures and symbols, events covering history till the close of time.

The Great Results of True Health Reform

When the time came for the Hebrew youth to be examined for the service of the kingdom, "among them all was found none like Daniel, Hananiah, Mishael, and Azariah." Their keen comprehension, their wide knowledge, their exact language, testified to the unimpaired strength and vigor of their mental powers. "Therefore stood they before the king."

At the court of Babylon were gathered from all lands men of the highest talent, richly endowed with natural gifts, and possessed of the broadest culture the world could bestow. Among them all, the Hebrew youth were without a peer in physical strength, mental vigor, and literary attainment. The erect form, the firm step, the fair countenance, the undimmed senses, the untainted breath—all were insignia of the nobility with which nature honors those who are obedient to her laws.

In acquiring the wisdom of the Babylonians, Daniel and his companions were far more successful than their fellow students. They obtained their knowledge under the guidance of the Holy Spirit, making the knowledge of God the foundation of their education. They prayed for wisdom, and they improved every opportunity to become intelligent in all lines of learning. They followed the rules of life that could not fail to give them strength of intellect. Constantly praying, conscientiously studying, keeping in touch with the Unseen, they walked with God as did Enoch.

True success in any line of work is not the result of chance or accident or destiny. It is the outworking of God's providences, the reward of faith and discretion, of virtue and perseverance. Fine mental qualities and a high moral tone are not the result of accident. God gives opportunities; success depends on the use made of them.

Herein is revealed the divine principle of cooperation. To make God's grace our own, we must act our part. His grace is given to work in us to will and to do, but never as a substitute for our effort.

As the Lord cooperated with Daniel, so He will cooperate with all who strive to do His will. By His Spirit He will strengthen every true purpose, every noble resolution. Those who walk in the path of obedience will encounter many hindrances, but the Lord is able to render futile every agency that works for the defeat of His chosen ones. In His strength they may overcome every temptation, conquer every difficulty.

The Secret of Daniel's Success

God brought Daniel and his associates into connection with the great men of Babylon that they might represent His character. Faithfulness in little things gave complexion to their whole life. They honored God in the smallest duties as well as in larger responsibilities.

As God called Daniel He calls us to be His witnesses in the world today. He desires us to reveal the principles of His kingdom. Many are waiting for some great work while daily they fail of discharging with wholeheartedness the little duties of life. While they wait for some large work in which they may exercise supposedly great talents, their days pass away. We shall be judged by what we ought to have done but did not accomplish because we did not use our powers to glorify God.

A noble character is not the result of accident; it is the result of self-discipline, of subjection of the lower to the higher nature, of the surrender of self to the service of God and man.

Today there is need of men who like Daniel will do and dare for the cause of right. Pure hearts, strong hands, fearless courage are needed. To every soul Satan comes with temptation in many alluring forms on the point of indulgence of appetite.

The body is a most important medium through which the mind and soul are developed for the upbuilding of character. Hence the adversary directs his temptations to enfeebling and degrading the physical powers. Success here often means the surrender of the whole being to evil. The tendencies of the physical nature, unless under the dominion of a higher power, will work ruin and death. The passions are to be controlled by the will, which is itself to be under the control of God. The kingly power of reason, sanctified by grace, is to bear sway in the life. Intellectual power, physical stamina, and length of life depend upon immutable laws. Through obedience to these laws, man may stand conqueror of himself, conqueror of his own inclinations, conqueror of "the rulers of the darkness of this world." Ephesians 6:12.

The Hebrew worthies were men of like passions with ourselves; yet they stood firm, because they depended on a strength that is infinite. In them a heathen nation beheld an illustration of the beneficence of God and the love of Christ. And in their experience we have an instance of the triumph of principle over temptation, of purity over depravity, of devotion and loyalty over atheism and idolatry.

The youth of today may draw from the same source of strength, and reveal the same grace in their lives, even under circumstances as unfavorable. Though surrounded by temptations, especially in large cities where sensual gratification is made easy and inviting, by divine grace they may withstand every temptation that assails the soul. But only by him who determines to do right will the victory be gained.

As these noble Hebrews bade farewell to their childhood home, little did they dream what a high destiny was to be theirs. They yielded to the divine guiding so that through them God could fulfill His purpose!

The life of Daniel and his fellows is a demonstration of what God will do for youth and children today who yield themselves to Him and with the whole heart seek to accomplish His purpose.

40 / Nebuchadnezzar's Dream of World Empires

Soon after Daniel and his companions entered Nebuchadnezzar's service, events occurred that revealed to an idolatrous nation the power of God. Nebuchadnezzar had a dream by which "his spirit was troubled, and his sleep brake from him." But the king found it impossible, when he awoke, to recall the particulars.

In his perplexity Nebuchadnezzar assembled his wise men—"the magicians, and the astrologers, and the sorcerers"—and requested them to reveal to him that which would bring relief to his mind.

The wise men responded, "Tell thy servants the dream, and we will show the interpretation." Dissatisfied with their evasive answer, the king commanded his wise men to tell him not only the interpretation but the dream itself. "If ye will not make known unto me the dream, with its interpretation thereof, ye shall be cut in pieces. . . . But if ye show the dream, and the interpretation thereof, ye shall receive of me gifts and rewards and great honor."

Still the wise men answered, "Let the king tell his servants the dream, and we will show the interpretation of it."

Nebuchadnezzar, now thoroughly angered by the apparent perfidy of those whom he had trusted, declared, "Ye have prepared lying and corrupt words to speak before me, till the time be changed: therefore tell me the dream, and I shall know that ye can show me the interpretation thereof."

This chapter is based on Daniel 2.

The magicians endeavored to show the king that his request was unreasonable. "There is no king, lord, nor ruler, that asked such things at any magician, or astrologer, or Chaldean. . . . And there is none other that can show it before the king, except the gods, whose dwelling is not with flesh."

Then "the king was angry and very furious, and commanded to destroy all the wise men of Babylon."

Daniel's Opportunity Has Come

When told that according to the decree Daniel and his friends also must die, "with counsel and wisdom" Daniel inquired of Arioch, the captain of the king's guard, "Why is the decree so hasty from the king?" Arioch told him the story of the king's failure to secure help. Upon hearing this, Daniel, taking his life in his hands, ventured into the king's presence and begged for time that he might petition his God to reveal to him the dream and its interpretation.

To this request the monarch acceded. "Then Daniel went to his house, and made the thing known to Hananiah, Mishael, and Azariah, his companions." Together they sought wisdom from the Source of knowledge. Their faith was strong that God had placed them where they were, that they were doing His work. In times of perplexity they had always turned to Him for guidance; now they submitted themselves anew to the Judge of the earth, pleading that He would grant deliverance. And the God whom they had honored, now honored them. To Daniel "in a night vision" was revealed the king's dream and its meaning.

"Blessed be the name of God forever and ever," Daniel exclaimed. "He revealeth the deep and secret things. . . . I thank Thee, and praise Thee, O Thou God of my fathers, who hast given me wisdom and might, and hast made known unto me now what we desired of Thee: for Thou hast now made known unto us the king's matter."

Going immediately to Arioch, Daniel said, "Destroy

not the wise men of Babylon: bring me in before the king, and I will show unto the king the interpretation." Quickly the officer ushered Daniel in before the king, with the words, "I have found a man of the captives of Judah, that will make known unto the king the interpretation."

Daniel's Refreshing Honesty

In his first words the Jewish captive disclaimed honor for himself and exalted God as the source of all wisdom. To the inquiry of the king, "Art thou able to make known unto me the dream which I have seen, and the interpretation thereof?" he replied: "There is a God in heaven that revealeth secrets, and maketh known to the king Nebuchadnezzar what shall be in the latter days. . . . As for me, this secret is not revealed to me for any wisdom that I have more than any living, but . . . that thou mightest know the thoughts of thy heart.

"Thou, O king, sawest, and behold a great image. This great image, whose brightness was excellent, stood before thee; and the form thereof was terrible. This image's head was of fine gold, his breast and his arms of silver, his belly and his thighs of brass, his legs of iron, his feet part of iron and part of clay.

"Thou sawest till that a stone was cut out without hands, which smote the image upon his feet that were of iron and clay, and brake them to pieces. Then was the iron, the clay, the brass, the silver, and the gold, broken to pieces together, and became like the chaff of the summer threshing floors; and the wind carried them away, that no place was found for them: and the stone that smote the image became a great mountain, and filled the whole earth."

"This is the dream," confidently declared Daniel; and the king, listening with closest attention, knew it was the very dream which had troubled him. Thus his mind was prepared to receive with favor the interpretation. He was to be awakened, if possible, to a sense of his responsibility to Heaven. The events of the future down to the end of time were to be opened before him.

"Thou, O king, art a king of kings: for the God of heaven hath given thee a kingdom, power, and strength, and glory. . . . Thou art this head of gold.

"And after thee shall arise another kingdom inferior to thee, and another third kingdom of brass, which shall bear rule over all the earth.

"And the fourth kingdom shall be strong as iron: forasmuch as iron breaketh in pieces and subdueth all things: and as iron that breaketh all these, shall it break in pieces and bruise.

"And whereas thou sawest the feet and toes, part of potters' clay, and part of iron, the kingdom shall be divided; but there shall be in it of the strength of the iron, forasmuch as thou sawest the iron mixed with miry clay. And as the toes of the feet were part of iron, and part of clay, so the kingdom shall be partly strong, and partly broken. And whereas thou sawest iron mixed with miry clay, they shall mingle themselves with the seed of men: but they shall not cleave one to another, even as iron is not mixed with clay."

"In the days of these kings shall the God of heaven set up a kingdom, which shall never be destroyed: and the kingdom shall not be left to other people, but it shall break in pieces and consume all these kingdoms, and it shall stand forever. . . . The dream is certain, and the interpretation thereof sure."

The King Is Humbled

The king was convinced. In humility he "fell upon his face, and worshiped," saying, "Your God is a God of gods, and a Lord of kings, and a revealer of secrets, seeing thou couldest reveal this secret."

Nebuchadnezzar revoked the decree for the destruction of the wise men. Their lives were spared because of Daniel's connection with the Revealer of secrets. And "the king made Daniel a great man, and gave him many great gifts, and made him ruler over the whole province of Babylon. . . . Then Daniel requested of the king, and he set Shadrach, Meshach, and Abednego, over the affairs of the province of Babylon: but Daniel sat in the gate of the king.''

In history, the growth of nations, the rise and fall of empires, appear as if dependent on the will and prowess of man. But in the Word of God the curtain is drawn aside, and we behold the agencies of the All-merciful One, silently, patiently working out the counsels of His will.

Hundreds of years before certain nations came on the stage of action, the Omniscient One looked down the ages and predicted the rise and fall of the universal kingdoms. God declared to Nebuchadnezzar that Babylon should fall and a second kingdom would arise. Failing to exalt the true God, its glory would fade. A third kingdom also would pass away; and a fourth, strong as iron, would subdue the nations of the world.

Why Nations and Empires Fail

Had the rulers of Babylon kept always before them the fear of the Lord, they would have been given wisdom and power which would have kept them strong. But they made God their refuge only when perplexed. At such times, failing to find help in their great men, they sought it from men like Daniel who honored the living God and were honored by Him. Though the rulers of proud Babylon were of the highest intellect, they had separated themselves so far from God that they could not understand the revelations and warnings given them concerning the future.

Babylon, shattered and broken at last, passed away because in prosperity its rulers regarded themselves as independent of God and ascribed the glory of their kingdom to human achievement. The Medo-Persian realm was visited by the wrath of Heaven because in it God's law had been trampled underfoot. The fear of the Lord found no place in the hearts of the vast majority of people. Wickedness and corruption prevailed.

The kingdoms that followed were even more base and corrupt; and these sank lower and still lower in the scale of moral worth.

The power exercised by every ruler on earth is Heaven-imparted, and upon his use of this power his success depends. To each the word is "I girded thee, though thou hast not known Me." Isaiah 45:5.

In the Word of God only is it shown that the strength of nations, as of individuals, is not found in the opportunity or facilities that appear to make them invincible; it is not found in their boasted greatness. It is measured by the fidelity with which they fulfill God's purpose.

41 / Three Hebrews in the Fiery Furnace

The dream of the great image had been given that Nebuchadnezzar might understand the relation that his kingdom should sustain to the kingdom of heaven. In the interpretation of the dream, he had been plainly instructed regarding the establishment of God's everlasting kingdom.

The king had acknowledged God, saying to Daniel, "Of a truth it is, that your God is a God of gods, . . . and a revealer of secrets." Daniel 2:47. For a time Nebuchadnezzar was influenced by the fear of God, but his heart was not yet cleansed from a desire for self-exaltation. Filled with pride, in time he resumed his idol worship with increased zeal. The words "Thou art this head of gold" had made a deep impression on the ruler's mind. The wise men of his realm, taking advantage of this, proposed that he make an image similar to the one in his dream and set it up where all might behold the head of gold, interpreted as representing his kingdom.

Pleased, he determined to go even farther. His image should not deteriorate in value from the head to the feet, but be entirely of gold—symbolic of Babylon as an indestructible, all-powerful kingdom.

Establishing a dynasty that should endure forever appealed strongly to the ruler before whose arms the nations of earth had been unable to stand. Forgetting the remarkable providences connected with the dream

This chapter is based on Daniel 3.

of the great image, and that in connection with the interpretation the great men of the realm had been saved an ignominious death, the king and his counselors determined that they would endeavor to exalt Babylon as supreme.

Daniel's interpretation was to be rejected and forgotten; truth was to be misapplied. The symbol designed of Heaven to unfold to men important events of the future was to be used to hinder the knowledge God desired the world to receive. Satan knew that truth unmixed with error is a power mighty to save, but when used to exalt self it becomes a power for evil.

The Golden Image: The Eternal Glory of Babylon

From his rich treasure, Nebuchadnezzar made a great golden image, similar to what he had seen in vision, save in the one particular of the material of which it was composed. The Chaldeans had never before produced anything so imposing as this resplendent statue. It is not surprising that in a land where idol worship was of universal prevalence, the priceless image on the plain of Dura should be consecrated as an object of worship. A decree went forth that on the day of the dedication all should show their supreme loyalty to Babylon by bowing before the image.

A vast concourse from all "people, nations, and languages" assembled. When the sound of music was heard, the whole company "fell down and worshiped the golden image." The powers of darkness seemed to be gaining a triumph, connecting permanently the worship of the golden image with the established forms of idolatry recognized as the state religion. Satan hoped thereby to defeat God's purpose of making captive Israel in Babylon a means of blessing to all nations.

But God decreed otherwise. Not all had bowed to the idolatrous symbol of human power. Three men firmly resolved not to dishonor the God of heaven. Their God was King of kings; they would bow to none other.

To Nebuchadnezzar was brought word that some dared disobey his mandate. Certain wise men, jealous of the faithful companions of Daniel, reported to the king: "There are certain Jews whom thou hast set over the affairs of the province of Babylon, Shadrach, Meshach, and Abednego; these men, O king, have not regarded thee: they serve not thy gods, nor worship the golden image which thou hast set up."

The King Tries to Pressure the Hebrews

The king commanded that the men be brought before him. Pointing to the fiery furnace, he reminded them of the punishment awaiting them if they should persist in their refusal to obey his will. But firmly the Hebrews testified to their allegiance to the God of heaven and their faith in His power to deliver.

As the three Hebrews stood before the king, he was convinced that they possessed something the other wise men did not have. He would give them another trial. If only they would unite with the multitude in worshiping the image, all would be well. "But if ye worship not," he added, "ye shall be cast the same hour into the midst of a burning fiery furnace." Then with his hand stretched upward in defiance, he demanded, "Who is that God that shall deliver you out of my hands?"

In vain were the king's threats. Calmly facing the furnace, the three Hebrews said, "O Nebuchadnezzar, we are not careful to answer thee in this matter. If it be so [if this is your decision], our God whom we serve is able to deliver us from the burning fiery furnace, and He will deliver us out of thine hand, O king." Their faith strengthened as they declared that God would be glorified by delivering them, and with assurance born of implicit trust in God, they added, "But if not, be it known unto thee, O king, that we will not serve thy gods, nor worship the golden image which thou hast set up."

The king's wrath knew no bounds. "Full of fury,"

"the form of his visage was changed against Shadrach, Meshach, and Abednego," representatives of a despised, captive race. Directing that the furnace be heated seven times hotter than usual, he commanded the mighty men of his army to bind the worshipers of Israel's God.

"Then these men were bound in their coats, their trousers, and their turbans, and their other garments, and were cast into the midst of the burning fiery furnace." (Verse 21, NKJV.) And "the flame of the fire slew those men that took up Shadrach, Meshach, and Abednego."

God in the Furnace

But as the Lord's witnesses were cast into the furnace, the Saviour revealed Himself to them in person, and together they walked in the midst of the fire. In the presence of the Lord of heat and cold, the flames lost their power to consume.

From his royal seat the king looked on, expecting to see the men who had defied him utterly destroyed. But his face grew pale as he started from the throne and looked intently into the glowing flames. In alarm he asked, "Did not we cast three men bound into the midst of the fire? . . . Lo, I see four men loose, walking in the midst of the fire, and they have no hurt; and the form of the fourth is like the Son of God."

How did that heathen king know what the Son of God was like? The Hebrew captives in Babylon had in character represented before him the truth. When asked for a reason of their faith, they had given it without hesitation, teaching those around them of the God whom they worshiped. They had told of Christ, the Redeemer to come; and in the form of the fourth in the midst of the fire the king recognized the Son of God.

His greatness and dignity forgotten, Nebuchadnezzar cried out, "Ye servants of the most high God, come forth." Then Shadrach, Meshach, and Abednego came forth before the vast multitude, showing themselves unhurt. The presence of their Saviour had guarded them from harm, and only their fetters had been burned.

Forgotten was the great image, set up with such pomp. "Blessed be the God of Shadrach, Meshach, and Abednego," the humbled king acknowledged, "who hath sent His angel, and delivered His servants that trusted in Him, and have changed the king's word, and yielded their bodies, that they might not serve nor worship any god, except their own God." "There is no other god that can deliver after this sort."

The king of Babylon endeavored to spread before all the peoples of earth his conviction that the God of the Hebrews was worthy of supreme adoration. And God was pleased with the effort of the king to make the royal confession as widespread as was the Babylonian realm.

By the deliverance of His faithful servants, the Lord declared that He takes His stand with the oppressed and rebukes all earthly powers that rebel against the authority of Heaven.

In the hour of their trial the three Hebrews remembered the promise, "When thou passest through the waters, I will be with thee; and through the rivers, they shall not overflow thee: when thou walkest through the fire, thou shalt not be burned; neither shall the flame kindle upon thee." Isaiah 43:2. The tidings of their wonderful deliverance were carried to many countries by representatives of the nations that had been invited by Nebuchadnezzar to the dedication.

A Time of Trouble Such as Never Was

Important are the lessons to be learned from the experience on the plain of Dura. In our day many of God's servants will suffer humiliation and abuse at the hands of those who are filled with envy and religious bigotry. Especially will wrath be aroused against those who hallow the Sabbath of the fourth commandment, and at last a universal decree will denounce these as deserving of death. God's people must make it manifest that no consideration can induce them to make the least concession to false worship. To the loyal heart the commands of men will sink into insignificance beside the word of the eternal God. Truth will be obeyed though the result be death.

The Lord will work mightily in behalf of those who stand for the right. He who walked with the Hebrews in the fiery furnace will be with His followers wherever they are. In the time of trouble His chosen ones will stand unmoved. In their behalf Jehovah will reveal Himself as a "God of gods," able to save to the uttermost those who put their trust in Him.

42 / Nebuchadnezzar's Seven Years of Madness

After Nebuchadnezzar's dream of the great image, his mind had been profoundly influenced by the thought that the Babylonian Empire was finally to fall. At last all earthly kingdoms were to be superseded by a kingdom set up by God.

Nebuchadnezzar's noble conception of God's purpose concerning the nations was lost sight of later, yet when his proud spirit was humbled on the plain of Dura, he once more acknowledged that God's kingdom is "an everlasting kingdom." Daniel 7:27. He had an innate sense of justice and right, and God was able to use him as an instrument for the punishment of the rebellious and for the fulfillment of the divine purpose. As he added nation after nation to the Babylonian realm, he added more and more to his fame as the greatest ruler of the age.

It was not surprising that the successful, proud-spirited monarch should be tempted to turn aside from the path of humility, which alone leads to true greatness. Between his wars of conquest he gave much thought to the beautifying of his capital, until the city of Babylon became "the golden city," "the praise of the whole earth." Isaiah 14:4; Jeremiah 51:41. His success in making Babylon one of the wonders of the world ministered to his pride, until he was in grave danger of spoiling his record as a ruler whom God could use.

In mercy God gave the king another dream to warn

This chapter is based on Daniel 4.

him of his peril. In vision Nebuchadnezzar saw a great tree, its top towering to the heavens and its branches stretching to the ends of the earth. Flocks and herds enjoyed shelter beneath its shadow, and birds built their nests in its boughs. "And all flesh was fed of it."

As the king gazed upon the tree, he saw "a Watcher," even "an Holy One," who approached the tree and in a loud voice cried: "Hew down the tree, and cut off his branches, shake off his leaves, and scatter his fruit: . . . nevertheless leave the stump of his roots in the earth, . . . and let it be wet with the dew of heaven, and let his portion be with the beasts in the grass of the earth: let his heart be changed from man's, and let a beast's heart be given unto him; and let seven times pass over him. This matter is by the decree of the watchers . . . to the intent that the living may know that the most High ruleth in the kingdom of men, and giveth it to whomsoever He will."

The Attempt to Discover the Meaning

Greatly troubled, the king repeated the dream to the wise men; but although the dream was very explicit, none could interpret it. The king in his perplexity sent for Daniel, esteemed for his integrity and unrivaled wisdom.

After relating the dream, Nebuchadnezzar said: "Declare the interpretation thereof, forasmuch as all the wise men of my kingdom are not able to make known unto me the interpretation: but thou art able; for the spirit of the holy gods is in thee."

To Daniel the meaning of the dream was plain, and its significance startled him. Seeing Daniel's hesitation and distress, the king expressed sympathy for his servant. "Let not the dream, or the interpretation thereof, trouble thee."

The prophet realized that God had laid on him the solemn duty of revealing to Nebuchadnezzar the judgment about to fall upon him because of his pride and arrogance. Although its dreadful import had made him hesitate, he must state the truth, whatever the consequences to himself.

"The tree that thou sawest," he said, "is thou, O king, . . . for thy greatness is grown . . . to the end of the earth. And whereas the king saw a Watcher and an Holy One, . . . saying, Hew the tree down, and destroy it; yet leave the stump . . . ; this is the interpretation . . . : They shall drive thee from men, and thy dwelling shall be with the beasts of the field, and they shall make thee to eat grass as oxen, and they shall wet thee with the dew of heaven, and seven times shall pass over thee, till thou know that the most High ruleth in the kingdom of men, and giveth it to whomsoever He will. And whereas they commanded to leave the stump of the tree roots; thy kingdom shall be sure unto thee, after that thou shalt have known that the Heavens do rule."

Daniel urged the proud monarch to repent, that he might avert the threatened calamity. "Break off thy sins by righteousness, and thine iniquities by showing mercy to the poor; if it may be a lengthening of thy tranquillity."

Nebuchadnezzar's Short-lived Repentance

For a time the counsel of the prophet was strong on Nebuchadnezzar; but self-indulgence and ambition had not yet been eradicated from the king's heart, and later these traits reappeared. His rule which heretofore had been to a great degree just and merciful became oppressive. He used his God-given talents for self-glorification, exalting himself above the God who had given him life and power.

For months the judgment of God lingered. But instead of being led to repentance by this forbearance, the king indulged his pride until he lost confidence in the interpretation of the dream and jested at his former fears.

A year after the warning, Nebuchadnezzar, walking in his palace and thinking with pride of his power as a ruler and of his success as a builder, exclaimed, "Is not this great Babylon, which I have built by my mighty power as a royal residence and for the glory of my majesty?" RSV.

While the proud boast was yet on the king's lips, a voice from heaven announced that God's appointed time of judgment had come: "O king Nebuchadnezzar, to thee it is spoken; The kingdom is departed from thee. And they shall drive thee from men, and thy dwelling shall be with the beasts of the field: they shall make thee to eat grass as oxen, and seven times shall pass over thee, until thou know that the most High ruleth in the kingdom of men, and giveth it to whomsoever He will."

In a moment the once mighty ruler was a maniac. His hand could no longer sway the scepter. Stripped of the power his Creator had given him, and driven from men, Nebuchadnezzar "did eat grass as oxen, and his body was wet with the dew of heaven, till his hairs were grown like eagles' feathers, and his nails like birds' claws."

For seven years Nebuchadnezzar was an astonishment to all his subjects, humbled before all the world. Then his reason was restored and he recognized the divine hand in his chastisement. In a public proclamation he acknowledged the great mercy of God in his restoration: "I Nebuchadnezzar lifted up mine eyes unto heaven, and mine understanding returned unto me, and I blessed the Most High, and I praised and honored Him that liveth forever. . . .

"And for the glory of my kingdom, mine honor and brightness returned unto me; and my counselors and my lords sought unto me; and I was established in my kingdom, and excellent majesty was added unto me."

The once proud monarch had become a humble child of God, a wise and compassionate king. He now acknowledged the power of the Most High and earnestly sought to promote the fear of Jehovah and the happiness of his subjects. Nebuchadnezzar had learned at last the lesson which all rulers need to learn—that true greatness consists in true goodness. He acknowledged the living God, saying, ''I Nebuchadnezzar praise and extol and honor the King of heaven, all whose works are truth, and His ways judgment: and those that walk in pride He is able to abase.''

God's purpose was now fulfilled. This public proclamation, in which Nebuchadnezzar acknowledged the goodness and authority of God, was the last act of his life recorded in sacred history.

43 / Belshazzar's Feast: Babylon's Last Night

Great changes were taking place in the land to which Daniel and his companions had been carried captive more than sixty years before. Nebuchadnezzar had died, and Babylon had passed under the unwise rule of his successors. Gradual but sure dissolution was resulting.

Belshazzar, the grandson of Nebuchadnezzar, gloried in his power and lifted up his heart against the God of heaven. He had known of his grandfather's banishment by the decree of God from the society of men. He was familiar with Nebuchadnezzar's conversion and miraculous restoration. But he allowed pleasure and self-glorification to efface the lessons he should never have forgotten. He neglected to use the means within his reach for becoming more fully acquainted with truth.

It was not long before reverses came. Babylon was besieged by Cyrus, commanding general of the Medes and Persians. But within its massive walls and gates of brass, protected by the river Euphrates and stocked with provision in abundance, the voluptuous monarch felt safe and passed his time in mirth and revelry.

In his pride and arrogance, with a reckless feeling of security, Belshazzar "made a great feast to a thousand of his lords, and drank wine before the thousand." Beautiful women with their enchantments were among the guests. Men of genius and education were there.

This chapter is based on Daniel 5.

Princes and statesmen drank wine and reveled under its maddening influence.

With reason dethroned through intoxication and with lower impulses and passions in the ascendancy, the king himself took the lead in the riotous orgy. He "commanded to bring the golden and silver vessels which . . . Nebuchadnezzar had taken out of the temple which was in Jerusalem." The king would prove that nothing was too sacred for his hands to handle. "They brought the golden vessels . . . ; and the king, and his princes, his wives, and his concubines, drank in them. They drank wine, and praised the gods of gold, and of silver, of brass, of iron, of wood and of stone."

A Portent of Doom to the King and Guests

A divine Watcher, unrecognized, looked upon the scene, heard the sacrilegious mirth, beheld the idolatry. Soon the uninvited Guest made His presence felt. When the revelry was at its height, a bloodless hand traced on the palace walls characters that gleamed like fire—words which were a portent of doom.

Hushed was the boisterous mirth, while men and women, seized with terror, watched the hand slowly tracing the mysterious characters. Before them passed, as in panoramic view, the deeds of their evil lives. They seemed to be arraigned before the judgment bar of the eternal God whose power they had just defied. Where a few moments before had been hilarity and blasphemous witticism, were pallid faces and cries of fear.

Belshazzar was the most terrified of them all. Conscience was awakened, and "his knees smote one against another." Now he realized that for his wasted opportunities and defiant attitude he could offer no excuse.

In vain the king tried to read the burning letters. Turning to the wise men for help his wild cry rang out in the assembly: "Whosoever shall read this writing, and show me the interpretation thereof, shall be clothed with scarlet, and have a chain of gold about his neck, and shall be the third ruler in the kingdom." But heavenly wisdom cannot be bought or sold. "All the king's wise men . . . could not read the writing, nor make known to the king the interpretation thereof." They were no more able than had been the wise men of a former generation to interpret the dreams of Nebuchadnezzar.

Then the queen mother remembered Daniel. "O king," she said, "let not thy thoughts trouble thee, nor let thy countenance be changed: There is a man in thy kingdom, in whom is the spirit of the holy gods; and in the days of thy father light and understanding and wisdom, like the wisdom of the gods, was found in him; whom the king Nebuchadnezzar . . . made master of the magicians, astrologers, Chaldeans, and soothsayers; . . . now let Daniel be called, and he will show the interpretation."

"Then was Daniel brought in before the king." Making an effort to regain his composure, Belshazzar said to the prophet: "I have heard of thee, that thou canst make interpretations, and dissolve doubts: now if thou canst read the writing and make known to me the interpretation thereof, thou shalt be clothed with scarlet, and have a chain of gold about thy neck, and shalt be the third ruler in the kingdom."

Unmoved by the promises of the king, Daniel stood in the quiet dignity of a servant of the Most High. "Give thy rewards to another," he said, "yet I will read the writing unto the king, and make known to him the interpretation."

Daniel Holds the King's Sin up Before Him

The prophet first reminded Belshazzar of Nebuchadnezzar's sin and fall, of the divine judgment for his pride, and his subsequent acknowledgment of the power and mercy of the God of Israel. Then in bold, emphatic words he rebuked Belshazzar for his great wickedness and showed him the lessons he might have learned but did not. Belshazzar had not heeded the warning of events so significant to himself. He was about to reap the consequence of his rebellion.

"Thou . . . , O Belshazzar, . . . hast lifted up thyself against the Lord of heaven; and they have brought the vessels of His house before thee, and thou, and thy lords, thy wives, and thy concubines, have drunk wine in them; and thou hast praised the gods of silver, and gold, of brass, iron, wood, and stone. . . : and the God in whose hand thy breath is, and whose are all thy ways, hast thou not glorified: then was the part of the hand sent from Him; and this writing was written."

Interpretation of the Writing on the Wall

Turning to the message on the wall, the prophet read, "MENE, MENE, TEKEL, UPHARSIN." The hand was no longer visible, but these words were still gleaming with terrible distinctness; and now with bated breath the people listened while the aged prophet declared: "This is the interpretation of the thing: MENE; God hath numbered thy kingdom, and finished it. TEKEL; Thou art weighed in the balances, and art found wanting. PERES; thy kingdom is divided, and given to the Medes and Persians."

God's Restraining Hand Removed

In that last night of mad folly Belshazzar and his lords had filled up the measure of the guilt of the Chaldean kingdom. No longer could God's restraining hand ward off the impending evil. "We would have healed Babylon," God declared of those whose judgment was now reaching unto heaven, "but she is not healed." Jeremiah 51:9. God had at last found it necessary to pass the irrevocable sentence. Belshazzar's kingdom was to pass into other hands.

As the prophet ceased speaking, the king commanded that he be awarded the promised honors.

More than a century before, Inspiration had foretold that "the night of . . . pleasure" (Isaiah 21:4), during

which king and counselors would blaspheme God
would suddenly be changed into a season of fear and
destruction. And now, while still in the festal hall, the
king is informed that "his city is taken" by the enemy.
Jeremiah 51:31. Even while he and his nobles were
drinking from the sacred vessels and praising their
gods of silver and gold, the Medes and Persians, having
turned the Euphrates out of its channel, were marching
into the heart of the unguarded city. The army of Cyrus
now stood under the walls of the palace. The city was
filled with the soldiers of the enemy, "as many as locusts" (RSV), and their triumphant shouts could be
heard above the despairing cries of the astonished rev-
elers.

"In that night was Belshazzar the king of the Chaldeans slain," and an alien monarch sat upon the throne.

Prophecy Fulfilled

The Hebrew prophets had spoken clearly concerning the manner in which Babylon should fall:

"Suddenly Babylon has fallen and been broken."
"The Lord is a God of recompense, He will surely re-
quite. I will make drunk her princes and her wise men,
her governors, her commanders, and her warriors;
they shall sleep a perpetual sleep and not wake, says
the King, whose name is the Lord of hosts." Jeremiah
51:8, 56, 57, RSV.

Thus did "Babylon, the glory of kingdoms, the
beauty of the Chaldees' excellency," become as
Sodom and Gomorrah—a place forever accursed. "It
shall never be inhabited, neither shall it be dwelt in
from generation to generation: neither shall the Ara-
bian pitch tent there; neither shall the shepherds make
their fold there. But wild beasts of the desert shall lie
there; and their houses shall be full of doleful crea-
tures; and owls shall dwell there, and satyrs shall
dance there. And the wild beasts of the islands shall
cry in their desolate towers, and dragons in their pleasant palaces." Isaiah 13:19-22.

Come down and sit in the dust,
  O virgin daughter of Babylon;
Sit on the ground without a throne. . . .
You said, "I shall be mistress forever,"
  So that you did not lay these things to heart
  Or remember their end.
Now therefore hear this, you lover of pleasures,
  Who sit securely,
Who say in your heart,
  "I am, and there is no one besides me;
I shall not sit as a widow
  Or know the loss of children":
These two things shall come to you
  In a moment, in one day;
The loss of children and widowhood
  Shall come upon you in full measure. . . .
You felt secure in your wickedness,
  You said, "No one sees me."
                Isaiah 47:1, 7-10, RSV

Prophecy has traced the rise and progress of the world's great empires—Babylon, Medo-Persia, Greece, and Rome. With each, as with nations of less power, history has repeated itself. Each has had its period of test; each has failed, its glory faded, its power departed. Nations have rejected God's principles and have wrought their own ruin, yet a divine, overruling purpose has been at work throughout the ages.

A Power Overrides the Affairs of Men

It was this that the prophet Ezekiel saw when before his astonished gaze were portrayed symbols that revealed a Power overruling the affairs of earthly rulers. Wheels intersecting one another were moved by four living beings. High above all these "was the likeness of a throne, in appearance like sapphire; and seated above the likeness of a throne was a likeness as it were of a human form." Ezekiel 1:26, RSV.

The wheels, so complicated that at first sight they appeared to be in confusion, moved in perfect harmony. Heavenly beings were impelling those wheels. The complicated play of human events is under divine control. Amidst the strife and tumult of nations He that sits above the cherubim still guides the affairs of this earth. To every nation and individual God has assigned a place in His great plan. Today men and nations are by their own choice deciding their destiny, and God is overruling all for the accomplishment of His purposes.

The prophecies which the great I AM has given in His Word tell us where we are in the procession of the ages. All that prophecy has foretold until the present time has been traced on the pages of history, and all which is yet to come will be fulfilled in its order.

The signs of the times declare that we are standing on the threshold of great and solemn events. Everything in our world is in agitation. The Saviour prophesied of events to precede His coming: "Ye shall hear of wars and rumors of wars. . . . Nation shall rise against nation, and kingdom against kingdom: and there shall be famines, and pestilences, and earthquakes, in divers places." Matthew 24:6, 7. Rulers and statesmen recognize that something great and decisive is about to take place—that the world is on the verge of a stupendous crisis.

The Bible, and the Bible only, gives a correct view of events that already are casting their shadows before, the sound of their approach causing the earth to tremble and men's hearts to fail them for fear. "Behold, the Lord will lay waste the earth and make it desolate, and He will twist its surface and scatter its inhabitants." "For they have transgressed the laws, violated the statutes, broken the everlasting covenant. Therefore a curse devours the earth, and its inhabitants suffer for their guilt." Isaiah 24:1, 5, 6, RSV.

"Alas! for that day is great, so that none is like it: it is even the time of Jacob's trouble; but he shall be saved out of it." Jeremiah 30:7.

Because thou hast made the Lord, which is
    my refuge,
  Even the most High, thy habitation;
There shall no evil befall thee,
    Neither shall any plague come nigh thy
      dwelling.
              Psalm 91:9, 10

God will not fail His church in the hour of her greatest peril. He has promised deliverance. The principles of His kingdom will be honored by all beneath the sun.

44 / Daniel in the Lions' Den

Darius the Median at once proceeded to reorganize the government. He "set over the kingdom an hundred and twenty princes, . . . and over these three presidents; of whom Daniel was first: that the princes should give accounts unto them, and the king should have no damage. Then this Daniel was preferred above the presidents and princes, because an excellent spirit was in him; and the king thought to set him over the whole realm."

The honors bestowed on Daniel excited the jealousy of the leading men of the kingdom. But they could find no occasion of complaint against him, because "he was faithful, neither was there any error or fault found in him."

"We shall not find any occasion against this Daniel," they acknowledged, "except we find it against him concerning the law of his God."

Thereupon the presidents and princes asked the king to sign a decree forbidding any person to ask anything of God or man, except of Darius the king, for thirty days. Violation of this decree should be punished by casting the offender into a den of lions.

Appealing to Darius's vanity, they pursuaded him that carrying out this edict would add greatly to his authority. Ignorant of the subtle purpose of the princes, the king signed it.

Satanic agencies had stirred the princes to envy.

This chapter is based on Daniel 6.

They had inspired the plan for Daniel's destruction; and the princes, yielding themselves as instruments of evil, carried it into effect.

The prophet's enemies counted on Daniel's firm adherence to principle for the success of their plan. He quickly read their malignant purpose but did not change his course. Why should he cease to pray now, when he most needed to pray? He performed his duties as chief of the princes and at the hour of prayer went to his chamber to offer his petition to the God of heaven. He did not try to conceal his act. Before those plotting his ruin he would not allow it even to appear that his connection with Heaven was severed. Thus the prophet boldly yet humbly declared that no earthly power has a right to interpose between the soul and God. His adherence to right was a bright light in the moral darkness of that heathen court.

For an entire day the princes watched Daniel. Three times they saw him go to his chamber and heard his voice lifted in prayer. The next morning they laid their complaint before the king. Daniel had set the royal decree at defiance! "Hast thou not signed a decree," they reminded him, "that every man that shall ask a petition of any god or man within thirty days, save of thee, O king, shall be cast into the den of lions?"

"The thing is true," the king answered, "according to the law of the Medes and Persians, which altereth not." Exultantly they now informed Darius: "That Daniel, which is of the children of the captivity of Judah, regardeth not thee, O king, nor the decree that thou hast signed, but maketh his petition three times a day."

A Vain King's Remorse

The monarch saw at once the snare that had been set. Not zeal for kingly honor but jealousy against Daniel had led to the royal decree. "Sore displeased with himself" he "labored till the going down of the sun" to deliver his friend. The princes came to him with the words, "Know, O king, that the law of the Medes and Persians is, That no decree nor statute which the king establisheth may be changed." The decree must be carried into effect.

Daniel Is Thrown in the Lions' Den

"Then the king commanded, and they brought Daniel and cast him into the den of lions. Now the king spake and said unto Daniel, Thy God whom thou servest continually, He will deliver thee." A stone was laid on the mouth of the den, and the king himself "sealed it with his own signet. . . . Then the king went to his palace, and passed the night fasting."

God permitted evil angels and wicked men thus far to accomplish their purpose; but through the courage of this one man who chose to follow right, Satan was to be defeated and the name of God to be exalted.

Early the next morning King Darius hastened to the den and "cried with a lamentable voice," "O Daniel, servant of the living God, is thy God, whom thou servest continually, able to deliver thee from the lions?"

God Is Able to Deliver

The prophet replied: "My God hath sent His angel, and hath shut the lions' mouths, that they have not hurt me: forasmuch as before Him innocency was found in me; and also before thee, O king, have I done no hurt.

"Then was the king exceedingly glad for him, and commanded that they should take Daniel up out of the den. So Daniel was taken up out of the den, and no manner of hurt was found upon him, because he believed in his God.

"And the king commanded, and they brought those men which had accused Daniel, and they cast them into the den of lions."

The wicked opposition to God's servant was now completely broken. "Daniel prospered in the reign of Darius, and in the reign of Cyrus the Persian." And through association with him these heathen monarchs were constrained to acknowledge his God as the "living God, and steadfast forever, and His kindgom that which shall not be destroyed."

Daniel the Same in Adversity or Prosperity

A man whose heart is stayed on God will be the same in the hour of his greatest trial as he is in prosperity. Faith grasps eternal realities. Christ identifies with His faithful people; He suffers in the person of His chosen ones. It is possible for the servant of God to maintain his integrity under all circumstances and to triumph through divine grace.

The experience of Daniel reveals that a businessman is not necessarily a designing, policy man. He may be instructed by God at every step. A man of like passions as ourselves, Daniel is described by the pen of inspiration as without fault. His business transactions, when subjected to the closest scrutiny of his enemies, were found without flaw. He was an example of what every businessman may become when his heart is converted.

Daniel, by his noble dignity and unswerving integrity, while young won the "favor and tender love" of the heathen officer in whose charge he had been placed. Daniel 1:9. He rose speedily to the position of prime minister of Babylon. Such were his wisdom and his courtesy, his fidelity to principle, that even his enemies were forced to confess that "they could find none occasion nor fault; forasmuch as he was faithful."

Daniel was honored by God as His ambassador and was given many revelations of the mysteries of ages to come. His prohecies in chapters 7 to 12 were not fully understood even by the prophet himself, but he was given assurance that in the closing period of this world's history he would again be permitted to stand in his lot and place. "Shut up the words, and seal the book," he was directed concerning his prohetic writings, "even to the time of the end." Daniel 12:4.

The prophecies of Daniel demand our special attention, as they relate to the time in which we are living. With them should be linked the last book of the New Testament. The promise is plain that special blessing will accompany the study of these prophecies. "The wise shall understand." Verse 10. And of the revelation that Christ gave to John the promise is, "Blessed is he that readeth, and they that hear the words of this prohecy, and keep those things which are written therein." Revelation 1:3.

From the books of Daniel and Revelation we need to learn how worthless is worldly glory. Babylon, with all its power and magnificence, how completely has it passed away! So perished Medo-Persia, Grecia, and Rome. And so perishes all that has not God for its foundation.

A careful study of God's purpose in the history of nations and in the revelation of things to come will help us to learn what is the true aim of life. Viewing time in the light of eternity, we may, like Daniel, live for that which is true and enduring. Learning the principles of the kingdom of our Lord and Saviour, we may at His coming enter into its possession.

45 / Cyrus Sets the Exiles Free

More than a century before the birth of Cyrus, Inspiration had mentioned the work he should do in taking Babylon unawares and in preparing the way for the release of the children of the captivity: "Thus saith the Lord to His anointed, to Cyrus, whose right hand I have holden, to subdue nations before him; . . . to open before him the two-leaved gates; and the gates shall not be shut; I will go before thee, and make the crooked places straight: I will break in pieces the gates of brass, and cut in sunder the bars of iron." Isaiah 45:1, 2.

In the unexpected entry of the army of the Persian conqueror into the Babylonian capital by way of the river whose waters had been turned aside, and through the inner gates that in careless security had been left open and unprotected, the Jews had abundant evidence of the literal fulfillment of Isaiah's prophecy. This should have been to them an unmistakable sign that God was shaping the affairs of nations in their behalf, for inseparably linked with the prophecy outlining Babylon's capture and fall were the words:

"Thus saith the Lord . . . of Cyrus, He is My shepherd, and shall perform all My pleasure: even saying to Jerusalem, Thou shalt be built; and to the temple, Thy foundation shall be laid." "He shall build My city, and he shall let go My captives, not for price nor reward, saith the Lord of hosts." Isaiah 44:24, 28; 45:13.

In the writings of Jeremiah was set forth plainly the time for the restoration of Israel: "When seventy years are accomplished, that I will punish the king of Babylon, and that nation, . . . for their iniquity, and the land of the Chaldeans." Jeremiah 25:12. "I will turn away your captivity, and I will gather you from all the nations, and from all the places whither I have driven you, saith the Lord; and I will bring you again into the place whence I caused you to be carried away captive." Jeremiah 29:14.

Daniel had gone over these and similar prophecies. Now, as events betokened the hand of God at work, Daniel gave special thought to the promises made to Israel. The Lord had declared, "Then shall ye call upon Me, and ye shall go and pray unto Me, and I will hearken unto you. And ye shall seek Me, and find Me, when ye shall search for Me with all your heart." Verses 12, 13.

Shortly before the fall of Babylon, when Daniel was meditating on these prophecies and seeking God for understanding, a series of visions was given him concerning the rise and fall of kingdoms. With the first vision, recorded in the seventh chapter of Daniel, an interpretation was given, yet not all was made clear to the prophet. "My cogitations much troubled me," he wrote, "and my countenance changed in me: but I kept the matter in my heart." Daniel 7:28.

The Time Prophecy Unfolds

Another vision threw further light on the events of the future. At the close of this vision Daniel heard "a holy one speaking; and another holy one said to the one that spoke, 'For how long is the vision?' " Daniel 8:13, RSV. The answer was given: "Unto two thousand and three hundred days; then shall the sanctuary be cleansed." Verse 14.

Filled with perplexity, he sought for the relation sustained by the seventy years' captivity to the 2300 years that should elapse before the cleansing of God's sanctuary. When the prophet heard the words, "The vision . . . shall be for many days," he fainted "and was sick certain days." He records of his experience: "Afterward I rose up, and did the king's business; and I was astonished at the vision, but none understood it." Verses 26, 27.

The prophecies of Jeremiah were so plain that he understood "the number of the years, whereof the word of the Lord came to Jeremiah the prophet, that He would accomplish seventy years in the desolations of Jerusalem." Daniel 9:2.

Faithful Daniel Identifies Himself With Unfaithful Israel

Daniel pleaded with the Lord for the speedy fulfillment of these promises and for the honor of God to be preserved. He identified himself fully with those who had fallen short of the divine purpose, confessing their sins as his own. Though Daniel had been spoken of by heaven as "greatly beloved," he now appeared before God as a sinner, urging the need of the people he loved. His prayer was eloquent in its simplicity:

"O Lord, . . . we have sinned, . . . neither have we hearkened unto Thy servants the prophets, which spake in Thy name to our kings, our princes, and our fathers."

"O Lord, according to all Thy righteousness, I beseech Thee, let Thine anger and Thy fury be turned away from Thy city Jerusalem, Thy holy mountain: because for our sins, and for the iniquities of our fathers, Jerusalem and Thy people are become a reproach to all that are about us."

"O Lord, hearken and do; defer not, for Thine own sake, O my God." Verses 4-6, 16, 19.

Even before the prophet had finished his plea, Gabriel again appeared to him, called his attention to the vision he had seen, and outlined in detail the seventy weeks which were to begin at "the going forth of the commandment to restore and to build Jerusalem." Verse 25.

The beginning of Cyrus's reign marked the completion of the seventy years since the first company of Hebrews had been taken by Nebuchadnezzar to Babylon.

The deliverance of Daniel from the den of lions had been used of God to create a favorable impression on the mind of Cyrus. The sterling qualities of the man of God as a statesman of farseeing ability led the Persian ruler to show him marked respect and to honor his judgment. And now God moved upon Cyrus to discern the prophecies concerning himself and to grant the Jewish people their liberty.

The king saw the words foretelling more than a hundred years before his birth the manner in which Babylon should be taken. He read the message addressed to him by the Ruler of the universe: "I girded thee, though thou hast not known Me: that they may know from the rising of the sun, and from the west, that there is none beside Me." "I have surnamed thee, though thou hast not known Me." As he traced the inspired record, "He shall build My city, and he shall let go My captives, not for price nor reward," his heart was profoundly moved, and he determined to fulfill his divinely appointed mission. Isaiah 45:5, 6, 4, 13. He would let the Judean captives go free!

In a proclamation published "throughout all his kingdom," Cyrus made known his desire: "The Lord God of heaven . . . hath charged me to build Him an house at Jerusalem, which is in Judah. Who is there among you of all His people? his God be with him, and let him go up to Jerusalem, . . . and build the house of the Lord God of Israel, (He is the God,) which is in Jerusalem. And whosoever remaineth in any place where he sojourneth, let the men of his place help him with silver, and with gold, and with goods, and with beasts, beside the freewill offerings for the house of God that is in Jerusalem." Ezra 1:1-4.

"Let the house be builded," he further directed regarding the temple, "the place where they offered sacrifices, . . . and let the expenses be given out of the king's house: and also let the golden and silver vessels of the house of God, which Nebuchadnezzar took forth out of the temple which is in Jerusalem, and brought unto Babylon, be restored, and brought again unto the temple which is at Jerusalem." Ezra 6:3-5.

Tidings of this decree reached the farthermost provinces, and there was great rejoicing. Many, like Daniel, had been studying the prophecies and had been seeking God for His promised intervention in behalf of Zion. And now their prayers were being answered!

When the Lord turned again the captivity of Zion,
We were like them that dream.
Then was our mouth filled with laughter,
And our tongue with singing.
Psalm 126:1, 2

About fifty thousand from the Jews in exile determined to take advantage of the wonderful opportunity "to build the house of the Lord which is in Jerusalem." Their friends "aided them with vessels of silver, with gold, with goods, with beasts, and with costly wares." "Cyrus the king also brought out the vessels of the house of the Lord." Ezra 1:5-7, RSV.

The long journey across the desert was accomplished in safety, and the happy company at once undertook the work of reestablishing that which had been destroyed. "The chief of the fathers" (Ezra 2:68) led in offering of their substance to help defray the expense of rebuilding the temple, and the people, following their example, gave freely of their meager store. See verses 64-70.

An altar was erected on the site of the ancient altar in the temple court. The people "gathered themselves together as one man" and united in reestablishing the sacred services interrupted at the destruction of Jerusalem, and "they kept also the feast of tabernacles." Ezra 3:1, 4. Setting up the altar greatly cheered the faithful remnant. They gathered courage as preparations for rebuilding the temple advanced from month to month. Surrounded by many sad reminders of the apostasy of their fathers, they longed for some abiding token of divine forgiveness and favor. Above regaining personal property, they valued the approval of God. They felt the assurance of His presence with them; yet they desired greater blessings. They looked forward to the time when they might behold the shining forth of His glory from within the rebuilt temple.

The workmen found among the ruins some of the immense stones brought to the temple site in the days of Solomon. These were made ready for use, and much new material was provided. Soon the foundation stone was laid in the presence of many thousands assembled to witness the progress of the work. While the cornerstone was being set in position, the people "sang together by course in praising and giving thanks unto the Lord." Verse 11.

A Carryover From Israel's Ancient Unbelief

All present should have entered heartily into the spirit of the occasion. Yet mingled with the music and shouts of praise heard on that glad day was a discordant note: "Many of the . . . ancient men, that had seen the first house, . . . wept with a loud voice." Verse 12. These aged men thought of the results of long-continued impenitence. Had they and their generation carried out God's purpose for Israel, the temple built by Solomon would not have been destroyed and the captivity would not have been necessary.

But conditions were now changed. The Lord had allowed His people to return to their own land. Sadness should have given way to joy. God had moved upon Cyrus to aid them in rebuilding the temple! But instead of rejoicing, some cherished thoughts of discontent and discouragement. They had seen the glory of Solomon's temple and lamented because of the inferiority of the building now to be erected.

The murmuring and complaining had a depressing influence on many. The workmen were led to question whether they should proceed with the erection of a building that was so freely criticized and was the cause of so much lamentation. Many, however, did not view this lesser glory with such dissatisfaction. They "shouted aloud for joy: so that the people could not discern the noise of the shout of joy from the noise of the weeping of the people: for the people shouted with a loud shout, and the noise was heard afar off." Verses 12, 13.

Little did those who failed to rejoice at the laying of the foundation stone realize the weight of their words of disapproval and disappointment. Little did they know how much their dissatisfaction would delay the completion of the Lord's house.

The magnificence of the first temple had been a source of pride to Israel before their captivity; but the glory of the first temple could not recommend them to God, for they did not bring Him the sacrifice of a humble and contrite spirit. When the vital principles of the kingdom of God are lost sight of, ceremonies become multitudinous and extravagant. When the simplicity of godliness is despised, pride and love of display demand magnificent church edifices, splendid adornings, and imposing ceremonials.

But God values His church for the sincere piety which distinguishes it from the world. He estimates it according to the growth of its members in the knowledge of Christ, their progress in spiritual experience. He looks for love and goodness. Beauty of art cannot compare with beauty of character revealed in Christ's representatives. A congregation may be the poorest in the land, but if the members possess the principles of the character of Christ, angels will unite in their worship.

Give thanks unto the Lord, for He is good:
    For His mercy endureth forever.
Let the redeemed of the Lord say so,
    Whom He hath redeemed from the hand of the
    enemy.
            Psalm 107:1, 2

46 / Bitter Opposition Fails

Close by the Israelites dwelt the Samaritans, a race that had sprung up through intermarriage of heathen colonists from Assyria with the remnant of the ten tribes left in Samaria and Galilee. In heart and practice they were idolaters. True, they held that their idols were but to remind them of the living God, but the people were prone to reverence images.

These Samaritans came to be known as "the adversaries of Judah and Benjamin." Hearing that the "children of the captivity builded the temple unto the Lord God of Israel," they expressed a desire to unite in its erection. "Let us build with you," they proposed, "for we seek your God, as ye do." But the leaders of the Israelites declared, "We ourselves together will build unto the Lord God of Israel, as King Cyrus the king of Persia hath commanded us." Ezra 4:1-3.

Only a remnant had chosen to return from Babylon, and now, as they undertook a work seemingly beyond their strength, their nearest neighbors came with an offer of help. "We seek your God, as ye do," the Samaritans declared; "let us build with you." But had the Jewish leaders accepted this offer, they would have opened a door for idolatry. They discerned the insincerity of the Samaritans.

Regarding the relation that Israel should sustain to surrounding peoples, the Lord had declared through Moses: "Thou shalt make no covenant with them, nor show mercy unto them: . . . for they will turn away thy son from following Me, that they may serve other gods." "The Lord hath chosen thee to be a peculiar people unto Himself, above all the nations that are upon the face of the earth." Deuteronomy 7:2-4; 14:2.

The result that would follow a covenant with surrounding nations was plainly foretold: "The Lord shall scatter thee among all people, from the one end of the earth even unto the other; and there thou shalt serve other gods. . . . And among these nations shalt thou find no ease." Deuteronomy 28:64, 65.

Why the Samaritans' Help Was Refused

Zerubbabel and his associates were familiar with these and many like scriptures; and in the recent captivity they had many evidences of their fulfillment. And now, having turned with all the heart to God and renewed their covenant relationship with Him, they had been permitted to return to Judea, that they might restore that which had been destroyed. Should they at the beginning of their undertaking enter into a covenant with idolaters? Those who had rededicated themselves to the Lord at the altar set up before the ruins of His temple refused to enter into alliance with those who, though familiar with God's law, would not yield to its claims. Never can God's people afford to compromise principle by entering into alliance with those who do not fear Him.

God's People Must Guard Against Subtle Influences

God's people must strictly guard against every subtle influence that seeks entrance by flattering inducements from enemies of truth. They are pilgrims and strangers in this world. It is not the open and avowed enemies of the cause of God that are most to be feared. Those who come with smooth words and fair speeches, apparently seeking friendly alliance with God's children, have greater power to deceive. Every soul should be on the alert lest some concealed and masterly snare take him unaware. The Lord requires a vigilance that knows no relaxation.

But none are left to struggle alone. Angels protect those who walk humbly before God. As His children draw near to Him for protection from evil, in love He lifts up for them a standard against the enemy. Touch them not, He says, for they are Mine.

Untiring in their opposition, the Samaritans "discouraged the people of Judah, and made them afraid to build, and hired counselors against them to frustrate their purpose, all the days of Cyrus king of Persia, even until the reign of Darius king of Persia." Ezra 4:4, 5, RSV. But for many years the powers of evil were held in check, and the people in Judea had liberty to continue their work.

The Battle Behind the Scenes

While Satan was striving to influence Medo-Persia to show disfavor to God's people, angels worked in behalf of the exiles. Through Daniel we are given a glimpse of this struggle between good and evil. For three weeks Gabriel wrestled with the powers of darkness seeking to counteract the influences at work on the mind of Cyrus; and before the contest closed, Christ Himself came to Gabriel's aid. "The prince of the kingdom of Persia withstood me one and twenty days," Gabriel declared; "but, lo, Michael, one of the chief princes, came to help me; and I remained there with the kings of Persia." Daniel 10:13. The victory was finally gained; the forces of the enemy were held in check all the days of Cyrus, and all the days of his son Cambyses.

The highest agencies of heaven were working on the hearts of kings, and the people of God should have spared no effort to restore the temple and its services and to reestablish themselves in their Judean homes. But the opposition of their enemies was determined, and gradually the builders lost heart. Some could not forget the scene at the laying of the cornerstone, when many had expressed lack of confidence in the enterprise. And as the Samaritans grew more bold, many questioned whether the time had come to rebuild. The feeling soon became widespread. Workmen, discouraged and disheartened, took up the ordinary pursuits of life.

During the reign of Cambyses work on the temple progressed slowly. And during the reign of the false Smerdis the Samaritans induced the impostor to issue a decree forbidding the Jews to rebuild their temple and city.

For more than a year the temple was well-nigh forsaken. The people dwelt in their homes and strove to attain temporal prosperity, but they did not prosper. Nature seemed to conspire against them. Because they had let the temple lie waste, the Lord sent drought. God had bestowed on them the fruits of field and garden as a token of His favor, but because they had used these gifts selfishly, the blessings were removed.

God's Work Grinds to a Halt

Such were the conditions during the early part of the reign of Darius Hystaspes. The Israelites were in a pitiable state. They murmured and doubted and chose to make personal interests first, while viewing with apathy the Lord's temple in ruins. Many had lost sight of God's purpose in restoring them to Judea, and these were saying, "The time is not come, the time that the Lord's house should be built." Haggai 1:2.

But the prophets Haggai and Zechariah were raised up to meet the crisis. These appointed messengers revealed to the people the cause of their troubles. The lack of temporal prosperity was the result of a neglect to put God's interests first. Had the Israelites honored God by making the building of His house their first work, they would have invited His presence and blessing.

Haggai addressed the searching inquiry, "Is it time for you, O ye, to dwell in your cieled houses, and this house lie waste?" verse 4. Why do you feel concern for your own buildings and unconcern for the Lord's building? The desire to escape poverty has led you to neglect the temple, but this neglect has brought upon you that which you feared.

"Ye have sown much, and bring in little; ye eat, but ye have not enough; ye drink, but ye are not filled with drink; ye clothe you, but there is none warm; and he that earneth wages earneth wages to put it into a bag with holes." Verse 6.

Then the Lord revealed the cause that had brought them to want: "Ye looked for much, and, lo, it came to little; and when ye brought it home, I did blow upon it. Why? saith the Lord of hosts. Because of Mine house that is waste, and ye run every man unto his own house. Therefore . . . I called for a drought upon the land." Verses 9-11.

"Consider your ways. Go up to the mountain, and bring wood, and build the house; and I will take pleasure in it, and I will be glorified." Verses 7, 8.

The message given through Haggai was taken to heart. The leaders and people dared not disregard the instruction sent—that prosperity, both temporal and spiritual, was dependent on faithful obedience to God's commands. Aroused, Zerubbabel and Joshua, "with all the remnant of the people, obeyed the voice of the Lord their God, and the words of Haggai the prophet." Verse 12.

God Sends a Comforting Message

Less than a month after work on the temple was resumed, the builders received a comforting message: "Take courage, O Zerubbabel, . . . take courage, O Joshua, . . . take courage all you people of the land, says the Lord; work, for I am with you, says the Lord of hosts." Haggai 2:4, RSV.

To His children today the Lord declares, "Take courage, . . . work, for I am with you." The earnest pleadings and encouragement given through Haggai were added to by Zechariah, whom God raised up to stand by his side. Zechariah's first message was an assurance that God's word never fails and a promise of blessing [is reserved] to those who would hearken to the sure word of prophecy.

With their scant store of provisions rapidly failing and surrounded by unfriendly peoples, the Israelites moved forward by faith and labored diligently to restore the ruined temple. Message after message was given through Haggai and Zechariah, with assurances that their faith would be rewarded and that the future glory of the temple whose walls they were rearing would not fail. In this very building would appear in the fullness of time, the Desire of all nations as the Saviour of mankind.

The Promise of Temporal Prosperity

With repentance and willingness to advance by faith, came the promise of temporal prosperity: "From this day will I bless you." Verse 19. To Zerubbabel their leader, who had been so sorely tried through all the years since their return from Babylon, was given a precious message. The day was coming when the enemies of God's people would be cast down. "In that day, saith the Lord of hosts, will I take thee, O Zerubbabel, My servant, . . . and will make thee as a signet: for I have chosen thee." Verse 23.

Now the governor of Israel could see the meaning of the providence that had led him through discouragement and perplexity. God never leads His children otherwise than they would choose to be led if they could see the end from the beginning and discern the glory of the purpose that they are fulfilling.

Haggai and Zechariah roused the people to put forth every possible effort for rebuilding the temple, but the Samaritans and others devised many hindrances. On one occasion the provincial officers of Medo-Persia visited Jerusalem and requested the name of the one who had authorized the restoration of the building. If the Jews had not been trusting in the Lord for guidance, this inquiry might have resulted disastrously.

But the officers were answered so wisely that they decided to write to Darius Hystaspes, directing his attention to the original decree made by Cyrus, which commanded that the house of God at Jerusalem be rebuilt and the expenses be paid from the king's treasury.

Darius searched for this decree and found it, whereupon he directed those who had made the inquiry to allow the rebuilding of the temple to proceed. "Let the work of this house of God alone," he commanded; "let the governor of the Jews and the elders of the Jews build this house of God in His place.

"Moreover, I make a decree what ye shall do to the elders of these Jews for the building of this house of God: that of the king's goods, even of the tribute beyond the river, forthwith expenses be given unto these men, that they be not hindered." Ezra 6:7, 8.

The king further decreed that severe penalties be meted out to those who should alter the decree, and he closed with the remarkable statement: "May the God who has caused His name to dwell there overthrow any king or people that shall put forth a hand to alter this, or to destroy this house of God which is in Jerusalem." Verse 12, RSV. For months before this decree was made, the Israelites had kept on working by faith, the prophets helping them by means of timely messages.

The Encouraging Visions of Zechariah

Two months after Haggai's last recorded message, Zechariah had a series of visions regarding the work of God in the earth. These messages, given in the form of parables and symbols, came at a time of great anxiety and were of peculiar significance to the men advancing in the name of God. It seemed as if permission to rebuild was about to be withdrawn; the future appeared dark.

Zechariah heard the angel of the Lord inquiring, "O Lord of hosts, how long wilt Thou not have mercy on Jerusalem and on the cities of Judah, against which Thou hast had indignation these three score and ten years? And the Lord answered the angel that talked with me," Zechariah declared, "with good words and comfortable words.

"So the angel that communed with me said unto me, . . . Thus saith the Lord of hosts; . . . I am very sore displeased with the heathen that are at ease: for I was but a little displeased, and they helped forward the affliction. Therefore thus saith the Lord; I am returned to Jerusalem with mercies: My house shall be built in it." Zechariah 1:12-16.

The prophet was now directed to predict, "The Lord shall yet comfort Zion, and shall yet choose Jerusalem." Verse 17.

Zechariah then saw the powers that had "scattered Judah, Israel, and Jerusalem," symbolized by four horns. Immediately afterward he saw four carpenters—agencies used by the Lord in restoring His people and the house of His worship. See verses 18-21. "Jerusalem shall be inhabited as towns without walls for the multitude of men and cattle therein: for I, saith the Lord, will be unto her a wall of fire round about, and will be the glory in the midst of her." Zechariah 2:4, 5.

God had commanded that Jerusalem be rebuilt; the vision was an assurance that He would give comfort and strength to His afflicted ones and fulfill the promises of His everlasting covenant. That which He was accomplishing for His people was to be known in all the earth. "Cry out and shout, thou inhabitant of Zion: for great is the Holy One of Israel in the midst of thee." Isaiah 12:6.

47 / Satan, the Accuser; Christ, the Defender

Because Israel had been chosen to preserve the knowledge of God in the earth, Satan was determined to cause their destruction. While they were obedient he could do them no harm; therefore he had bent all his power and cunning to entice them into sin. Ensnared, they had transgressed and had become the prey of their enemies.

Yet God did not forsake them. He sent His prophets with warnings and aroused them to see their guilt. When they returned to Him with true repentance, He sent messages of encouragement, declaring that He would deliver them from captivity and once more establish them in their own land. Now that this restoration had begun and a remnant had already returned to Judea, Satan was determined to frustrate the divine purpose. To this end he was seeking to move upon the heathen nations to destroy them.

But in this crisis the Lord strengthened His people with "good words and comfortable words." Zechariah 1:13. Through an impressive illustration He showed the power of Christ their Mediator to vanquish Satan, the accuser of His people.

"Joshua the high priest," "clothed with filthy garments" (Zechariah 3:1, 3), stands before the Angel of the Lord. As he pleads for the fulfillment of God's promises, Satan points to the transgressions of Israel as a reason why they should not be restored to the favor of God. He claims them as his prey and demands that they be given into his hands.

The high priest does not claim that Israel is free from fault. In filthy garments, symbolizing the sins of the people which he bears as their representative, he stands before the Angel, confessing their guilt yet pointing to their repentance, and in faith relying on the mercy of a sin-pardoning Redeemer.

Then the Angel, who is Christ the Saviour of sinners, puts to silence the accuser: "The Lord rebuke thee, O Satan; even the Lord that hath chosen Jerusalem rebuke thee: is not this a brand plucked out of the fire?" Verse 2. Because of their sins Israel had been well-nigh consumed in the flame kindled by Satan and his agents for their destruction, but God had now set His hand to bring them forth.

As the intercession of Joshua is accepted, the command is given, "Take away the filthy garments from him"; and to Joshua the Angel says, "I have caused thine iniquity to pass from thee, and I will clothe thee with change of raiment. . . . So they . . . clothed him with garments." Verses 4, 5. His sins and those of his people were pardoned. Israel was clothed with "change of raiment"—the righteousness of Christ imputed to them. Notwithstanding Joshua's former transgressions, he was now qualified to minister before God in His sanctuary. If obedient, he should be honored as the judge, or the ruler, over the temple and should walk among attending angels even in this life. At last he should join the glorified throng around the throne of God.

"Hear now, O Joshua the high priest, . . . I will bring forth My Servant the Branch." Verse 8. In the "Branch," the Deliverer to come, lay the hope of Israel. By faith in the coming Saviour Joshua and his people had received pardon and had been restored to God's favor. By virtue of His merits they would be honored as the chosen of Heaven among the nations of earth.

In all ages Satan is "the accuser of our brethren, . . . which accused them before our God day and night." Revelation 12:10. Over every soul rescued from the power of evil the controversy is repeated. Never is one received into the family of God without exciting the determined resistance of the enemy. But He who was the defense of Israel, their justification and redemption, is the hope of the church today.

How Satan Works

Satan's accusations against those who seek the Lord are not prompted by displeasure at their sins. He exults in their defective characters, for he knows that only through their transgression of God's law can he obtain power over them. His accusations arise solely from enmity to Christ. As he beholds the evidences of Christ's supremacy, he works to wrest from Him those who have accepted salvation. He leads men to lose confidence in God and separate from His love. He tempts them to break the law and then claims them as his captives, contesting Christ's right to take them from him.

Satan knows that those who ask for pardon will obtain it; therefore he presents their sins before them to discourage them. Even their best service he seeks to make appear corrupt. By countless devices, subtle and cruel, he endeavors to secure their condemnation.

In his own strength, man cannot meet the charges of the enemy. But Jesus our Advocate presents an effectual plea in behalf of all who by repentance and faith commit their souls to Him. By the mighty arguments of Calvary He vanquishes their accuser. His perfect obedience to God's law has given Him all power in heaven and earth, and to the accuser of His people He declares: "The Lord rebuke thee, O Satan. These are the purchase of My blood, brands plucked from the burning." See Zechariah 3:2. And to those who rely on Him in faith He gives the assurance: "I have caused thine iniquity to pass from thee, and I will clothe thee with change of raiment." Verse 4.

All who have put on the robe of Christ's righteousness will stand faithful and true. The promise given to

Joshua is given to all: "If you will . . . keep My charge, . . . I will give you the right of access among those who are standing here." Verse 7, RSV. Angels will walk on either side of them even in this world, and they will stand at last among the angels that surround the throne of God.

Zechariah's vision applies with peculiar force to God's people in the closing scenes of the great day of atonement. The remnant will then be brought into great distress. Those who keep the commandments of God and the faith of Jesus will feel the ire of the dragon and his hosts. Here is a little company resisting his supremacy. If he could blot them from the earth, his triumph would be complete. In the near future he will stir up the wicked powers of earth to destroy the people of God.

Those who are true to God will be denounced and proscribed. They will be "betrayed both by parents, and brethren, and kinsfolks, and friends," even unto death. Luke 21:16. As Joshua pleaded before the Angel, so the remnant church, with brokenness of heart and unfaltering faith, will plead for pardon and deliverance through Jesus their Advocate. They are fully conscious of their sinfulness and unworthiness, and they are ready to despair.

Satan Tries to Discourage God's People

The tempter stands by to accuse them. He points to their filthy garments, their defective characters, their weakness and folly, their sins of ingratitude, their unlikeness to Christ, which have dishonored their Redeemer. He endeavors to frighten them with the thought that their case is hopeless. He hopes that they will yield to his temptations and turn from their allegiance to God.

Satan has an accurate knowledge of the sins he has tempted God's people to commit, and he urges his accusations against them. He declares that by their sins they have forfeited divine protection; they are as deserving as himself of exclusion from the favor of God. "Are these," he says, "to take my place in heaven, and the place of the angels who united with me? They profess to obey the law of God, but have they not been lovers of self? Have they not placed their own interests above God's service? Have they not loved the things of the world? Look at their selfishness, their malice, their hatred of one another. Justice demands that sentence be pronounced against them."

But the followers of Christ have repented of their sins and sought the Lord in contrition, and the divine Advocate pleads in their behalf. He who has been most abused by their ingratitude declares: "I gave My life for these souls. They may have imperfections of character, but they have repented, and I have forgiven and accepted them."

The assaults of Satan are strong. The flames of the furnace seem about to consume God's people, but Jesus will bring them forth as gold tried in the fire. Their earthliness will be removed, that through them the image of Christ may be perfectly revealed.

At times the Lord may seem to have forgotten His church, but nothing in the world is so dear to the heart of God. He does not leave His people to be overcome by Satan's temptations. He will punish those who misrepresent Him, but He will be gracious to all who repent.

In the time of the end the people of God will sigh and cry for the abominations done in the land. With tears they will warn the wicked of their danger in trampling on the divine law, and they will humble themselves before the Lord in penitence. The wicked will ridicule their solemn appeals. But the anguish of God's people is evidence that they are regaining the nobility of character lost in consequence of sin. It is because they are drawing nearer to Christ, because their eyes are fixed on His perfect purity, that they discern clearly the sinfulness of sin. A crown of glory awaits those who bow at the foot of the cross.

God's faithful, praying ones know not how securely they are shielded. Urged on by Satan, the rulers of this world seek to destroy them, but could the eyes of God's children be opened, they would see angels encamped about them.

As the people of God plead for purity of heart, the spotless robe of Christ's righteousness is placed on them. The despised remnant are clothed in glorious apparel, nevermore to be defiled by the corruptions of the world. Their names are retained in the Lamb's book of life. They have resisted the wiles of the deceiver. Now they are eternally secure, their sins transferred to the originator of sin.

The Blotting out of Sins

While Satan has been urging his accusations, holy angels, unseen, have been placing on the faithful ones the seal of God. These stand on Mount Zion, having the Father's name written in their foreheads. They sing that song which no one can learn save the 144,000 redeemed from the earth. "In their mouth was found no guile: for they are without fault." Revelation 14:5.

Now is reached the complete fulfillment of the words of the Angel to Joshua: "I will bring forth My Servant the Branch." Christ is revealed as the Redeemer and Deliverer of His people. Now are the remnant "men wondered at" (Zechariah 3:8) as the tears and humiliation of their pilgrimage give place to joy and honor in the presence of God and the Lamb. See Isaiah 4:2, 3.

48 / The Secret of Success in God's Work

After Zechariah's vision of Joshua and the Angel, the prophet received a message regarding Zerubbabel: "The Angel that talked with me came again, and waked me, . . . and behold a candlestick all of gold, . . . and seven pipes to the seven lamps, . . . and two olive trees by it. . . .

"So I . . . spake to the Angel, . . . What are these, my Lord? . . . Then He answered, . . . This is the word of the Lord unto Zerubbabel, saying, Not by might, nor by power, but by My Spirit, saith the Lord of hosts." "And I answered again, and said unto Him, What be these two olive branches which through the two golden pipes empty the golden oil out of themselves? . . . Then said He, These are the two anointed ones, that stand by the Lord of the whole earth." Zechariah 4:1-6, 12-14.

From the anointed ones that stand in God's presence divine light, love, and power are imparted to His people, that they may impart to others light and joy and refreshing. Those who are enriched are to enrich others with God's love.

In rebuilding the house of the Lord, Zerubbabel had labored in the face of manifold difficulties. Adversaries had "discouraged the people of Judah, and made them afraid to build," "and by force and power made them cease." Ezra 4:4, 23, RSV. But the Lord now spoke through His prophet to Zerubbabel, "Who art thou, O great mountain? before Zerubbabel thou shalt become a plain: and he shall bring forth the headstone thereof with shoutings, crying, Grace, grace unto it.'' Zechariah 4:7. Throughout history, great mountains of apparently insurmountable difficulty have loomed up before those trying to carry out the purposes of Heaven. Such obstacles are permitted by the Lord as a test of faith. This is the time to trust in God. The exercise of living faith means an increase of spiritual strength and the development of unfaltering trust. Before the demand of faith, obstacles placed by Satan will disappear: "Nothing shall be impossible unto you." Matthew 17:20.

Man's Way Contrasted With God's Way

The way of the world is to begin with pomp and boasting. God's way is to make the day of small things the beginning of the glorious triumph of truth. Sometimes He trains His workers by disappointment and apparent failure. It is His purpose that they shall learn to master difficulties.

Often men are tempted to falter before perplexities and obstacles. But if they will hold their confidence steadfast, God will make the way clear. Success will come. Mountains of difficulty will become a plain; and He whose hands have laid the foundation, even "his hands shall also finish it." Zechariah 4:9.

Human power did not establish the church of God. Not on the rock of human strength, but on Christ Jesus, the Rock of Ages, was the church founded, "and the gates of hell shall not prevail against it." Matthew 16:18. God's glorious work will never come to nought. It will go on "not by might, nor by power, but by My Spirit, saith the Lord of hosts." Zechariah 4:6.

The promise to Zerubbabel was literally fulfilled. See verse 9. "The elders of the Jews builded, . . . and finished it, according to the commandment of the God of Israel, and according to the commandment of Cyrus, and Darius, and Artaxerxes king of Persia. And this house was finished on the third day of the month Adar." Ezra 6:14, 15.

The second temple did not equal the first in magnificence, nor was it hallowed by those visible tokens of the divine presence which pertained to the first temple. No supernatural power marked its dedication—no cloud of glory filled the newly erected sanctuary, no fire from heaven consumed the sacrifice on its altar. The Shekinah no longer abode in the most holy place. The ark, the mercy seat, and the tables of testimony were not found there.

The True Glory of the Second Temple

And yet this was the building concerning which the Lord had declared, "The glory of this latter house shall be greater than of the former." "The Desire of all nations shall come." Haggai 2:9, 7. Jesus, the Desire of all nations, by His personal presence hallowed the temple. Yet many have refused to see in His advent any special significance. Their minds have been blinded to the true meaning of the prophet's words.

The second temple was honored, not with the cloud of God's glory, but with the presence of the One in whom dwelt "all the fullness of the Godhead bodily"—God "manifest in the flesh." Colossians 2:9; 1 Timothy 3:16. In this alone did the second temple exceed the first in glory. The "Desire of all nations" had indeed come to His temple, when the Man of Nazareth taught and healed in the sacred courts.

49 / Esther, the Hebrew Girl Who Became Queen

Nearly 50,000 children of the captivity had taken advantage of the decree permitting their return. These, however, were but a mere remnant. Hundreds of thousands of Israelites had chosen to remain in Medo-Persia rather than undergo the hardships of the return journey and the reestablishment of their desolated cities and homes.

A score or more years passed when a decree was issued by Darius Hystaspes, the monarch then ruling. Thus did God in mercy provide another opportunity for the Jews to return to the land of their fathers. The Lord foresaw the troublous times that were to follow during the reign of Xerxes (Ahasuerus of the book of Esther), and He inspired Zechariah to plead with the exiles to return:

"Escape to Zion, you who dwell with the daughter of Babylon. For thus said the Lord of hosts, after His glory sent me to the nations who plundered you, for he who touches you touches the apple of His eye: 'Behold, I will shake My hand over them, and they shall become plunder for those who served them. Then you will know that the Lord of hosts has sent me.'" Zechariah 2:7-9, RSV.

It was still the Lord's purpose that His people should glorify His name. He had given them many opportunities to return to Him. Some had chosen to listen, and some had found salvation in the midst of affliction. Many of these were among the remnant that should return.

Those "whose spirit God had raised" (Ezra 1:5) returned under the decree of Cyrus. But God ceased not to plead with those who voluntarily remained in the land of exile, and through manifold agencies He made it possible for them also to return. However, the larger number of those who failed to respond to the decree, remained unimpressible, and even when Zechariah warned them to flee from Babylon, they did not heed the invitation.

The Death Decree Against God's People

Meanwhile conditions in Medo-Persia were changing rapidly. Darius Hystaspes was succeeded by Xerxes the Great. During his reign those who had failed to flee were called on to face a terrible crisis. Having refused the way of escape God had provided, now they were brought face to face with death.

Through Haman the Agagite, an unscrupulous man high in authority in Medo-Persia, Satan worked to counterwork the purposes of God. Haman cherished bitter malice against Mordecai, a Jew. Mordecai had done Haman no harm but had simply refused to show him worshipful reverence. Scorning to "lay hands on Mordecai alone," Haman plotted "to destroy all the Jews that were throughout the whole kingdom of Ahasuerus." Esther 3:6.

Misled by Haman, Xerxes was induced to decree the massacre of all Jews "scattered abroad and dispersed among the people in all the provinces" of Medo-Persia. Verse 8. A certain day was appointed on which the Jews were to be destroyed and their property confiscated. Satan, the instigator of the scheme, was trying to rid the earth of those who preserved the knowledge of the true God.

"In every province, whithersoever the king's commandment and his decree came, there was great mourning among the Jews, and fasting, and weeping, and wailing; and many lay in sackcloth and ashes." Esther 4:3.

The decree of the Medes and Persians could not be revoked; apparently all the Israelites were doomed to destruction. But in the providence of God, Esther had been made queen. Mordecai was her near relative. In their extremity they decided to appeal to Xerxes in behalf of their people. Esther was to venture into his presence as an intercessor. "Who knoweth," said Mordecai, "whether thou art come to the kingdom for such a time as this?" Verse 14.

The Great Prayer Meeting

The crisis Esther faced demanded quick action; but both she and Mordecai realized that unless God should work in their behalf, their efforts would be unavailing. So Esther took time for communion with God. "Go," she directed Mordecai, "gather together all the Jews that are present in Shushan, and fast ye for me, and neither eat nor drink three days, night or day: I also and my maidens will fast likewise; and so will I go in unto the king, which is not according to the law: and if I perish, I perish." Verse 16.

The events that followed—the appearance of Esther before the king, the favor shown her, the banquets of the king and queen with Haman as the only guest, the troubled sleep of the king, the public honor shown Mordecai, and the humiliation and fall of Haman—all these are parts of a familiar story. God wrought marvelously for His people. A counter decree issued by the king, allowing God's people to fight for their lives, was communicated to the realm by mounted couriers who "rode out in haste, urged by the king's command." "There was gladness and joy among the Jews, a feast and a holiday. And many from the peoples of the country declared themselves Jews, for the fear of the Jews had fallen upon them." Esther 8:14, 17, RSV.

On the day appointed for their destruction, "the Jews gathered themselves together in their cities throughout all the provinces of the king Ahasuerus, to lay hand on such as sought their hurt: and no man could withstand them; for the fear of them fell upon all people.'' Esther 9:2. Angels had been commissioned by God to protect His people while they "gathered to defend their lives." Verse 16, RSV.

Mordecai "was [elevated to be] next in rank to King Ahasuerus, and he was great among the Jews and popular with the multitude of his brethren." Esther 10:3, RSV. He sought to promote the welfare of Israel. Thus did God bring His chosen people once more into favor at the Medo-Persian court, making possible His purpose to restore them to their own land. But not until the seventh year of Artaxerxes I did any considerable number return to Jerusalem, under Ezra.

The experiences that came to God's people in the days of Esther were not peculiar to that age. The revelator, looking down the ages, declared, "The dragon was wroth with the woman, and went to make war with the remnant of her seed, which keep the commandments of God, and have the testimony of Jesus Christ." Revelation 12:17. Some today will see these words fulfilled. The spirit that in ages past led men to persecute the true church will lead to a similar curse toward those who maintain their loyalty to God. Even now preparations are being made for this last great conflict.

The final decree against the remnant people of God will be similar to that issued by Ahasuerus against the Jews. The enemies of the true church see in the little company keeping the Sabbath commandment a Mordecai at the gate. The reverence of God's people for His law is a constant rebuke to those who have cast off the fear of the Lord and are trampling on His Sabbath.

Satan will arouse indignation against the minority who refuse to accept popular traditions. Men of position and reputation will join the lawless and the vile against the people of God. Wealth, genius, education will combine to cover them with contempt. Persecuting rulers, ministers, and church members will conspire against them. With voice and pen, by threats and ridicule, they will seek to overthrow their faith. By false representations and angry appeals, men will stir up the passions of the people. Not having a "Thus saith the Scriptures" to bring against the Bible Sabbath, they will resort to oppressive enactments to supply the lack. Legislators will yield to the demand for Sunday laws. But those who fear God cannot accept an institution that violates a precept of the Decalogue. On this battlefield will be fought the last great conflict in the controversy between truth and error. As in the days of Esther and Mordecai, the Lord will vindicate His truth and His people.

50 / Ezra, the King's Trusted Friend

About seventy years after the return of the first exiles, Artaxerxes Longimanus came to the throne of Medo-Persia. During his reign Ezra and Nehemiah lived and labored. In 457 B.C. he issued the third decree for the restoration of Jerusalem. During his long rule he often showed favor to God's people, and in his trusted Jewish friends, Ezra and Nehemiah, he recognized men of God's appointment.

Ezra, living among the Jews who remained in Babylon, attracted the favorable notice of King Artaxerxes with whom he talked freely regarding the power of God and the divine purpose in restoring the Jews to Jerusalem.

Ezra had been given priestly training, and in addition had acquired familiarity with the writings of the wise men of the Medo-Persian realm. But he was not satisfied with his spiritual condition. He longed to be in full harmony with God. And so he "prepared his heart to seek the law of the Lord, and to do it." Ezra 7:10. This led him to search the books of the Bible to learn why the Lord had permitted Jerusalem to be destroyed and His people carried captive into a heathen land.

Ezra Studies to Show Himself Approved

Ezra studied the promise made to Abraham and the instruction given at Mount Sinai and through the wilderness wandering. Ezra's heart was stirred, and he experienced a thorough conversion. As he learned to yield his mind and will to divine control, there were brought into his life the principles of true sanctification. In later years these had a molding influence upon all associated with him.

God chose Ezra that He might put honor upon the priesthood, the glory of which had been eclipsed during the captivity. Ezra developed into a man of extraordinary learning and became "skilled in the law of Moses." Verse 6, RSV. These qualifications made him an eminent man in the kingdom.

Ezra Becomes a Mouthpiece for the Lord

During the remaining years of his life, whether near the court of Medo-Persia or at Jerusalem, he communicated to others the truths he learned. He was the Lord's witness to the world of the power of Bible truth to ennoble daily life.

The efforts of Ezra to revive interest in the study of the Scriptures were given permanency by his painstaking, lifelong work of preserving and multiplying the Sacred Writings. He gathered all the copies he could find and had these transcribed and distributed. The pure Word, placed in the hands of many people, gave knowledge that was of inestimable value.

Ezra's faith led him to tell Artaxerxes of his desire to return to Jerusalem to assist his brethren in restoring the Holy City. As he declared his perfect trust in God, the king was deeply impressed. So great was his confidence in Ezra that he granted his request, bestowing on him rich gifts for the temple, and conferring on him extensive powers for carrying out the purposes in his heart.

The Third Decree Makes Complete Provision

The decree of Artaxerxes for restoring and building Jerusalem, the third since the close of the 70 years' captivity, is remarkable for its expressions regarding God and for the liberality of the grants to the people of God. The king offered freely "unto the God of Israel, whose habitation is in Jerusalem," and he made provision for meeting many heavy expenses "out of the king's treasure house." Verses 15, 20.

"Thou art sent of the king," Artaxerxes declared to Ezra, "to enquire concerning Judah and Jerusalem, according to the law of thy God which is in thine hand." "Whatsoever is commanded by the God of heaven, let it be diligently done for the house of the God of heaven." Verses 14, 23.

Artaxerxes arranged for the restoration of the members of the priesthood to their ancient privileges. "It shall not be lawful to impose toll, tribute, or custom, upon them." He also arranged for civil officers to govern the people. "Thou, Ezra, after the wisdom of thy God, that is in thine hand," he directed, "set magistrates and judges, which may judge all the people that are beyond the river, all such as know the laws of thy God; and teach ye them that know them not." Verses 24, 25.

Thus Ezra had persuaded the king to make provision for the return of all the people of Israel and of the priests and Levites in the Medo-Persian realm, who were minded "of their own freewill to go up to Jerusalem." Verse 13.

This decree brought great rejoicing to those who had been studying with Ezra God's purposes concerning His people. "Blessed be the Lord God of our fathers," Ezra exclaimed, "which hath put such a thing as this in the king's heart. Verse 27.

God's Providence Manifest in Artaxerxes' Decree

In this decree by Artaxerxes, God's providence was manifest. Some discerned this and gladly took advantage of the privilege of returning under circumstances so favorable. A general place of meeting was named, and at the appointed time those going to Jerusalem assembled for the long journey.

But the number who responded was disappointingly small. Many who had acquired houses and lands were satisfied to remain. Their example proved a hindrance to others who might have chosen to advance by faith.

As Ezra looked over the company assembled, he was surprised to find none of the sons of Levi, the tribe set apart for the service of the temple. The Levites should have been the first to respond. During the captivity, they had enjoyed liberty to minister to their brethren in exile. Synagogues had been built; the priests conducted the worship of God and instructed the people. Observance of the Sabbath had been freely allowed.

But after the close of the captivity, conditions changed. The temple at Jerusalem had been rebuilt and dedicated, and more priests were needed as teachers of the people. Besides, the Jews in Babylon were in danger of having their religious liberty restricted. During the troublous times of Esther and Mordecai, the Jews in Medo-Persia had been plainly warned to return to their own land. It was perilous for them to dwell longer in the midst of heathen influences. In view of these changed conditions, the priests in Babylon should have been quick to discern in the decree a special call to return to Jerusalem.

The king and his princes had provided abundant means, but where were the sons of Levi? A decision to accompany their brethren would have led others to follow their example. Their strange indifference is a sad revelation of the attitude of the Israelites in Babylon toward God's purpose for his people.

Once more Ezra sent the Levites an urgent invitation to unite with his company. Trusted messengers hastened with the plea, ''Bring unto us ministers for the house of our God.'' Ezra 8:17. Some who had been halting decided to return. In all, about 40 priests and 220 ministers, teachers, and helpers were brought to the camp.

All were now ready. Before them was a journey of several months. The men were taking their wives and children, their substance, and treasure for the temple. Enemies lay in wait, ready to plunder and destroy Ezra and his company, yet he had asked from the king no armed force for protection. "I was ashamed," he explained, "to ask the king for a band of soldiers and horsemen to protect us against the enemy on our way; since we had told the king, 'The hand of our God is for good upon all that seek Him, and the power of His wrath is against all that forsake Him.' " Verse 22, RSV.

They therefore determined to put their trust wholly in God. They would ask for no soldiers. They would not arouse in the minds of their heathen friends one doubt as to the sincerity of their dependence on God. Strength would be gained not through the power of men, but through the favor of God. Only by striving to obey the law of the Lord would they be protected.

This knowledge lent solemnity to the consecration service held by Ezra and his company just before their departure. "I proclaimed a fast there, at the river of Ahava," Ezra declared, "that we might afflict ourselves before our God, to seek of Him a right way for us, and for our little ones, and for all our substance. . . . So we fasted and besought our God for this: and He was intreated of us." Verses 21-23.

Only the Trustworthy Are Chosen

The blessing of God, however, did not make unnecessary the exercise of prudence and forethought. In safeguarding the treasure, Ezra "separated twelve of the chief of the priests . . . and weighed unto them the silver, and the gold, and the vessels, even the offering of the house of our God." Verses 24, 25. These men were solemnly charged to act as vigilant stewards over the treasure. "Guard them and keep them until you weigh them before the chief priests and the Levites and the heads of fathers' houses in Israel at Jerusalem." Verse 29, RSV.

Only those whose trustworthiness had been proved were chosen. Ezra recognized the necessity of order and organization in the work of God.

"We departed," Ezra writes, "on the twelfth day of the first month, to go unto Jerusalem: and the hand of our God was upon us, and He delivered us from the hand of the enemy, and of such as lay in wait by the way." Verse 31. About four months were occupied on the journey. Their enemies were restrained from harming them, and on the first day of the fifth month, in the seventh year of Artaxerxes, they reached Jerusalem.

51 / Ezra Sparks a Spiritual Revival

Ezra's arrival in Jerusalem brought courage and hope to many who had long labored under difficulties. Since the return of the first exiles more than seventy years before, much had been accomplished. The temple had been finished, the walls of the city had been partially repaired. Yet much remained undone.

Many of the exiles had remained true to God, but a considerable number of the children and grandchildren lost sight of the sacredness of God's law. Even some entrusted with responsibilities were living in open sin. Their course was largely neutralizing efforts to advance the cause of God, for so long as flagrant violations of the law were unrebuked, the blessing of Heaven could not rest on the people.

Those who returned with Ezra had had special seasons of seeking the Lord. Their journey from Babylon, unprotected by any human power, had taught them rich spiritual lessons. Many had grown strong in faith, and as these mingled with the discouraged and indifferent in Jerusalem, their influence was a powerful factor in the reform soon instituted.

Soon a few of the chief men of Israel approached Ezra with a serious complaint. Some of "the people of Israel, and the priests, and the Levites" had so far disregarded the holy commands of Jehovah as to intermarry with the surrounding peoples. "They have taken of their daughters for themselves, and for their sons," Ezra was told, "so that the holy seed have mingled themselves with the people" of heathen lands; "yea, the hand of the princes and rulers hath been chief in this trespass.'' Ezra 9:1, 2.

Ezra had learned that Israel's apostasy was largely traceable to their mingling with heathen nations. He had seen that if they had kept separate, they would have been spared many sad experiences. Now when he learned that men of prominence had dared transgress the laws given as a safeguard against apostasy, his heart was stirred. He was overwhelmed with righteous indignation. "When I heard this, I rent my garment and my mantle. . . . Then all who trembled at the words of the God of Israel, because of the faithlessness of the returned exiles, gathered round me." Verses 3, 4, RSV.

At the time of the evening sacrifice Ezra fell on his knees and unburdened his soul to Heaven. "O my God, I am ashamed and blush to lift my face to Thee," he exclaimed. Verse 6. "From the days of our fathers to this day we have been in great guilt; and for our iniquities we, our kings, and our priests have been given into the hand of the kings of the lands, to the sword, to captivity, to plundering, and to utter shame, as at this day." "For we are bondmen; yet our God has not forsaken us in our bondage, but has extended to us His steadfast love before the kings of Persia, to grant us some reviving to set up the house of our God, to repair its ruins, and to give us protection in Judea and Jerusalem." "Shall we break Thy commandments again and intermarry with the peoples who practice these abominations?" Verses 7, 9, 14, RSV.

The Beginning of Reformation

The sorrow of Ezra and his associates wrought repentance. Many who had sinned were deeply affected. "The people wept very sore." Ezra 10:1. They saw the sacredness of the law spoken at Sinai, and many trembled at the thought of their transgressions.

One of those present, Shechaniah, acknowledged as true the words spoken by Ezra. "We have broken faith with our God," he confessed, "and have married foreign women from the peoples of the land." Shechaniah proposed that all who had transgressed should forsake their sin and be adjudged "according to the law." "Arise," he told Ezra, "for it is your task, and we are with you; be strong and do it." Verses 2-4, RSV.

This was the beginning of a wonderful reformation. With tact and careful consideration for the rights and welfare of every individual concerned, Ezra and his associates strove to lead Israel into the right way. Ezra gave personal attention to every case. He sought to impress the people with the holiness of the law and the blessings to be gained through obedience.

Wherever Ezra labored, there sprang up a revival in the study of the Scriptures. The law of the Lord was exalted and made honorable. The passages in the books of the prophets foretelling the coming of the Messiah brought hope to many a heart.

In this age of the world, when Satan is seeking to blind the eyes of men and women to the claims of the law of God, there is need of men who can cause many to "tremble at the commandment of our God." Verse 3. There is need of men mighty in the Scriptures, men who seek to strengthen faith. Teachers are needed who will inspire hearts with love for the Scriptures!

The Cause of Corruption: Setting Aside God's Law

When the Word of God is set aside, its power to restrain the evil passions of the natural heart is rejected. Men sow to the flesh and of the flesh reap corruption. With setting aside the Bible has come a turning away from God's law, weakening the force of moral obligation and opening the floodgates of iniquity. Lawlessness and dissipation are sweeping in like an overwhelming flood. Everywhere are seen hypocrisy, estrangement, strife, and indulgence of lust. The whole system of religious principles, the foundation and framework of social life, seems ready to fall in ruins.

Man has set his will against the will of God, but the

human mind cannot evade its obligation to a higher power. Men may try to set science in opposition to revelation, and thus do away with God's law, but still stronger comes the command, *"Thou shalt worship the Lord thy God, and Him only shalt thou serve."* Matthew 4:10. There is no such thing as weakening or strengthening the law of God. It always has been, and always will be, holy, just, and good. It cannot be repealed or changed.

We Are Entering the Last Battle of the Controversy

We are now entering on the last great battle of the controversy between truth and error—a battle not between rival churches but between the religion of the Bible and the religions of tradition. God's Holy Word, which has been handed down to us at so great a cost of suffering and bloodshed, is little valued. Creation as presented by the inspired writers, the fall of man, the atonement, the perpetuity of the law—these doctrines are practically rejected by a large share of the professedly Christian world. Thousands regard it as weakness to place implicit confidence in the Bible, and a proof of learning to spiritualize and explain away its most important truths.

God calls for a revival and a reformation. The words of the Bible alone should be heard from the pulpit. In many sermons today there is not that divine manifestation which awakens the conscience and brings life to the soul. The hearers cannot say, "Did not our heart burn within us, while He talked with us by the way, and while He opened to us the Scriptures?" Luke 24:32. Let the word of God speak to the heart. Let those who have heard only tradition and human theories hear the voice of Him who can renew the soul unto eternal life.

The Reformers, whose protest has given us the name of Protestant, felt that God had called them to give the gospel to the world, and to do this they were ready to sacrifice possessions, liberty, even life itself. In the face of persecution and death, the Word of God was carried to all classes, high and low, rich and poor, learned and ignorant. Are we, in this last conflict of the great controversy, as faithful as the early Reformers?

"Blow the trumpet in Zion. . . . Let the priests, the ministers of the Lord, weep and say, 'Spare Thy people, O Lord, and make not Thy heritage a reproach.' " Joel 2:15-17, RSV.

52 / Nehemiah, Man of Prayer and Action

Nehemiah, one of the Hebrew exiles, occupied a position of influence in the Persian court and was admitted freely to the royal presence. He had become the monarch's friend and counselor. However, though surrounded by pomp and splendor, he did not forget God nor His people. His heart turned toward Jerusalem. Through this man God purposed to bring blessing to His people.

By messengers from Judea the Hebrew patriot learned that the returned exiles in the chosen city were suffering. The work of restoration was hindered, the temple services were disturbed, and the walls of the city were still largely in ruins. Overwhelmed with sorrow, Nehemiah could neither eat nor drink. In grief he turned to the divine Helper. "I prayed before the God of heaven." He pleaded that God would maintain the cause of Israel, restore their courage and strength, and help them build up the waste places.

As Nehemiah prayed, his faith and courage grew. He pointed to the dishonor that would be cast on God if His people should be left in weakness and oppression. He urged the Lord to bring to pass His promise given to Israel through Moses before they entered Canaan. See Deuteronomy 4:29-31. God's people had now returned to Him in penitence, and His promise would not fail.

Now Nehemiah resolved that if he could obtain the

This chapter is based on Nehemiah 1 and 2.

326 / FROM SPLENDOR TO SHADOW

consent of the king and the necessary material, he would himself undertake the task of rebuilding the walls of Jerusalem and restoring Israel's national strength. And he asked the Lord to grant him the king's favor that his plan might be carried out. "Prosper, I pray Thee, Thy servant this day," he entreated, "and grant him mercy in the sight of this man."

Nehemiah Waits for God's Opportunity

Four months Nehemiah waited to present his request to the king. Though his heart was heavy with grief, he endeavored to be cheerful in the royal presence. In those halls of luxury all must appear lighthearted and happy. But in Nehemiah's seasons of retirement, concealed from human sight, many were the prayers and tears heard and witnessed by God and angels.

At length sleepless nights and care-filled days left their trace on his countenance. The king, jealous for his own safety, was accustomed to read countenances and to penetrate disguises. He saw that some secret trouble was preying on his cupbearer. "Why is thy countenance sad," he inquired, "seeing thou art not sick? this is nothing else but sorrow of heart."

Would not the king be angry that while outwardly engaged in his service, the courtier's thoughts had been far away with his afflicted people? His cherished plan for restoring Jerusalem—was it about to be overthrown? "Then," he writes, "I was very sore afraid." With tearful eyes he revealed the cause of his sorrow: "Why should not my countenance be sad, when the city, the place of my fathers' sepulchers, lieth waste, and the gates thereof are consumed with fire?"

The sympathy of the monarch was awakened. "For what dost thou make request?"

The man of God did not venture to reply till he had sought direction from One higher than Artaxerxes. He required help from the king, and he realized that much depended on his presenting the matter in such a way as to enlist his aid. "I prayed," he said, "to the God of heaven." In that brief prayer Nehemiah pressed into the presence of the King of kings and won to his side a power that can turn hearts as the rivers of waters are turned.

Toilers in the busy walks of life, almost overwhelmed with perplexity, can send up a petition to God for divine guidance. Travelers when threatened with some great danger can commit themselves to Heaven's protection. In times of sudden difficulty the heart may send up its cry for help to One who has pledged to come to the aid of His believing ones when they call on Him. The soul fiercely assailed by temptation may find support in the unfailing power and love of a covenant-keeping God.

God Gave Nehemiah Courage

In that brief moment of prayer Nehemiah gathered courage to ask Artaxerxes for authority to build up Jerusalem and make it once more a strong city. Momentous results to the Jewish nation hung on this request. "And," Nehemiah declared, "the king granted me what I asked, for the good hand of my God was upon me." RSV.

Nehemiah proceeded to make arrangements to ensure the success of the enterprise. While he knew that many of his countrymen would rejoice in his success, he feared that some might arouse the jealousy of their enemies and perhaps bring about the defeat of the undertaking.

His request to the king had been so favorably received that Nehemiah was encouraged to ask for still further assistance. He asked for a military escort to give authority to his mission. He obtained royal letters to the governors of the territory through which he must pass on his way to Judea and a letter to the keeper of the king's forest in Lebanon directing him to furnish timber. Nehemiah was careful to have the authority accorded him clearly defined. God's children are not only to pray for faith but to work with diligent and provident care.

Nehemiah did not regard his duty done when he had wept and prayed before the Lord. He united his petitions with holy endeavor. The means that Nehemiah lacked he solicited from those able to bestow. And the Lord is still willing to move on the hearts of those in possession of His goods, in behalf of the cause of truth. Those who labor for Him are to avail themselves of these gifts by which the light of truth shall go to many benighted lands. The donors may have no faith in Christ, no acquaintance with His Word; but their gifts are not on this account to be refused.

53 / Nehemiah Accomplishes the "Impossible"

The royal letters to the governors of the provinces along Nehemiah's route secured him prompt assistance. No enemy dared molest the official guarded by the power of the Persian king!

However, his arrival in Jerusalem with a military escort, showing that he had come on some important mission, excited the jealousy of heathen tribes who had often heaped on the Jews injury and insult. Foremost in this evil work were certain chiefs of these tribes, Sanballat, Tobiah, and Geshem. These leaders watched Nehemiah with critical eyes and endeavored to thwart and hinder his work.

Knowing that bitter enemies stood ready to oppose him, Nehemiah concealed his mission from them until a study of the situation should enable him to form his plans. He hoped to set the people at work before his enemies could be aroused.

Choosing a few men whom he knew, Nehemiah told them of the object that he wished to accomplish and the plans he proposed. Their interest and assistance were at once enlisted.

On the third night after his arrival Nehemiah rose at midnight and with a few trusted companions went out to view the desolation of Jerusalem. On his mule, he passed from one part of the city to another, surveying the broken-down walls and gates of the city. Painful reflections filled his sorrow-stricken heart as he gazed

This chapter is based on Nehemiah 2, 3, and 4.

on the ruined defenses of Jerusalem. Memories of Israel's past greatness stood in sharp contrast with the evidences of her humiliation.

In secrecy and silence Nehemiah completed his circuit. "And the officials did not know where I had gone or what I was doing; and I had not yet told the Jews, the priests, the nobles, the officials, and the rest that were to do the work." RSV. The remainder of the night he spent in prayer, for the morning would call for earnest effort to arouse his dispirited countrymen.

Nehemiah bore a royal commission requiring the inhabitants to cooperate in rebuilding the walls of the city, but he sought rather to gain the sympathy of the people, knowing that a union of hearts was essential in the work. When he called the people together he presented arguments calculated to unite their scattered numbers.

Nehemiah's hearers did not know of his midnight circuit the night before. But the fact that he was able to speak of the condition of the city with accuracy and minuteness astonished them.

How Nehemiah Won Support

Nehemiah presented before the people their reproach among the heathen—their religion dishonored, their God blasphemed. He told them that in a distant land he had entreated the favor of Heaven in their behalf and had determined to ask permission from the king to come to their assistance. He had asked God that the king might also invest him with authority and give him the help needed for the work. And his prayer had been answered in such a way as to show that the plan was of the Lord!

Then Nehemiah asked the people directly whether they would take advantage of this opportunity and arise and build the wall. With new courage they said with one voice, "Let us rise up and build. So they strengthened their hands for this good work."

Nehemiah's enthusiasm and determination were

contagious. Each man became a Nehemiah in his turn and helped to make stronger the heart and hand of his neighbor.

When Israel's enemies heard what the Jews were hoping to accomplish, they laughed. "What is this thing that ye do? Will ye rebel against the king?" But Nehemiah answered, "The God of heaven, He will prosper us; therefore we His servants will arise and build."

Nehemiah's Example Wins the Day

Among the first to catch Nehemiah's spirit were the priests. Because of their influential position, these men could advance or hinder the work; and their cooperation at the outset contributed not a little to its success. The majority came up nobly to their duty, and these faithful men have honorable mention in the book of God. But a few, the Tekoite nobles, "put not their necks to the work of their Lord." In every religious movement some hold themselves aloof, refusing to help. In the record kept on high every neglected opportunity to do service for God is recorded; and there, too, every deed of faith and love is held in everlasting remembrance.

The people in general were animated by patriotism and zeal. Men of ability organized the citizens into companies, each a leader responsible for a certain part of the wall. Some built "each one opposite his own house." RSV. With tireless vigilance Nehemiah superintended the building, noting the hindrances and providing for emergencies. Along the whole of that three miles of wall his influence was constantly felt. He encouraged the fearful, aroused the laggard, and approved the diligent. And ever he watched the movements of their enemies at a distance engaged in conversation, as if plotting mischief.

Nehemiah did not forget the Source of his strength. His heart was constantly uplifted to the great Overseer of all. "The God of heaven," he exclaimed, "He will prosper us." The words thrilled the hearts of all the workers on the wall.

But Sanballat, Tobiah, and Geshem endeavored to cause division among the workmen. They ridiculed the efforts of the builders, predicting failure. "What are these feeble Jews doing?" exclaimed Sanballat mockingly. "Will they restore things? . . . Will they revive the stones out of the heaps of rubbish, and burned ones at that?" Tobiah added, "Yes, what they are building—if a fox goes up on it he will break down their stone wall!" RSV.

The builders were soon compelled to guard continually against the plots of their adversaries, who formed conspiracies to draw Nehemiah into their toils. Falsehearted Jews aided the treacherous undertaking. The report was spread that Nehemiah was plotting against the Persian monarch, intending to exalt himself as king over Israel and that all who aided him were traitors.

But "the people had a mind to work." The enterprise went forward until the gaps were filled and the entire wall built up to half its intended height.

Building With One Hand, Fighting With the Other

The enemies of Israel were filled with rage. They had not dared employ violent measures, for they knew of the king's commission and feared that active opposition against Nehemiah might bring on them the monarch's displeasure. But now they themselves became guilty of the crime of which they had accused Nehemiah. They "conspired all of them together to come and to fight against Jerusalem." At the same time some of the leading Jews, disaffected, sought to discourage Nehemiah. "The strength of the bearers of burdens is decayed, and there is much rubbish; so that we are not able to build the wall."

Discouragement came from still another source: "The Jews who lived by them," taking no part in the work, gathered up the reports of their enemies to create disaffection. But ridicule and threats only inspired Nehemiah to greater watchfulness. His courage was undaunted. "We prayed to our God," he declares, "and set a guard as a protection against them day and night." "So in the lowest parts of the space behind the wall, in open places, I stationed the people according to their families, with their swords, their spears, and their bows. And I . . . said to the nobles and to the officials and to the rest of the people, 'Do not be afraid of them. Remember the Lord, who is great and terrible, and fight for your brethren, your sons, your daughters, your wives, and your homes.' " RSV.

"We all returned to the wall, each to his work. From that day on, half of my servants worked on construction, and half held the spears, shields, bows, and coats of mail. . . . Those who carried burdens were laden in such a way that each with one hand labored on the work and with the other held his weapon." RSV.

On different parts of the wall were stationed priests bearing the sacred trumpets. On the approach of danger at any point a signal was given. "So we labored in the work: and half of them held the spears from the rising of the morning till the stars appeared."

Those who had been living outside Jerusalem were now required to lodge within the walls, to guard the work and to be ready for duty in the morning. This would prevent the enemy from attacking the workmen as they went to and from their homes. Not even during the short time given to sleep did Nehemiah and his companions put off their clothing or lay aside their armor.

The opposition that the builders in Nehemiah's day met from open enemies and pretended friends is typical of the experience that those today will have who work for God. Derision and reproach are hurled at them, and at a favorable opportunity, the enemy uses more cruel and violent measures.

Among those who profess to support God's cause are those who lay His cause open to the attacks of His bitterest foes. Even some who desire the work of God to prosper will weaken the hands of His servants by reporting and half believing the slanders of His adversaries. But, like Nehemiah, God's people are neither to fear nor to despise their enemies. Putting their trust in God, they are to go steadily forward, committing to His providence the cause for which they stand.

In every crisis God's people may confidently declare, "If God be for us, who can be against us?" Romans 8:31. However craftily the plots of Satan may be laid, God can bring to nought all their counsels. He is in the work, and no man can prevent its ultimate success.

54 / Nehemiah Bravely Rebukes Selfishness

Nehemiah's attention was called to the unhappy condition of the poorer classes of people. There was a scarcity of grain. In order to obtain food the poor were obliged to buy on credit at exorbitant prices. They also were compelled to borrow on interest to pay the heavy taxes imposed by Persia. To add to the distress, the more wealthy among the Jews had taken advantage of their necessities, thus enriching themselves.

The Lord had commanded that every third year a tithe be raised for the benefit of the poor and that every seventh year the spontaneous products of the land be left to those in need. Faithfulness in devoting these offerings to the relief of the poor would have kept fresh before the people God's ownership of all, eradicating selfishness and developing character. "Thou shalt not lend upon usury to thy brother; usury of money, usury of victuals, usury of anything." Deuteronomy 23:19. "For the poor shall never cease out of the land: therefore I command thee, saying, Thou shalt open thine hand wide unto thy brother, to thy poor, and to thy needy, in thy land." Deuteronomy 15:11.

Wealthy Jews had gone directly contrary to these commands. When the poor were obliged to borrow to pay tribute to the king, the wealthy had exacted high interest. By taking mortgages they had reduced the debtors to deep poverty. Many had been forced to sell their sons and daughters into servitude, and there

This chapter is based on Nehemiah 5.

seemed no prospect before them but perpetual want and bondage.

At length the people presented their condition before Nehemiah: "Some of our daughters have already been enslaved; but it is not in our power to help it, for other men have our fields and our vineyards." RSV.

Nehemiah's soul was filled with indignation. "I was very angry when I heard their cry and these words." He saw that he must take a decided stand for justice.

The oppressors were men of wealth whose support was needed in restoring the city. But Nehemiah sharply rebuked the nobles and rulers, and he set before the people the requirements of God. He called their attention to events in the reign of King Ahaz. Because of their idolatry, Judah had been delivered into the hands of still more idolatrous Israel. The latter had seized women and children, intending to keep them as slaves or sell them to the heathen. Because of the sins of Judah, the Lord had not interposed, but by the prophet Oded He rebuked the victorious army: "You intend to subjugate the people of Judah and Jerusalem, male and female, as your slaves. Have you not sins of your own against the Lord your God?" 2 Chronicles 28:10, RSV.

Upon hearing these words, the armed men left the captives and spoil before the congregation. Then leading men of Ephraim "took the captives, and with the spoil clothed all that were naked among them, and arrayed them, and shod them, and gave them to eat and to drink, and anointed them, and carried all the feeble of them upon asses, and brought them to Jericho . . . to their brethren." Verse 15.

Nehemiah and others had ransomed certain Jews who had been sold to the heathen, and he now placed this course in contrast with the conduct of those who for gain were enslaving their brethren. He himself, invested with authority from the Persian king, might have demanded large contributions for his personal benefit. But instead he had given liberally to relieve the poor. He urged those guilty of extortion to restore the lands of the poor and the increase of money exacted from them, and to lend to them without security or usury.

"We will restore them," the rulers declared, "and will require nothing of them; so will we do as thou sayest." "And all the congregation said, Amen, and praised the Lord. And the people did according to this promise."

The Gospel Can Cure Modern Economic Injustice

This record teaches an important lesson. In this generation wealth is often obtained by fraud. Multitudes are struggling with poverty, compelled to labor for small wages, unable to secure even the necessities of life. Careworn and oppressed, they know not where to turn for relief. And all this that the rich may support their extravagance or indulge their desire to hoard!

Love of money and display has made this world a den of thieves. "Come now, you rich," James wrote. "You have laid up treasure for the last days. Behold, the wages of the laborers who mowed your fields, which you kept back by fraud, cry out; and the cries of the harvesters have reached the ears of the Lord of hosts. You have lived on the earth in luxury and in pleasure; you have fattened your hearts in a day of slaughter." James 5:1, 3-5, RSV.

Even some who profess to fear God are acting over again the course pursued by the nobles of Israel. Because it is in their power to do so, they become oppressors. And because avarice is seen in the lives of those who have named the name of Christ, the religion of Christ is held in contempt. Extravagance and extortion are corrupting the faith of many and destroying their spirituality. The church gives countenance to evil if she fails to lift her voice against it.

Every unjust act is a violation of the golden rule—done to Christ Himself in the person of His saints. Every attempt to take advantage of the ignorance or misfortune of another is registered as fraud in the ledger of heaven. Just to the extent that a man would gain advantage for himself at the disadvantage of another, will his soul become insensible to the influence of the Spirit of God.

The Son of God paid the price of our redemption. He became poor that through His poverty we might be rich. By deeds of liberality to the poor we may prove the sincerity of our gratitude: ''Let us do good unto all men, especially unto them who are of the household of faith.'' Galatians 6:10. ''Whatsoever ye would that men should do to you, do ye even so to them: for this is the law and the prophets.'' Matthew 7:12.

55 / Union With the World Hinders God's Cause

Sanballat and his confederates with increasing malice continued their secret efforts to discourage and injure the Jews. When the wall about Jerusalem should be finished and its gates set up, these enemies could not force an entrance into the city. They were eager, therefore, to stop the work. At last they devised a plan to draw Nehemiah from his station and to kill or imprison him.

Pretending to desire a compromise, they invited him to meet them in a village on the plain of Ono. But enlightened by the Holy Spirit as to their real purpose, he refused. "I sent messengers unto them," he writes, "saying, I am doing a great work, so that I cannot come down: why should the work cease, whilst I leave it, and come down to you?" Four times the tempters sent a message of similar import, and each time received the same answer.

Finding this unsuccessful, they resorted to a more daring stratagem. Sanballat sent an open letter which said: "It is reported among the heathen, and Gashmu saith it, that thou and the Jews think to rebel: for which cause thou buildest the wall, that thou mayest be their king. . . . And thou hast also appointed prophets to preach of thee at Jerusalem, saying, There is a king in Judah: and now shall it be reported to the king according to these words. Come now therefore, and let us take counsel together."

Nehemiah was convinced that the reports mentioned in the letter were wholly false. This conclusion was strengthened by the fact that the letter was sent open,

This chapter is based on Nehemiah 6.

evidently that the people might read the contents and become alarmed and intimidated. He promptly returned the answer: "No such things as you say have been done, for you are inventing them out of your own mind." RSV. Nehemiah knew that these attempts were made in order to weaken the hands of the builders and thus to frustrate their efforts.

Now Satan laid a still more subtle and dangerous snare for the servant of God. Sanballat hired men who professed to be friends of Nehemiah, to give him evil counsel as the word of the Lord. The chief one was Shemaiah, previously held in good repute by Nehemiah. This man shut himself in a chamber near the sanctuary as if fearing that his life was in danger. The temple was protected by walls and gates, but the gates of the city were not yet set up. Professing great concern for Nehemiah's safety, Shemaiah advised him, "Let us meet together in the house of God, within the temple, and let us shut the doors of the temple: for . . . in the night they will come to slay thee."

Had Nehemiah followed this treacherous counsel, he would have sacrificed his faith in God and would have appeared cowardly. In view of the confidence he professed to have in the power of God, it would have been inconsistent for him to hide. The alarm would have spread among the people, each would have sought his own safety, and the city would have been left to its enemies. That one unwise move on the part of Nehemiah would have been a virtual surrender of all that had been gained.

God's Servant Sees Through the Plot

Nehemiah penetrated the true object of his counselor. "I perceived that God had not sent him," he says, "but that he pronounced this prophecy against me: for Tobiah and Sanballat had hired him . . . that I should be afraid, and do so, and sin, and that they might have matter for an evil report."

Shemaiah's counsel was seconded by more than one

of Nehemiah's "friends" who were secretly in league with his enemies. But Nehemiah's fearless answer was: "Should such a man as I flee? And who is there, that, being as I am, would go into the temple to save his life? I will not go in."

Notwithstanding enemies, in less than two months from Nehemiah's arrival in Jerusalem the builders could walk on the walls and look down on their defeated and astonished foes. "When all our enemies heard thereof," Nehemiah writes, "they were much cast down in their own eyes: for they perceived that this work was wrought of our God."

Yet even this evidence of the Lord's controlling hand was not sufficient to restrain rebellion and treachery among the Israelites. "The nobles of Judah sent many letters unto Tobiah, and the letters of Tobiah came unto them. For there were many in Judah sworn unto him, because he was the son-in-law of Shechaniah." A family of Judah had intermarried with the enemies of God, and the relation had proved a snare. Others had done the same. These were a source of constant trouble.

The nobles of Judah who had become entangled in idolatrous marriages and who had held traitorous correspondence with Tobiah now represented him as a man of ability and foresight, an alliance with whom would be to the advantage of the Jews. At the same time they betrayed Nehemiah's plans to him. Thus opportunity was given to misconstrue Nehemiah's words and acts and to hinder his work.

Satan's assaults have ever been directed against those who advance the work of God. Though often baffled, he renews his attacks with fresh vigor, using means hitherto untried. But it is his secret working through the "friends" of God's work that is most to be feared. Open opposition may be fierce and cruel, but it is fraught with far less peril to God's cause than is the secret enmity of those who, while professing to serve God, are at heart the servants of Satan.

Every device that the prince of darkness can suggest will be employed to induce God's servants to form a confederacy with the agents of Satan. But, like Nehemiah, they should reply, "I am doing a great work, so that I cannot come down." God's workers must refuse to be diverted from their work by threats or mockery or falsehood. Enemies are continually on their track. Ever they must "set a watch against them day and night." Nehemiah 4:9.

As the time of the end draws near, Satan will employ human agents to mock and revile those who "build the wall." The builders should endeavor to defeat the purposes of their adversaries, but they should not allow anything—neither friendship nor sympathy—to call them from their work. He who by any unguarded act weakens the hands of fellow workers brings on his own character a stain not easily removed and places a serious obstacle in the way of his future usefulness.

"They that forsake the law praise the wicked." Proverbs 28:4. When those who are uniting with the world plead for union with those who have ever been the opposers of the cause of truth, we should shun them as decidedly as did Nehemiah. Such counsel should be resisted resolutely. Whatever influence would tend to unsettle the faith of God's people in His guiding power should be steadfastly withstood.

In Nehemiah's firm reliance on God lay the reason of the failure of his enemies to draw him into their power. In the life that has a noble aim, an absorbing purpose, evil finds little foothold. God's true servants work with a determination that will not fail, because the throne of grace is their constant dependence. God gives the Holy Spirit to help in every strait. If His people are watching the indications of providence and are ready to cooperate, they will see mighty results.

56 / The Joy of Forgiveness and Healing

It was the time of the Feast of Trumpets. Many were gathered at Jerusalem. The wall had been rebuilt and the gates set up, but a large part of the city was still in ruins.

On a platform erected in one of the broadest streets, surrounded by sad reminders of Judah's departed glory, stood Ezra, now an aged man. At his right and left were gathered his brother Levites. From all the surrounding country the children of the covenant had assembled. "And Ezra blessed the Lord, the great God. And all the people answered, Amen, . . . and they bowed their heads, and worshiped the Lord."

Yet even here was evidence of sin. Through intermarriage of the people with other nations, the Hebrew language had become corrupted, and great care was necessary on the part of the speakers to explain the law in language understood by all. Certain priests united with Ezra in explaining its principles. "They read in the book in the law of God distinctly, and gave the sense, and caused them to understand the reading."

The people listened, intent and reverent, to the words of the Most High. They were convinced of their guilt and mourned because of their transgressions. But this was a day of rejoicing, a holy convocation which the Lord had commanded the people to keep with gladness and to rejoice because of God's great mercy to them. "This day is holy unto the Lord your God; mourn not, nor weep. . . . Send portions unto them for whom nothing is prepared: for this day is holy unto our

This chapter is based on Nehemiah 8, 9, and 10.

Lord: neither be ye sorry; for the joy of the Lord is your strength.''

Part of the day was devoted to religious exercises. The remainder of the time was spent enjoying the bounties God had provided. Portions were also sent to the poor. The words of the law had been read and understood.

On the tenth day of the seventh month the services of the Day of Atonement were performed. From the fifteenth to the twenty-second of the month the people and their rulers kept the Feast of Tabernacles. ''In all their towns and in Jerusalem . . . the people . . . made booths for themselves, each on his roof, and in their courts and in the courts of the house of God. . . . And there was very great rejoicing. And day by day, from the first day to the last day, . . . [Ezra] read from the book of the law of God.'' RSV.

As they had listened from day to day to the words of the law, the people had been convicted of the sins of their nation in past generations. It was because of departure from God that His protecting care had been withdrawn and the children of Abraham had been scattered in foreign lands. They determined to pledge themselves to walk in His commandments. Before entering on this solemn service, they separated themselves from the heathen among them.

Their leaders encouraged them to believe that God, according to His promise, heard their prayers. They must not only repent, they must believe that God pardoned them. They must show their faith by praising Him for His goodness. ''Stand up,'' said these teachers, ''and bless the Lord your God.''

Then from the assembled throng, as they stood with outstretched hands toward heaven, arose the song:

Blessed be Thy glorious name,
Which is exalted above all blessing and praise.
Thou, even Thou, art Lord alone; . . .
And the host of heaven worshipeth Thee.

The song ended, the leaders related the history of Israel, showing how great had been God's goodness and how great their ingratitude. They had suffered punishment for their sins. Now they acknowledged God's justice and pledged to obey His law. A memorial of the obligation they had taken on themselves was written out, and the priests, Levites, and princes signed it as a reminder of duty and a barrier against temptation. The people took a solemn oath "to observe and do all the commandments of the Lord our Lord, and His judgments and His statutes." The oath included a promise not to intermarry with the people of the land.

The people still further manifested their determination to return to the Lord by pledging to cease from desecrating the Sabbath. In an effort to save the people from yielding to temptation, Nehemiah bound them by a solemn covenant not to transgress the Sabbath by purchasing from the heathen traders, hoping that this would put an end to the traffic.

Provision was also made to support the public worship of God. In addition to the tithe the congregation pledged to contribute yearly a stated sum for the service of the sanctuary. "We cast the lots," Nehemiah writes, "to bring the first fruits of our ground, and the first fruits of all fruit of all trees, year by year, unto the house of the Lord."

Israel had returned to God with deep sorrow for backsliding. Now they must manifest faith in His promises. God had accepted their repentance; they were now to rejoice in the assurance of sins forgiven and their restoration to divine favor.

Nehemiah's efforts had been crowned with success. As long as the people were obedient to God's word, so long would the Lord fulfill His promise by pouring rich blessings on them.

For those who are convicted of sin and weighed down with a sense of unworthiness, there are lessons of faith and encouragement in this record. The Bible faithfully presents Israel's apostasy, but it portrays also the deep repentance, the earnest devotion and sacrifice, that marked their return to the Lord.

When a sinner yields to the Holy Spirit, he sees himself as a transgressor. But he is not to give way to despair, for his pardon has already been secured. It is God's glory to encircle repentant human beings in the arms of His love, to bind up their wounds, to cleanse them, and to clothe them with salvation.

57 / Nehemiah's Painful Work of Reformation

The people of Judah had pledged to obey the law of God. But when the influence of Ezra and Nehemiah was for a time withdrawn, many departed from the Lord. Nehemiah had returned to Persia. During his absence from Jerusalem, evils crept in that threatened to pervert the nation. Idolaters contaminated the very precincts of the temple. Through intermarriage, a friendship had been brought about between Eliashib, the high priest, and Tobiah, the Ammonite, Israel's bitter enemy. As a result of this unhallowed alliance, Tobiah occupied an apartment connected with the temple, which had been used as a storeroom for tithes and offerings.

Because of the treachery of the Ammonites toward Israel, God had declared that they should be forever shut out from the congregation of His people. See Deuteronomy 23:3-6. In defiance of this the high priest had cast out the offerings stored in God's house to make a place for this enemy of God and His truth. Greater contempt for God could not have been shown!

On returning from Persia, Nehemiah took prompt measures to expel the intruder. "I cast forth all the household stuff of Tobiah out of the chamber. Then I commanded, and they cleansed the chambers: and thither brought I again the vessels of the house of God."

The temple had been profaned and the offerings

This chapter is based on Nehemiah 13.

misapplied. This had discouraged the liberality of the people. The treasuries of the Lord's house were poorly supplied; many employed in the temple, not receiving sufficient support, had left the work of God to labor elsewhere.

Nehemiah set to work to correct these abuses. This inspired the people with confidence, and all Judah brought "the tithe of the corn and the new wine and the oil." Men who "were counted faithful" were made treasurers, "and their office was to distribute unto their brethren."

Another result of mingling with idolaters was a disregard of the Sabbath. Nehemiah found that the heathen merchants coming to Jerusalem had induced many Israelites to engage in traffic on the Sabbath. Some could not be persuaded to sacrifice principle, but many dared openly to violate the Sabbath. "In those days," Nehemiah writes, "I saw in Judah men treading wine presses on the Sabbath, and bringing in heaps of grain and loading them on asses; and also wine, grapes, figs, and all kinds of burdens, which they brought into Jerusalem on the Sabbath day. . . . Men of Tyre also, who lived in the city, brought in fish and all kinds of wares and sold them on the Sabbath to the people of Judah." RSV.

The Leaders Had Favored Wrong

A desire to advance their own interests had led the rulers to favor the ungodly. "What evil thing is this that ye do, and profane the Sabbath day?" Nehemiah sternly demanded. "Did not your fathers thus . . . ? yet ye bring more wrath upon Israel by profaning the Sabbath." He then gave command that the gates of Jerusalem should be shut "before the Sabbath" and not opened again till the Sabbath was past.

"The merchants and sellers of all kind of ware lodged without Jerusalem once or twice," hoping to traffic with the people. Nehemiah warned them: "Why lodge ye about the wall? If ye do so again, I will lay hands on you. From that time forth came they no more on the Sabbath.''

Now Nehemiah turned to the danger from intermarriage and association with idolaters. "In those days,'' he writes, "saw I Jews that had married wives of Ashdod, of Ammon, and of Moab: and their children spake half in the speech of Ashdod, and could not speak in the Jews' language.''

Some men who entered into unlawful alliances were rulers to whom the people had a right to look for counsel and example. Foreseeing the ruin before the nation if this evil continued, Nehemiah pointed to the case of Solomon. Among all the nations there had risen no king like this man, yet idolatrous women had turned his heart from God, and his example had corrupted Israel. "Shall we then hearken unto you,'' Nehemiah sternly demanded, "to do all this great evil, to transgress against our God in marrying strange wives?'' Their consciences were aroused, and a work of reformation was begun that brought God's approval and blessing.

Some in sacred office pleaded that they could not bring themselves to separate from their heathen wives. But no respect was shown for rank or position. Whoever refused to sever his connection with idolaters was immediately separated from the service of the Lord. A grandson of the high priest, having married a daughter of the notorious Sanballat, was not only removed from office but banished from Israel.

Constant Struggle With Opposing Elements

How much anguish of soul this needed severity cost the faithful worker for God, the judgment alone will reveal. Only by fasting, humiliation, and prayer was advancement made.

Many who had married idolaters chose to go with them into exile and join the Samaritans. Some who had occupied high positions in the work of God cast in their lot fully with them. The Samaritans promised to adopt more fully the Jewish faith, and the apostates, determined to outdo their former brethren, erected a temple on Mount Gerizim in opposition to the house of God at Jerusalem. Their religion continued to be a mixture of Judaism and heathenism, and their claim to be the people of God was the source of enmity between the two nations from generation to generation.

In the work of reform today, there is need of men who, like Ezra and Nehemiah, will not excuse sin, men who will not hold their peace when wrong is done, nor cover evil with a false charity. Severity to a few may prove mercy to many. They will remember also that in the one who rebukes evil the spirit of Christ should ever be revealed.

Ezra and Nehemiah confessed their sins and the sins of their people as if they themselves were the offenders. Patiently they toiled and suffered. That which made their work most difficult was the secret opposition of pretended friends who lent their influence to the service of evil. These traitors furnished the Lord's enemies with material to use in their warfare on His people. Their rebellious wills were ever at war with the requirements of God.

Nehemiah's success shows what prayer, faith, and wise action will accomplish. Nehemiah was not a priest; he was not a prophet. He was a reformer. It was his aim to set his people right with God. As he came into contact with evil and opposition to right he took so determined a stand that the people could not but recognize his loyalty, his patriotism, and his deep love for God. Seeing this, they were willing to follow where he led.

Industry in a God-appointed duty is an important part of true religion. Decisive action at the right time will gain glorious triumphs, while delay and neglect result in failure and dishonor to God. If the leaders show no zeal, if they are indifferent, the church will be indolent and pleasure-loving; but if they are filled with a holy purpose to serve God and Him alone, the people will be united, hopeful, eager. The pages of God's

Word that describe the hatred, falsehood, and treachery of Sanballat and Tobiah, describe also the devotion and self-sacrifice of Ezra and Nehemiah. We are left free to copy either, as we choose.

"Nehemiahs" Today Lead Out in Sabbath Reformation

The work of reform carried on by Zerubbabel, Ezra, and Nehemiah presents a picture of a work of spiritual restoration in the closing days of this earth's history. Through the remnant of Israel God purposed to preserve in the earth a knowledge of Himself. They were the guardians of true worship, the keepers of the holy oracles. Strong was the opposition they had to meet, heavy the burdens borne by the leaders. But these men moved forward in firm reliance on God, believing that He would cause His truth to triumph.

The spiritual restoration of which the work in Nehemiah's day was a symbol is outlined in the words of Isaiah: "Your ancient ruins shall be rebuilt; you shall raise up the foundations of many generations; you shall be called the repairer of the breach, the restorer of streets to dwell in." Isaiah 58:12, RSV.

A breach has been made in God's law—the wall that He placed around His chosen ones for their protection, and obedience to whose precepts of justice, truth, and purity is to be their perpetual safeguard. The prophet points out the specific work of this remnant people who built the wall: "If you turn back your foot from the Sabbath, from doing your pleasure on My holy day, and call the Sabbath a delight and the holy day of the Lord honorable; if you honor it, not going your own ways, or seeking your own pleasure, or talking idly; then you shall take delight in the Lord, and I will make you ride upon the heights of the earth." Isaiah 58:13, 14, RSV.

In the time of the end every divine institution is to be restored. The breach made in the law at the time the Sabbath was changed by man is to be repaired. God's remnant people are to show that the law of God is the foundation of all enduring reform. In clear, distinct lines they are to present the necessity of obedience to all the precepts of the Decalogue. Constrained by the love of Christ, they are to cooperate with Him in building up the waste places. They are to be repairers of the breach, restorers of paths to dwell in.

58 / Darkness Precedes the Dawn

Through the long centuries from the day our first parents lost their Eden home, to the time the Son of God appeared as the Saviour, the hope of the fallen race was centered in the coming of a Deliverer to free men and women from the bondage of sin and the grave.

Hope was given first to Adam and Eve in Eden when the Lord declared to Satan, ''I will put enmity between thee and the woman, and between thy seed and her seed; it shall bruise thy head, and thou shalt bruise his heel.'' Genesis 3:15. As the guilty pair listened, they were inspired with hope, for they discerned a promise of deliverance from ruin. They need not yield to despair. The Son of God was to atone with His own blood for their transgression. Through faith in the power of Christ to save, they might become once more the children of God.

By turning man from obedience Satan became ''the god of this world.'' 2 Corinthians 4:4. But the Son of God proposed not only to redeem man but to recover the dominion forfeited. ''O Tower of the flock, . . . unto Thee shall it come, even the first dominion.'' Micah 4:8.

This hope of redemption has never become extinct. From the beginning there have been some whose faith has reached out beyond the present to the future, Adam, Seth, Enoch, Methuselah, Noah, Shem, Abraham, Isaac, and Jacob. Through these the Lord has preserved the revealings of His will. To the chosen people through whom was to be given the promised

Messiah, God imparted a knowledge of salvation through the atoning sacrifice of His beloved Son.

The promise was made at the call of Abraham, and afterward repeated: "In thee shall all families of the earth be blessed." Genesis 12:3. The Sun of Righteousness shone upon Abraham's heart, and his darkness was scattered. When the Saviour Himself walked among the sons of men, He bore witness of the patriarch's hope: "Your father Abraham rejoiced to see My day: and he saw it, and was glad." John 8:56.

This same "blessed hope" was foreshadowed in the benediction pronounced by Jacob on Judah:

> The scepter shall not depart from Judah,
> Nor the ruler's staff from between his feet,
> Until He comes to whom it belongs;
> And to Him shall be the obedience of the peoples.
> Genesis 49:10, RSV

Again, the coming of the world's Redeemer was foretold by Balaam:

> A star shall come forth out of Jacob,
> And a scepter shall rise out of Israel.
> Numbers 24:17, RSV

Through Moses also, God's purpose to send His Son as the Redeemer was kept before Israel. Moses declared, "The Lord thy God will raise up unto thee a Prophet from the midst of thee, of thy brethren . . . ; unto Him ye shall hearken." Deuteronomy 18:15.

How the Sanctuary Services Revealed the Saviour

The sacrificial offerings constituted a perpetual reminder of the coming of a Saviour. Throughout Israel's history each day the people were taught by types and shadows the great truths of Christ as Redeemer, Priest, and King. And once each year their minds were carried forward to the closing events of the great controversy between Christ and Satan. The earthly sanctuary was "a figure for the time then present." Its two holy places were "patterns of things in the heavens," for Christ is today "a minister of the sanctuary, and of the true tabernacle, which the Lord pitched, and not man." Hebrews 9:9, 23; 8:2.

When Adam and his sons began to offer ceremonial sacrifices ordained as a type of the coming Redeemer, Satan discerned in these a symbol of communion between earth and heaven. During the long centuries it has been his constant effort to intercept this communion, to misrepresent God and misinterpret the rites pointing to the Saviour. The archenemy of mankind has endeavored to represent God as one who delights in men's destruction. The sacrifices designed to reveal divine love have been perverted as means whereby sinners have vainly hoped to propitiate the wrath of an offended God. At the same time, Satan has sought to strengthen evil passions in order that through repeated transgression multitudes might be led far from God and hopelessly bound with the fetters of sin.

In the parchment rolls of the Old Testament Scriptures Satan traced the words that outlined Christ's work among men as a suffering sacrifice and as a conquering king. He read that the One who was to appear was to be "brought as a lamb to the slaughter," "His visage . . . so marred more than any man, and His form more than the sons of men." The promised Saviour was to be "despised and rejected of men; a man of sorrows, and acquainted with grief: . . . smitten of God, and afflicted." Isaiah 53:7; 52:14; 53:3, 4. These prophecies caused Satan to tremble, yet he determined to blind the people to their real significance in order to prepare the way for the rejection of Christ at His coming.

Preceding the Flood, success had attended Satan's efforts to bring about a worldwide rebellion against God. After the Flood, with artful insinuations he again led men into bold rebellion. He seemed about to triumph, but through the posterity of faithful Abraham, divinely appointed messengers were to be raised up to call attention to the meaning of the sacrificial ceremonies, and especially to the promise of the One toward whom all the ordinances pointed.

Not without determined opposition was the divine purpose carried out. In every way possible the enemy worked to cause the descendants of Abraham to forget their holy calling. For centuries preceding Christ's first advent, darkness covered the earth, and gross darkness the people. Multitudes were sitting in the shadow of death.

The True Character of the Messiah Revealed

With prophetic vision David had foreseen that the coming of Christ should be "as the light of the morning, when the sun riseth, even a morning without clouds." 2 Samuel 23:4. And Hosea testified, "His going forth is prepared as the morning." Hosea 6:3. Quietly and gently the daylight breaks on the earth, dispelling the darkness and waking the earth to life. Isaiah exclaimed:

> Unto us a Child is born,
> Unto us a Son is given:
> And the government shall be upon His shoulder:
> And His name shall be called
> Wonderful, Counselor, The mighty God,
> The everlasting Father, The Prince of Peace.
> Isaiah 9:6

The steadfast among the Jewish nation strengthened their faith by dwelling on these and similar passages. They read how the Lord would anoint One "to preach good tidings unto the meek," "to bind up the brokenhearted, to proclaim liberty to the captives," and to declare "the acceptable year of the Lord." Isaiah 61:1, 2. Yet with sadness and deep humiliation of soul they traced the words in the prophetic roll:

He is despised and rejected of men;
    A Man of Sorrows, and acquainted with grief:
And we hid as it were our faces from Him;
    He was despised, and we esteemed Him not.

Surely He hath borne our griefs,
And carried our sorrows:
    Yet we did esteem Him stricken,
    Smitten of God, and afflicted. . . .

All we like sheep have gone astray;
We have turned everyone to his own way;
    And the Lord hath laid on Him
    The iniquity of us all.
             Isaiah 53:3-6

As the substitute and surety for sinful man, Christ was to suffer under divine justice. Through the psalmist the Redeemer had prophesied of Himself:

Reproach hath broken My heart;
    And I am full of heaviness:
I looked for someone to take pity,
    But there was none;
And for comforters,
    But I found none.
They gave Me also gall for My meat;
    And in My thirst they gave Me vinegar to drink.
             Psalm 69:20, 21

He prophesied: "They pierced My hands and My feet. I may tell all My bones: they look and stare upon Me. They part My garments among them, and cast lots upon My vesture." Psalm 22:16-18.

These portrayals of the bitter suffering and cruel death of the Promised One, sad though they were, were rich in promise; for "it pleased the Lord to bruise Him" and put Him to grief, in order that He might become "an offering for sin." Isaiah 53:10.

Love for sinners led Christ to pay the price of redemption. None other could ransom men and women from the power of the enemy. In His life no self-assertion was mingled. The homage which the world gives to position, to wealth, and to talent, was to be foreign to the Son of God. None of the means that men employ to win allegiance was the Messiah to use. His renunciation of self was foreshadowed in the words:

> He shall not cry,
>> Nor lift up,
>> Nor cause His voice to be heard in the street.
> A bruised reed shall He not break,
> And the smoking flax shall He not quench.
>> Isaiah 42:2, 3

The Important Work: Deliverance From Sin

In marked contrast to the teachers of the day was the Saviour to conduct Himself among men. In His life no noisy disputation, no act to gain applause was ever to be witnessed. The Messiah was to be hid in God, and God was to be revealed in the character of His Son. Without divine help, men and women would sink lower and lower. Life and power must be imparted by Him who made the world.

The Son of God was to "magnify the law, and make it honorable." Verse 21. He was to free the divine precepts from the burdensome exactions placed on them by man, whereby many were discouraged in their efforts to serve God.

"And the Spirit of the Lord shall rest upon Him, the Spirit of wisdom and understanding, the Spirit of counsel and might, the Spirit of knowledge and of the fear of the Lord; . . . with righteousness shall He judge the poor, and reprove with equity for the meek of the earth." Isaiah 11:2-4.

A fountain was to be opened "for sin and for uncleanness." Zechariah 13:1. The sons of men were to hear the blessed invitation:

Incline your ear, and come unto Me:
  Hear, and your soul shall live;
And I will make an everlasting covenant with you,
  Even the sure mercies of David.
        Isaiah 55:3

In word and deed the Messiah was to reveal the glory of God the Father, to make known to fallen humanity the infinite love of God.

He shall feed His flock like a shepherd:
He shall gather the lambs with His arm,
And carry them in His bosom,
And shall gently lead those that are with young.
        Isaiah 40:11.

And those who err in spirit will come to understanding.
And those who murmur will accept instruction.
        Isaiah 29:24, RSV

Thus God spoke to the world concerning the coming of a Deliverer from sin. Inspired prophecy pointed to the advent of "the Desire of all nations." Haggai 2:7. Even the place of His birth and the time of His appearance were specified. The Son of David must be born in David's city. Out of Bethlehem "shall He come forth . . . that is to be ruler in Israel; whose goings forth have been from of old, from everlasting." Micah 5:2.

And thou Bethlehem, . . .
Out of thee shall come forth a Governor,
Which shall be Shepherd of My people Israel.
        Matthew 2:6, RV

The time of the first advent was made known to Daniel. "Seventy weeks," said the angel, "are determined upon thy people and upon thy holy city, to finish the transgression, and to make an end of sins, and to make reconciliation for iniquity, and to bring in everlasting righteousness, and to seal up the vision and prophecy, and to anoint the most Holy." Daniel 9:24.

The Time of Christ's First Coming Specified

A day in prophecy stands for a year. See Numbers 14:34; Ezekiel 4:6. The 70 weeks, or 490 days, represent 490 years. A starting point for this period is given: "Know therefore and understand, that from the going forth of the commandment to restore and to build Jerusalem unto the Messiah the Prince shall be seven weeks, and threescore [sixty] and two weeks" (Daniel 9:25)—69 weeks, or 483 years. The commandment to restore and build Jerusalem by the decree of Artaxerxes Longimanus went into effect in the autumn of 457 B.C. See Ezra 6:14; 7:1, 9. From this time, 483 years extend to the autumn of A.D. 27. According to the prophecy, this period was to reach to the Messiah, the Anointed One. In A.D. 27, Jesus at His baptism received the anointing of the Holy Spirit (see Acts 4:27; John 1:33), and soon afterward the message was proclaimed, "The time is fulfilled." Mark 1:15.

Then, said the angel, "He shall confirm the covenant with many for one week [seven years]." For seven years after the Saviour entered on His ministry, the gospel was to be preached especially to the Jews; for three and a half years by Christ Himself, and afterward by the apostles. "In the midst of the week He shall cause the sacrifice and the oblation to cease." Daniel 9:27. In the spring of A.D. 31, Christ, the true Sacrifice, was offered on Calvary. Then the veil of the temple was rent (see Mark 15:38), showing that the time had come for the earthly sacrifice to cease.

The one "week"—seven years—ended in A.D. 34. By the stoning of Stephen the Jews sealed their rejection of the gospel. The disciples "went everywhere preaching the word" (Acts 8:4), and shortly after, Saul the persecutor became Paul the apostle to the Gentiles.

The prophecies concerning the Saviour led the Hebrews to live in an attitude of constant expectancy. Many believed and confessed that they were "strangers and pilgrims on the earth." Hebrews 11:13. The promises repeated through patriarchs and prophets had kept alive the hope of His appearing.

Not at first had God revealed the exact time of the first advent; and even when the prophecy of Daniel made this known, not all rightly interpreted the message.

Century after century passed away. Finally the voices of the prophets ceased. As the Jews departed from God, hope well-nigh ceased to illuminate the future. Those whose faith should have continued strong were ready to exclaim, "The days are prolonged, and every vision faileth." Ezekiel 12:22. But in heaven's council the hour for the coming of Christ had been determined. "When the time had fully come, God sent forth His Son, born of woman." Galatians 4:4, 5, RSV.

Lessons must be given to humanity in the language of humanity. The Messenger of the covenant must be heard in His own temple. The author of truth must separate truth from the chaff of man's utterance. The plan of redemption must be clearly defined.

When the Saviour finally appeared "in the likeness of men" (Philippians 2:7), Satan could but bruise the heel, while by every act of suffering Christ was bruising the head of His adversary. The anguish that sin has brought was poured into the bosom of the Sinless. Yet Christ was breaking the bondage in which humanity had been held. Every pang of anguish, every insult was working out the deliverance of the race.

If Satan could have induced Christ by one act, or even thought, to stain His perfect purity, the prince of darkness would have triumphed and gained the whole human family. But while Satan could distress, he could not contaminate. He could cause agony, but not defilement. He made the life of Christ one long scene of conflict and trial, yet with every attack he was losing his hold on humanity.

In Gethsemane and on the cross, our Saviour measured weapons with the prince of darkness. When Christ hung in agony on the cross, then indeed His heel was bruised by Satan. But that very act was crushing the serpent's head. Through death He destroyed "him that had the power of death, that is, the devil." Hebrews 2:14. This act made forever sure the plan of salvation. In death, in rising again, He opened the gates of the grave to all His followers. Our Redeemer has opened the way so that the most sinful, the most needy, the most oppressed and despised may find access to the Father.

59 / Where Is God's True Israel?

In proclaiming the everlasting gospel to every nation, God's church is fulfilling the prophecy, "Israel shall blossom and bud, and fill the face of the world with fruit." Isaiah 27:6. As the result of the labors of the followers of Jesus, an abundant fruitage is developing, bringing the benefits foreshadowed in the promise to Abraham, "I will bless thee, . . . and thou shalt be a blessing." Genesis 12:2.

This promise of blessing should have met fulfillment in large measure during the centuries following the return of the Israelites from captivity. It was God's design that the whole earth be prepared for the first advent of Christ, even as today the way is preparing for His second coming. See Zechariah 8:3, 7, 8.

The sins that had characterized Israel prior to the captivity were not to be repeated. "Execute true judgment," the Lord exhorted those engaged in rebuilding. "Speak ye every man the truth to his neighbor; execute the judgment of truth and peace in your gates." Zechariah 7:9; 8:16.

Rich were the rewards promised those who should practice these principles: "As ye were a curse among the heathen, O house of Judah, and house of Israel; so will I save you, and ye shall be a blessing." Zechariah 8:13.

By the Babylonish captivity the Israelites were cured of the worship of images. After their return, under Zerubbabel, Ezra, and Nehemiah, they repeatedly covenanted to keep all the commandments of the

363

Lord. The seasons of prosperity that followed gave evidence of God's willingness to forgive. Yet with fatal shortsightedness they selfishly appropriated to themselves that which would have brought healing and life to multitudes.

This failure was apparent in Malachi's day. In his rebuke against transgressors, the prophet spared neither priests nor people. Only by heartfelt repentance could the blessing of God be realized. "I pray you," the prophet pleaded, "beseech God that He will be gracious unto us." Malachi 1:9.

However, the plan for the redemption of mankind was not to be frustrated by any temporary failure of Israel. "From the rising of the sun to its setting," the Lord declared through His messenger, "My name is great among the nations." Verse 11, RSV.

Malachi Reveals the Secret of Prosperity

Those who once had been spiritual leaders had through transgression become "contemptible and base before all the people." Malachi 2:9. Yet none were left without hope. Malachi's prophecies of judgment were accompanied by invitations to the impenitent to make peace with God. "Return unto Me," the Lord urged, "and I will return unto you." Malachi 3:7. The God of heaven is pleading with His erring children to cooperate with Him in carrying forward His work in the earth. The Lord holds out His hand to Israel to help them to the path of self-sacrifice, to share with Him the heirship as sons of God. Will they discern their only hope?

How sad that in Malachi's day the Israelites hesitated to yield their proud hearts in hearty cooperation! Self-vindication is apparent in their response, "Wherein shall we return?"

The Lord reveals to His people one of their special sins. "Will a man rob God?" He asks. "Yet ye have robbed Me." Still unconvicted of sin, the disobedient inquire, "Wherein have we robbed Thee?"

"In tithes and offerings. . . . Bring ye all the tithes into the storehouse, that there may be meat in Mine house, and prove Me now herewith, saith the Lord of hosts, if I will not open you the windows of heaven, and pour you out a blessing. . . . And I will rebuke the devourer for your sakes, and he shall not destroy the fruits of your ground. . . . And all nations shall call you blessed: for ye shall be a delightsome land, saith the Lord of hosts." Verses 7-12.

God gives the sunshine and the rain; He causes vegetation to flourish; He gives health and ability to acquire means; and He desires men and women to show their gratitude by returning tithes and offerings, that His vineyard may not remain a barren waste. They are to reveal an unselfish interest in building up His work in all the world.

Through messages such as those borne by Malachi, as well as through oppression from heathen foes, the Israelites finally learned that true prosperity depends on obedience to the law of God. But with many, obedience was not the outflow of faith. Their motives were selfish. Outward service was a means of attaining national greatness. The chosen people did not become the light of the world, but shut themselves away from the world as a safeguard against idolatry. The restrictions forbidding intermarriage with the heathen and joining in the idolatrous practices of surrounding nations were so perverted as to build up a wall of partition between the Israelites and all other peoples. This shut from others the blessings God had commissioned Israel to give to the world.

How the Sanctuary Services Were Perverted

At the same time the Jews were, by their sins, separating from God. They were unable to discern the spiritual significance of their symbolic service. In self-righteousness they trusted their own works—the sacrifices themselves—instead of relying on the merits of Him to whom these things pointed. "Seeking to establish their own . . . righteousness" (Romans 10:3, RSV), they built up a self-sufficient formalism. Not content with the ordinances God Himself had appointed, they devised countless exactions of their own. The greater their distance from God, the more rigorous their observance of these forms.

With all these burdensome exactions it was a practical impossibility for the people to keep the law. The glorious truths shadowed in the symbolic service were buried under a mass of human tradition. Those who were really desirous of serving God groaned under a heavy burden.

Israel Rejects Her Messiah

The people of Israel were separated so far from God that they could have no true conception of the character or mission of the promised Redeemer. Instead of desiring redemption from sin, their hearts were fixed on restoration to worldly power. They looked for Messiah to exalt Israel to dominion over all nations. Thus Satan had prepared the people to reject the Saviour when He should appear. Their pride and false conceptions would prevent them from honestly weighing the evidences of His Messiahship.

For more than a thousand years the Jewish people had awaited the coming of the promised Saviour. In song and prophecy, in temple rite and household prayer, His name had been enshrined. Yet when He came they did not recognize Him. "He came unto His own, and His own received Him not." John 1:11. They discerned in Him no beauty that they should desire Him. See Isaiah 53:2.

The life of Jesus among the Jewish people was a reproof to their selfishness. They hated His example of truthfulness, and when the test came they rejected the Holy One of Israel and became responsible for His crucifixion.

In the parable of the vineyard, Christ called the attention of the Jewish teachers to the blessings bestowed on Israel and showed God's claim to their obedience. Withdrawing the veil from the future, He showed how the whole nation was bringing ruin on itself:

"There was a householder who planted a vineyard, and set a hedge around it, and dug a wine press in it, and built a tower, and let it out to tenants, and went into another country.

"When the season of fruit drew near, he sent his servants to the tenants, to get his fruit; and the tenants took his servants and beat one, killed another, and stoned another. Again he sent other servants, more than the first; and they did the same to them. Afterward he sent his son to them, saying, 'They will respect my son.' But when the tenants saw the son, they said to themselves, 'This is the heir; come, let us kill him and have his inheritance.' And they took him and cast him out of the vineyard, and killed him."

Christ now put to them the question, "When therefore the owner of the vineyard comes, what will he do to those tenants?" The priests joined with the people in answering, "He will put those wretches to a miserable death, and let out the vineyard to other tenants who will give him the fruits in their seasons."

A Self Application

They had pronounced their own doom! Under Jesus' searching gaze they knew He read the secrets of their hearts. They saw in the husbandmen a picture of themselves.

Regretfully Christ asked: "Have you never read in the Scriptures: 'The very stone which the builders rejected has become the head of the corner; this was the Lord's doing, and it is marvelous in our eyes'? Therefore I tell you, the kingdom of God will be taken away from you and given to a nation producing the fruits of it." Matthew 21:33-44, RSV.

The Jewish nation determined they would not receive Jesus of Nazareth as the Messiah. Henceforth their lives were surrounded with darkness as the darkness of midnight. The doom foretold came on the Jewish nation. In their blind rage they destroyed one another. Their rebellious pride brought on them the wrath of their Roman conquerors. Jerusalem was destroyed, the temple laid in ruins, and its site plowed like a field. Millions were sold as bondmen in heathen lands.

The New Israel Which Replaces the Old

That which God purposed to do for the world through Israel, the chosen nation, He will finally accomplish through His church. He has "let out His vineyard to other tenants," who faithfully "give Him the fruits in their seasons." These witnesses for God are the spiritual Israel, and to them will be fulfilled all the covenant promises made to His ancient people.

For many centuries the preaching of the gospel in its purity was prohibited. As a consequence, the Lord's great moral "vineyard" was almost unoccupied. The people were deprived of the light of God's Word. Error and superstition threatened to blot out true religion. God's church was as verily in captivity during this long period of persecution as were the children of Israel in Babylon during the exile.

But, thank God, to spiritual Israel have been restored the privileges accorded the people of God at the time of their deliverance from Babylon. In every part of the earth, men and women are responding to the Heaven-sent message, "Fear God, and give glory to Him; for the hour of His judgment is come." Revelation 14:7.

"Fallen, fallen is Babylon the great," which hath "made all nations drink the wine of her impure passion." To spiritual Israel is given the message, "Come out of her, My people, lest you take part in her sins, lest you share in her plagues." Verse 8; 18:4, RSV. As the captive exiles heeded the message, "Flee out of the midst of Babylon" (Jeremiah 51:6), so those who fear

God are withdrawing from spiritual Babylon. Soon they are to stand as trophies of divine grace in the heavenly Canaan.

When the promised Messiah was about to appear, the message of the forerunner of Christ was: "Repent ye: for the kingdom of heaven is at hand." Matthew 3:2. Today in the spirit and power of John the Baptist, messengers of God's appointment call the attention of a judgment-bound world to the closing of probation and the appearance of Christ as King of kings and Lord of lords. On His church rests the responsibility of warning those standing on the brink of eternal ruin. To every human being who will give heed must be made plain the principles in the great controversy.

In these final hours the Lord expects His church to arouse to action as never before. Those who have been made free in Christ through precious truth are to show forth the praises of Him who has called them out of darkness into marvelous light. The blessings so liberally bestowed are to be communicated to every people. From every true disciple is to be diffused life, courage, and true healing.

Light Will Penetrate the World's Darkness

The coming of Christ will take place in the darkest period of earth's history, when Satan will work "with all deceivableness of unrighteousness." 2 Thessalonians 2:10. His working is revealed by the multitudinous heresies and delusions of these days. His deceptions are even leavening the professed churches of Christ. The great apostasy will develop into darkness deep as midnight. But out of that darkness God's light will shine. To His people God says, "Arise, shine; for thy light is come, and the glory of the Lord is risen upon thee." Isaiah 60:1.

At Nazareth Christ said, "The Spirit of the Lord is upon Me, because He has anointed Me to preach good news to the poor. He has sent Me to proclaim release to the captives and recovering of sight to the blind, to set at liberty those who are oppressed, to proclaim the acceptable year of the Lord." Luke 4:18, 19, RSV. This was the work He commissioned His disciples to do, "to share your bread with the hungry, and bring the homeless poor into your house. . . . Then shall your light break forth like the dawn, and your healing shall spring up speedily; your righteousness shall go before you, the glory of the Lord shall be your rear guard." Isaiah 58:7, 8, RSV.

Thus in the night of spiritual darkness God's glory is to shine forth through His church. All around us are heard the wails of a world's sorrow. On every hand are the needy and distressed. It is ours to aid in relieving life's hardships and misery. If Christ is abiding in us, our hearts will be full of divine sympathy.

There are many from whom hope has departed. Bring back the sunshine to them. Many have lost their courage. Pray for them. Read to them from the Word of God. Upon many is a soul sickness which no physician can heal. Bring them to Jesus.

The whole earth, wrapped in darkness and pain, is to be lighted with the knowledge of God's love. From no class of people is the light to be excluded. No longer are the heathen to be wrapped in midnight darkness.

Christ has made every provision that His church shall be a transformed body, every Christian surrounded with a spiritual atmosphere of light and peace. He desires that we shall reveal His own joy in our lives.

Christ is coming with power and great glory. While all the world is plunged in darkness, there will be light in every dwelling of the saints. They will catch the first light of His second appearing. While the wicked flee, Christ's followers will rejoice in His presence.

Then the redeemed will receive their promised inheritance. Thus God's purpose for Israel will meet with literal fulfillment. God's purposes have been moving steadily forward to their accomplishment. It was thus with Israel through the history of the divided monarchy; it is thus with spiritual Israel today.

The seer of Patmos testifies: "After this I looked, and behold, a great multitude which no man could number, from every nation, from all tribes and peoples and tongues, standing before the throne and before the Lamb, clothed in white robes, with palm branches in their hands, and crying out with a loud voice, 'Salvation belongs to our God who sits upon the throne, and to the Lamb!' "

"He is Lord of lords and King of kings, and those with Him are called and chosen and faithful." Revelation 7:9, 10; 17:14, RSV.

60 / Visions of a Glorious Future

In the darkest days of her long conflict with evil, the people of God have been given revelations of the eternal purpose of Jehovah. They have been permitted to look beyond the trials of the present to the triumphs of the future, when the redeemed will possess the Promised Land. Today the controversy of the ages is rapidly closing, and the promised blessings are soon to be realized. Despised, persecuted, forsaken, God's children in every age have looked forward to the time when He will fulfill His assurance, "I will make thee an eternal excellency, a joy of many generations." Isaiah 60:15.

Not without severe conflict is the church to triumph. "The bread of adversity," "the water of affliction" (Isaiah 30:20), these are the common lot of all; but none who put their trust in the One mighty to deliver will be overwhelmed. "Thus saith the Lord that created thee, . . . I have called thee by thy name; thou art Mine. When thou passest through the waters, I will be with thee; and through the rivers, they shall not overflow thee: when thou walkest through the fire, thou shalt not be burned; neither shall the flame kindle upon thee. For I am the Lord thy God, the Holy One of Israel, thy Saviour." Isaiah 43:1-3.

There is forgiveness with God; there is acceptance full and free through the merits of Jesus, our crucified and risen Lord. "I, even I, am He that blotteth out thy transgressions for Mine own sake, and will not remember thy sins." "Thou shalt know that I the Lord am thy Saviour." Verse 25; 60:16.

No weapon that is fashioned against you
    shall prosper,
And you shall confute every tongue
    that rises against you in judgment.
This is the heritage of the servants of the Lord
    And their vindication from Me, says the Lord.
              Isaiah 54:17, RSV

Clad in the armor of Christ's righteousness, the church is to enter on her final conflict. She is to go forth into all the world, conquering and to conquer. The darkest hour of the struggle immediately precedes the day of final deliverance. "When the blast of the terrible ones is as a storm against the wall," God will be to His church "a refuge from the storm." Isaiah 25:4.

The word of the Lord to His faithful ones is: "Come, My people, enter thou into thy chambers, and shut thy doors about thee: hide thyself as it were for a little moment, until the indignation be overpast. For, behold, the Lord cometh out of His place to punish the inhabitants of the earth for their iniquity." Isaiah 26:20, 21.

Human Pride Will Be Laid Low

In visions of the great judgment day, the inspired messengers of God were given glimpses of the consternation of those unprepared to meet their Lord. "Behold, the Lord will lay waste the earth and make it desolate, and He will twist its surface and scatter its inhabitants." "For they have transgressed the laws, violated the statutes, broken the everlasting covenant." Isaiah 24:1, 5, RSV.

"And the haughtiness of man shall be humbled, and the pride of men shall be brought low; and the Lord alone will be exalted in that day." "In that day men will cast forth their idols of silver and their idols of gold, which they made for themselves to worship, to the moles and to the bats, to enter the caverns of the rocks and the clefts of the cliffs, from before the terror of the Lord, and from the glory of His majesty, when

He rises to terrify the earth." Isaiah 2:17, 20, 21, RSV.

Of those times when the pride of man shall be laid low, Jeremiah testifies: "Alas! for that day is great, so that none is like it: it is even the time of Jacob's trouble; but he shall be saved out of it." Jeremiah 30:7.

The day of wrath to the enemies of God is the day of final deliverance to His church. The Lord "will swallow up death forever, and the Lord God will wipe away tears from all faces, and the reproach of His people He will take away from all the earth, for the Lord has spoken." Isaiah 25:8, RSV. And as the prophet beholds the Lord descending from heaven, with all the holy angels, to gather the remnant church from among the nations of earth, he hears the exultant cry:

> Lo, this is our God;
> We have waited for Him,
> And He will save us:
> This is the Lord;
> We have waited for Him,
> We will be glad and rejoice
> in His salvation.
> Verse 9

The Resurrection From the Dead

The voice of the Son of God calls forth the sleeping saints from the prison house of death. "Thy dead shall live, their bodies shall rise. O dwellers in the dust, awake and sing for joy!" Isaiah 26:19, RSV.

> Then the eyes of the blind shall be opened,
> And the ears of the deaf shall be unstopped.
> Then shall the lame man leap as an hart,
> And the tongue of the dumb sing.
> Isaiah 35:5, 6

Those who have triumphed over sin and the grave are now happy in the presence of their Maker, talking freely with Him as man talked with God in the beginning. "I will rejoice in Jerusalem, and joy in My people: and the voice of weeping shall be no more heard in her, nor the voice of crying." "The inhabitant shall not say, I am sick: the people that dwell therein shall be forgiven their iniquity." Isaiah 65:19; 33:24.

Waters shall break forth in the wilderness,
And streams in the desert;
The burning sand shall become a pool,
And the thirsty ground springs of water.

"Speak tenderly to Jerusalem, and cry to her that her warfare is ended, that her iniquity is pardoned, that she has received from the Lord's hand double for all her sins." Isaiah 35:6, 7; 40:2, RSV.

Violence shall no more be heard in your land,
    Devastation or destruction within your borders;
You shall call your walls Salvation,
    And your gates Praise.

Your people shall all be righteous;
They shall possess the land forever,
    The shoot of My planting,
    The work of My hands,
That I might be glorified.
                    Isaiah 60:18, 21, RSV

The prophet caught the sound of music there, such music and song as, save in the visions of God, no mortal ear has heard or mind conceived. "Joy and gladness shall be found therein, thanksgiving, and the voice of melody." Isaiah 51:3. "As well the singers as the players on instruments shall be there." Psalm 87:7.

What Life Will Be Like in the New Earth

In the earth made new, the redeemed will engage in the occupations and pleasures that brought happiness to Adam and Eve in the beginning. The Eden life will be lived, the life in garden and field. "They shall build houses and inhabit them; they shall plant vineyards and eat their fruit. They shall not build and another inhabit; they shall not plant and another eat; for like the days of a tree shall the days of My people be, and My chosen shall long enjoy the work of their hands." Isaiah 65:21, 22, RSV. Every power will be developed, every capability increased, the grandest enterprises carried forward, the highest ambitions realized.

The prophets to whom these scenes were revealed longed to understand their full import, inquiring "what person or time was indicated by the Spirit of Christ within them. . . . They were serving not themselves but you, in the things which have now been announced to you." 1 Peter 1:11, 12, RSV.

Fellow pilgrim, we are still amid the shadows and turmoil of earthly activities, but soon our Saviour is to appear. Soon we shall see Him in whom our hopes of eternal life are centered. And in His presence the trials of this life will seem as nothingness. The former things "shall not be remembered or come into mind." "Therefore do not throw away your confidence, which has a great reward. For you have need of endurance, so that you may do the will of God and receive what is promised. For yet a little while, and the coming One shall come and shall not tarry." Isaiah 65:17; Hebrews 10:35-37, RSV.

Look up and let your faith continually increase. Let this faith guide you along the narrow path that leads through the gates of the city into the wide, unbounded future of glory. "Be patient, therefore, brethren, until the coming of the Lord. Behold, the farmer waits for the precious fruit of the earth, being patient over it until it receives the early and the late rain. You also be patient. Establish your hearts, for the coming of the Lord is at hand." James 5:7, 8, RSV.

The nations of the saved will know no other law than the law of heaven. All will be a happy, united family. The morning stars will sing together, and the sons of

God will shout for joy, while God and Christ will unite in proclaiming, "There shall be no more sin, neither shall there be any more death."

"From new moon to new moon, and from Sabbath to Sabbath, all flesh shall come to worship before Me, says the Lord." "For the Lord will comfort Zion: He will comfort all her waste places, and will make her wilderness like Eden, her desert like the garden of the Lord."

"As the bridegroom rejoices over the bride, so shall your God rejoice over you." Isaiah 66:23; 51:3; 62:5, RSV.